D1055038

THE KNIGHTS TEMPLAR

By the same author

The Koh-i-Noor Diamond

271.
79
HOW

The Knights Templar

The Essential History

Stephen Howarth

FINKELSTEIN
MEMORIAL LIBRARY
SPRING VALLEY, N.Y.

continuum

3 2191 00778 3151

Continuum UK
The Tower Building
11 York Road
London SE1 7NX

Continuum US
80 Maiden Lane
Suite 704
New York, NY 10038

www.continuumbooks.com

Copyright © Stephen Howarth 1985
First published 1982 by William Collins & Sons
This edition 2006
Reprinted 2007

All rights reserved. No part of this publication may be reproduced or transmitted in any form or by any means, electronic or mechanical, including photocopying, recording or any information storage or retrieval system, without prior permission from the publishers.

British Library Cataloguing-in-Publication Data
A catalogue record for this book is available from the British Library.

ISBN 0 8264 8034 9

Typeset by MS Filmsetting Ltd, Frome Somerset
Printed and bound by Antony Rowe Ltd, Chippenham, Wilts

Contents

Illustrations

The chapter decoration, the Pegasus, was chosen as the Templars'
device. The story has it that with an eye to economy two men
mounted one horse; from a distance the impression was of a horse
with wings raised. A Pegasus with wings expanded is now
the arms of the Inner Temple, London.

The Masters of
the Order of the Temple
in Jerusalem

	Ruled
Hugh de Payens	1118/9–1136/7
Robert de Craon (the Burgundian)	1136/7–13 January 1149
Everard de Barres	1149–1152 (?)
Bernard de Trémélai	1152(?)–16 August 1153
André de Montbard	1153–17 January 1156
Bertrand de Blanquefort	1156–2 January 1169
Philippe de Milly of Nablus	1169–1171
Odo de Saint-Amand	1171–8 October 1179
Arnold de Torroges	1180–30 September 1184
Gerard de Ridefort	1185–4 October 1189
Robert de Sablé	1191–28 September 1193
Gilbert Erail	1194–21 December 1200
Philippe de Plessiez	1201–12 February 1209
William de Chartres	1210–25 August 1219
Pedro de Montaigu	1219–28 January 1232
Armand de Peragors	1232(?)–17 October 1244
Richard de Bures	1244/5–9 May 1247
William de Sonnac	1247–11 February 1250
Renaud de Vichiers	1250–20 January 1256
Thomas Berard	1256–25 March 1273
William de Beaujeu	May 1273–18 May 1291
Tibald Gaudin	1291–16 April 1293
Jacques de Molay	1293–18 March 1314

From Marie Luise Bulst-Thiele: *Sacrae Domus Militiae
Templi Hierosolymitani Magistri – Untersuchungen zur
Geschichte des Templerordens 1118/19–1314.* Published by
Vandenhoeck und Reprecht, Göttingen, 1974.

Preface

It is nearly seven hundred years since Pope Clement V dissolved the Order of the Knights of the Temple of Solomon. Since then their story has been told many times, and it will probably be told many times more, for it is a tale with all the elements of romantic history: it is set in exotic times and places, peopled with characters of the highest ideals and the deepest corruption, and imbued with mystery.

Much of the mystery surrounding the Templars springs from lack of knowledge, and from the many writers who have taken imaginative liberties with the known facts, presenting supposition under the guise of history. Secretive, elite societies – as the Templars' Order essentially was – have always exerted a peculiar fascination over the minds of people outside them: one may imagine what one likes, without fear of being disproved. This is fine for novels but as history it is, at best, a waste of time, and, at worst, downright misleading.

Yet because the Templars were an historical, and not a mythical phenomenon, new factual information is continually coming to light, dissolving some of the mysteries and uncertainties, though not all. And as more information slowly emerges from the dusty recesses of archives and libraries, the motives of the Templars – those strange men, at once knights and monks – become more understandable; and the story itself becomes more, not less, extraordinary.

A generation has passed since the last complete English account of Templar history was written. My own self-imposed brief has been to present, within the limitations of space, as accurate a picture as possible of the birth, life and sudden death of this unprecedented brotherhood, set against two centuries of changes in medieval society. If research into the Templars continues, then quite possibly the next generation will find that things which I believe to be true are mistaken; and so I think of this book rather as an interim report – the state of Templar knowledge at present.

Templar history, in any case, is so complex – and still, at times, so obscure – that it might be difficult to find two historians who agreed on every point. Researching this book, I sympathized deeply with Thomas Fuller. In 1639 he published *The Historie of the Holy Warre*, and at one point said despairingly, 'I must confess it passeth my chymistry to exact any agreement herein out of the contrariety of writers.'

I myself have exacted as much agreement as possible from other writers and scholars in this field; my debt to them will be apparent in the bibliography, and my thanks are due to them all.

Special words of thanks are due also to Frau Madeleine Kinsella and the staff of the Institut für Mittelalterliche Geschichte, Philipps-Universität, Marburg, West Germany, for their great help and co-operation in the making of this book; to my friends Bob Hannah and Andrew Motz for their valuable translations; and to Marianne, my wife, for her translations, and for her equally essential patience, love and support.

'And now,' as St Bernard wrote in *De Laude Novae Militiae*, 'now it is for my readers to judge me, since it is not possible that I should please everybody.' And I hope that readers will find it is a good story, accurately told; for that is all I have tried to do.

S.W.R.H.

ASHES TO ASHES

Paris, 18 March 1314

'So they went, talking earnestly of all
things, but, save in God, finding no
hope at all.'

The Brethren

THE MOOD OF THE CITY was shifting and uncertain. In the streets and inns, or in the greater safety of their homes, people speculated quietly and tensely on the events the afternoon would bring. Here and there a voice was raised to praise the virtues of the king, and few argued; a careless word could count as treason. Philip was a handsome man – as beautiful as a statue, people said – but there was no knowing his thoughts. His grandfather, Louis IX, had been a saint, and some of the awe and veneration accorded to Louis still clung to Philip; but when his subjects thought of Philip, awe was mingled with fear. His grip on the people of France was relentless, and in an age when travel was slow and communications poor, his police were ubiquitous and highly efficient. Through his agents, one pope had been kidnapped, and denounced in France as a black magician, and another had been elected to reign not in Rome, but in Avignon. Only eight years before – the memory was still fresh – every Jew in France had been arrested on the king's orders in a single night. Philip was a cold friend, a vicious, implacable enemy.

The Parisians were certain of one thing: on that March afternoon, neither winter nor yet spring, a war would be resolved – a war whose battles stretched over seven years of torture, trials and intrigue. The arrest and expulsion of the Jews had been only a rehearsal for a greater move. In France at the beginning of the fourteenth century there was one group whose power could match that of the king; the Poor Fellow-Soldiers of Jesus Christ, the Knights of the Temple of Solomon.

For nearly two hundred years the Templars, their white tunics emblazoned with the red cross of martyrdom, had represented the highest ideals of Christendom; they were the first military Order, a brotherhood of fighting monks, knights dedicated to Christ and to the three vows of poverty, chastity and obedience. Founded in Jerusalem in 1118 (or perhaps 1119: the exact date is uncertain), they had sworn in God's name to defend the holy places and to protect pilgrims on their long journeys. They had fought for Christ in every part of the Holy Land; under St Louis, Philip's grandfather, they had fought heretics in France and Saracens in the southern and eastern Mediterranean; and in Spain they were slowly but surely pushing back the Moors and restoring the land to the name of Christianity. Their houses and castles were the strongest and safest buildings known; their armies were the only disciplined, organized fighting units in the western world. Templar knights had frequently acted as confidential envoys for Philip himself; the Templar treasurer was the receiver and warden of the French royal revenues; once, indeed, it had even happened that Philip, fleeing from a rebellious mob, had taken refuge for three days in the Paris Temple.

But when he chose, the king's memory could be very short. Just fifteen months after the arrest of the Jews, every Templar in France had been arrested, again in a single night. Individually and as a group, the Knights Templar, the flower of Christian chivalry, were accused of appalling crimes; Philip denounced them as heretics, blasphemers, usurers, traitors, sodomites and idolators.

The mass arrest had taken place in 1307, and for seven years the trials had dragged on. At last, however, it seemed the end was imminent. Just before Christmas 1313 the pope, Clement V, had authorized three French cardinals to go to Paris, acting in his name, to accept the final confessions of the highest officers of the Temple. The cardinals were Arnold Novelli, a one-time monk of the abbey of Cîteaux: Nicolas de Fréanville, previously the king's confessor and one of his advisers; and Arnold de Farges, the pope's nephew. Clement's nepotism was notorious.

By March 1314 everything was ready, and on the morning of the eighteenth the carpenters were busy beside Notre-Dame. In the very shadow of the cathedral a macabre set was built for the afternoon's performance: a high platform for a scaffold; beside it, a pulpit, higher still; and close by, a group of carts, filled with faggots and brushwood.

At noon, the island was silent, the stage-set empty; but in the city all around the air was taut with apprehension. It seemed scarcely credible that the knights of the Temple could be guilty of the crimes imputed to them by the king. God knew, the king was hard enough, vindictive enough to use any means to further his own ends; and God only knew what designs were formed in his mind. Yet his ministers proclaimed him as a defender of the faith; through his influence, a French pope had been elected. And the Templars had confessed. Everyone had heard it from one source or another; that afternoon they would hear it for themselves, from the lips of the Temple's Grand Master, Jacques de Molay.

Shortly after noon the first members of the audience came over the bridges on to the island, glancing warily at the guards positioned around the scaffold. More came, and more, until the little island was full, and the guards had to hold the people back to keep a passage clear. The crowd was silent in the chilly air; then, in a stately procession, came the three cardinals, followed by the Archbishop of Sens and a swarm of other bishops and minor clerics. They all took their seats, confident in the power their vestments demonstrated. The men of the Church and the citizens of Paris faced each other, the one group seated, calm and sure of themselves, the other standing, tired, cold, suspicious and distrustful.

Then a tremor, an almost audible tremor, ran through the audience. The second procession was approaching: guards before and behind, and in the centre, four ragged, bearded figures, wasted bodies hung with chains. Hugh de Pairaud, treasurer of the Temple and Visitor of the Priory of France; Geoffrey de Gonneville, Preceptor of Aquitaine; Geoffrey de Charney, Preceptor of Normandy; and Jacques de Molay, Grand Master of the Temple. Seven years before, at the command of the pope, de Molay had arrived in Paris escorted by sixty knights. To those who had seen him then, he was barely recognizable. A swift murmur of shock and sympathy rippled through the assembled Parisians as they asked each other if these could be the holy knights they remembered. The isolated voices of those more hardy than the others jeered and shouted – traitors, heretics, idolators – but even they were hushed by the massive silence that hung over the watching crowd.

Slowly and painfully, carrying their chains, the prisoners climbed the steps of the scaffold and stood side by side. A preacher, spokesman for the papal delegation, swept up into the pulpit and began his oration. He spoke first of the pope's zeal in defending the Church against defilement by heretics; he reminded his listeners of the disinterest, even the altruism, of the king; and then he began the miserable catalogue of crime and sin. As the horrible list was read out, workmen beside the scaffold erected four stakes and piled brushwood around them. If the prisoners retracted their confessions, they knew the price. Hugh de Pairaud and Geoffrey de Gonneville listened dully and watched the growing heaps of firewood. Geoffrey de Charney stood as straight as he could under the weight of his chains. Only de Molay flashed a glance of contempt at the cardinals and their spokesman.

Finally the preacher's rhetoric reached its climax. The prisoners, he declared, were confessed heretics. They had defiled the Cross and reneged on their holy vows; instead of fighting for Christ, they had worked in every foul and subtle way imaginable for the anti-Christ. But the mercy of the pope was great; if the sinners would only confirm their confessions, the Holy Father would receive them into the Church again, and his servant Philip would undertake to hold the knights in perpetual imprisonment for the rest of their lives on earth. But for recanting heretics, the preacher concluded, there was only one fit punishment; and he pointed to the stakes below.

All attention turned to the scaffold as the prisoners were called to public confession. De Pairaud and de Gonneville affirmed their guilt, speaking so quietly they could scarcely be heard. And then Geoffrey de Charney and Jacques de Molay stepped forward to the front of the scaffold, and de Molay spoke.

'It is right,' he said, 'that on such a terrible day, and in the last moments of my life, that I should reveal all the iniquity of lies, and that I should let truth triumph; and so I declare, before heaven and earth, and I avow, even if it be to my eternal shame, that I have committed the greatest of all crimes.'

Everyone strained forward to hear, and the cardinals glanced in uneasy surprise at each other – this was more than the simple affirmation they had expected. De Molay continued, speaking clearly and loudly.

'But this is my crime: that I have agreed to the accusations brought with so much malice against an Order which truth forces me to recognize today as innocent. I gave the declaration demanded of me only to escape torture and suffering, and to move to pity those who made me suffer. I know the torments endured by those who had the courage to revoke such confessions, but the terrible spectacle before me cannot make me confirm a first lie by a second. In such a wretched state I renounce life willingly; it is already only too hateful to me. What use to me are such sad days, when I have only earned them by lies.'

With a great shout the crowd surged towards the scaffold; the guards leapt to hold them back. The cardinals jumped up in alarm and confusion – the provost and his men grabbed hold of the tattered, emaciated prisoners and bundled them down the scaffold steps. A new group formed, prisoners and churchmen in a ring of guardsmen, pushing through the roaring rabble, back over the bridge and into the city.

The king's response was immediate: burn them. Only the pope could authorize the burning of heretics; his delegates did not have the power. But the pope was far away in Avignon, and in any case Philip was not his servant – it was the pope who was the king's puppet. The cardinals retired, humiliated. That same evening de Charney and de Molay were dragged back to the Seine. An immense crowd surrounded every step of the way; it seemed all Paris had come to witness the final scene. On an island in the Seine close to Notre-Dame two pyres had been hastily erected. The prisoners were chained to the stakes, shouting their innocence and the innocence of the whole Order. Nothing, neither the entreaties of their friends nor the threats of the king's men, would move them; rather, they asked for the end to be swift. But to the last the king's ministers fought for a confession: before the wood was set alight, live coals were heaped around the men. Before thousands of onlookers they were being slowly roasted alive – yet they still persisted, crying against injustice, shrieking their innocence, cursing the king and the pope as instruments of the devil.

As the stinking smoke eddied around him Philip gazed

impassively at the two twisting bodies, listened as they spat out their hatred of him and roared their love of Christ and truth. He continued to watch, his expression changeless as stone, as the wood was lit and the flames curled up; and he stayed until all that was left, as night fell over Paris, was a smouldering, popping heap of coals. Only then did he leave, returning to his palace, perhaps to sleep. Guards were posted on the bridges to the island.

But if Philip slept, others were awake. During the night some monks slipped down to the river and swam to the island. There in the darkness they dug through the ashes and hot charcoal, and then swam back with the bitter, acrid bones of the Preceptor of Normandy and the last Grand Master held firmly in their mouths.

PART ONE

The First Crusade and the Birth of the Temple, 1095–1118

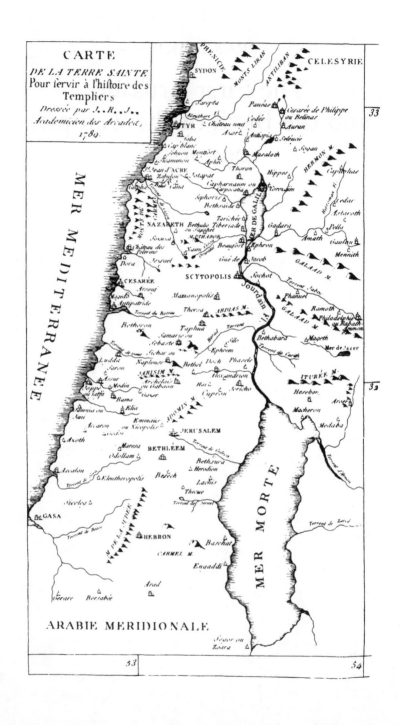

CHAPTER I

THE BLESSED SOLDIERS

'Will ye contend for God?'
Job XIII, 8

IN THE LAST WEEK of November 1095 a new age began in
Europe: the age of the crusades. For seven years, since his
election to the Holy See in 1088, Pope Urban II had worked
patiently towards the reunification of western Christendom.
Not only patience but tact had been necessary, for Gregory VII –
the most illustrious of Urban's immediate predecessors – had
repeatedly claimed temporal suzerainty over all the monarchs of
Christendom, and many of those monarchs had objected. Nor
had Urban's inheritance been made easier by the existence of a
rival – Guibert, the anti-pope, who reigned in Rome, illegally
elected by enemies of the dead Gregory. But Guibert's influence
was limited; and slowly, through diplomatic forbearance,
diligent organization and a consistent display of common sense,
Urban had won the spiritual allegiance of almost all the Christians
of the West. Having won that allegiance, he was going to use it.

For centuries western Christendom had been separated from
its source, the Holy City of Jerusalem. In AD 638 a Moslem army
had captured the city, and it had remained subject to Islam ever
since. Moreover, the Orthodox Christians of the East looked not
to the pope but to the Byzantine emperor in Constantinople for
spiritual leadership; and even before the conquest of Jerusalem
various unorthodox heretical sects had arisen which acknowledged neither pope nor emperor. Chief amongst these were the
Nestorians, the Jacobites and the Copts. The Nestorians, based in
Syria, and with missionaries as far east as India and China,
separated Christ's spiritual and human natures; the Jacobites and

21

the Copts stressed his spiritual nature so much that they virtually denied his humanity.

Both the Jacobites and the Copts sprang from a heretical sect, the Monophysites, founded in the fifth century; the main distinction between the two was that the Jacobites, like the Nestorians, were based in Syria, and the Copts in Egypt. There were others – the Manichaeans, the Gnostics, the Armenians – and with the combination of the eastern church, the heretical groups and the vast numbers of Muslims, there was no part of the eastern Mediterranean where the pope could claim authority.

Most of the eastern Christians found the arrangement quite satisfactory. The Orthodox had a lay protector in the Byzantine emperor, who was to them the symbol of Christian unity; and after the fall of Jerusalem, both they and the heretics, somewhat to their surprise, found that the infidel Moslem rulers were reasonable and just. Taxes were much lighter than they had been under Christian domination, and in accordance with the law of the Prophet Mohammed, the 'People of the Book' – the Christians and the Jews – were given freedom of worship.

For three and a half centuries, despite occasional bouts of war and mutual persecution, the people of the various religions found a tolerable *modus vivendi*; and then the Byzantine empire began to grow, as the armies of the emperors conquered Dalmatia, southern Italy, Syria, and even as far south as Caesarea.

In Europe such developments meant little to most people. Life was regulated by the seasons and, for the great majority, was a grim and constant struggle. In the year 1000 serfdom still existed. The peasantry, free men, were little better off than serfs; and even the rich, whose wealth was not in money but almost entirely in kind, led lives that we would see as brutal, harsh and precarious. Settlements were very small, separated by vast forest regions; travel was difficult, dangerous and extremely slow. A man would usually live and die in the village where he was born. His life was ordered by three major forces: the need for food, killed in the forest or dragged crudely and inefficiently from the soil; his duties to the local landowner; and the need to save his soul. For Christianity before the millenium was, for many people, a religion of guilt, and the Christian God a god of wrath and terror. There were those, such as St Augustine, who understood the beauty of Christ's love; but in AD 1000, the simple, brutish majority expected that Christ would descend at almost any moment to take vengeance on a sinful world.

However, when the millenium had passed without any obviously disastrous results, the eleventh century slowly brought some relief. In the first half of the century social organization became more formal, less based on ignorance, instinct and expediency. From the founding of Cluny in AD 910, the men of the churches and monasteries had tried to free themselves from secular intervention, and the feudal society of the eleventh century recognized at least three distinct social orders – the peasantry, the nobility and the clergy. And at least, by 1050 or so, it was possible to satisfy one basic need: everybody, or almost everybody, had enough to eat. But peace was still an unimaginable condition. With more food there were more people, and while the peasants worked and the clergy prayed, the knights and noblemen fought.

After his ceremonial entry into manhood and knighthood the only duty a knight acknowledged was strife. In theory this meant the defence and protection of the unarmed populace against a hostile foreign army. In practice, since invasions were not a daily event, it meant fighting practically everyone within sword's reach. The knight was trained only for war, and was taught at every step to regard anything else as beneath his status. Arms, armour and a horse visibly placed him above ordinary people. His training demanded an outlet, and though hunting could mimic the conditions of battle it was only mimicry; human opponents were necessary. Moreover, the gradual growth of primogeniture gave each succeeding generation of the eleventh-century nobility an increasing number of younger sons, landless, frequently penniless, and with only one trade: war.

The Church, trying to keep some vestige of order, introduced the 'Peace of God', which gave immunity from attack to peasants, the clergy and sacred places; and the 'Truce of God', which forbade any fighting on holy days and during Lent. Unfortunately, not everyone was prepared to fight to a timetable, and the theory of peace fell before violent practice.

Many people of all classes found escape from their constricting way of life by becoming pilgrims, visiting one or more of the five great centres of Christian shrines – St James of Compostela, St Michael of Monte Gargano, Rome, Jerusalem and

Constantinople. A journey to any one of these would probably take months, and a round trip to all of them would last several years; partly because of that, making a long pilgrimage became an accepted sentence for a malefactor. Not only did the wrongdoer expiate his sin, but the community which had sentenced him got rid of him for a long time. Indeed, there was a good chance that he might not come back alive at all.

Pilgrimages, whether voluntary or enforced, were blessed and encouraged by the Church; but they also served as reminders of two unpleasant problems. Firstly, the reason for the sanctity of Constantinople was that in that city, ten times larger than any European capital, were housed the major relics of the Passion of Christ – the crown of thorns and a cloth said to bear the imprint of Christ's face. Many a pope must have dreamt of the day when such relics might come to Rome, for their presence in Constantinople emphasized the discord between the churches of East and West. In the middle of the eleventh century the quarrel between the two became worse than usual, and Rome and Constantinople excommunicated each other.

Beyond Byzantium lay the second problem. Christian pilgrims arriving at Jerusalem could visit the holy shrines, but only on payment of a tax to the Moslems. International travel in the eleventh century was, by previous standards, a straightforward affair. By 1088, when Pope Urban II was elected, Islam had ruled Jerusalem for four hundred and fifty years. Those western Christians to whom it was important had tolerated the separation largely because there was little that could be done about it. But, as the century drew to a close, it seemed that something could be done; and Urban prepared to announce his plan.

The idea – that Jerusalem should belong exclusively to Christianity – was not new. In AD 614 a Persian army had taken the city, only to be ousted fifteen years later by the Byzantine Emperor Heraclius I; and in the second half of the tenth century, two further Byzantine emperors – Nicephorus Phocas in 964 and John Tzimisces in 974 – had attempted to repeat the achievement of Heraclius. Both employed a fine line in bombast: 'You living in the sands of the desert, beware!' said Nicephorus. 'I will move against Mecca leading masses of warriors like the darkness of the night. I will capture this city to erect there the throne of God. Then will I turn to Jerusalem, will conquer East and West and everywhere will I erect the symbol of the Cross.' 'Our desire,' said John Tzimisces ten years later, 'is to free the Holy Sepulchre from the outrages of the Muslims.' But though both enjoyed considerable success – Nicephorus in particular was an outstanding general – neither achieved the final goal, and Jerusalem remained with the Moslems.

Less than fifty years afterwards, in 1018, western Christendom began flexing its muscles, as French and Spanish noblemen and adventurers joined forces against the Moslems in Spain. The conflict soon gained the status of a holy war, and soldiers were tempted south with the hope of new lands and the promise of papal indulgences.

The Spanish war continued throughout the eleventh century. By the end of the century the Christian armies had gone no further than the towns of Huesca and Barbastro in Aragon – about fifty miles from the present French border. It was not far, but it was enough to make further progress seem possible; and it showed that the Moslems were not invincible. By 1075 Pope Gregory VII dreamed of complete papal supremacy in East and West. In his mind a new Rome arose, to rule the world through religion. Constantinople would rejoin the fold; Jerusalem would be Christian once more; and every monarch of Christendom would bow to the pontiff of Rome. However, Gregory was not a would-be world dictator; his ambition was not to rule the body politic – that, he always acknowledged, was the work of kings and ministers. He possessed an unshakeable belief that spiritual matters should guide the life of every person, and that the unity of Christianity should be a reality, not merely an ideal. In this belief he showed complete integrity, an integrity admitted even by his enemies. But when he died, in 1085, he had many enemies, for the very fire and simplicity of his view had made him a bad politician.

Perhaps fortunately for the Holy See Gregory was followed by the weak and colourless Victor III. Victor's pontificate lasted only two years – he died in September 1087 – but it gave time for much of the anger and indignation left by Gregory's uncompromising attitudes to die down. Even so, Gregory's antagonists still supported their own 'pope'; Victor's successor would have many problems.

There was no conclave during the winter of 1087, and it was

not until March 1088 that Urban II was elected. At first he had no thought of attempting to realize Gregory's dream; priority had to be given to western Christendom, still split by the turbulent reactions to Gregory's demands that all men should submit to papal authority. Like Gregory, Urban was a far-sighted man; but there the similarity ended. Urban's nature was meditative and patient; he sought his goals not through spiritual coercion but through persuasion. He was tall, handsome, courteous and gentle, though he could be stern and was, in his own way, relentless. He gave respect and did not demand devotion; and thus, in the way of human nature, he won at last the devotion of many and the respect of all.

The date of his birth is uncertain but it was about 1042. He came from the noble family de Lagery in Chatillon-sur-Marne, and was educated at St Bruno. After attaining, while still a very young man, the position of archdeacon in the cathedral of Reims, he joined the monastery at Cluny. By then it had become one of the greatest monasteries of the West, supporting and encouraging pilgrims to all the holy shrines and steadfastly opposing secular intrusions into religious life. Both of these influences stayed with Urban, and, in 1095, both were dramatically displayed.

The first was in March, at Piacenza in northern Italy. Just seven years after his election, this was the first great council that Urban had called. The delay was a measure of the difficulties he had experienced; his action was a measure of the strength he now felt – for at that council he and the assembled clergy formally excommunicated the anti-pope and all his followers. Quite apart from the rivalry and its disruption of Christendom, Guibert's election had been patronized by Henry IV of Germany, who had been Gregory's greatest opponent; and no Cluniac would tolerate such intervention for longer than necessary.

During the council of Piacenza, the foundation was laid for Urban's second great achievement – what he was to do would directly affect the lives of millions of people for at least two hundred years.

Envoys from the East came to the council – representatives of the Byzantine Emperor Alexius Comnenus. One of Urban's first deeds as pope had been to absolve the emperor from the excommunication imposed by Gregory; now all Christendom could benefit from the resulting good relationship between them. A decade earlier, in 1085, Alexius had started a war against the Seljuk Turks. It was going reasonably well, but slowly; more support was needed if the armies of the eastern Church were to succeed. And so the emperor's envoys spoke movingly of the dangers and difficulties faced by Christians in the East, and, in the name of Christian unity, appealed for aid from the West.

Urban and Alexius balanced each other in spiritual statesmanship. Each was aware of the other's ability, and both recognized the value of co-operation. And Urban especially could see one immediate practical advantage in providing military support: peace, or some degree of peace, could come to Europe. Instead of trying to curb the belligerent western knights, he could actively encourage them – and get rid of them. Instead of tearing the West apart they could fight – in the East – for the West; for the unity of Christendom; for the salvation of their souls; and with every chance of material gain as well.

It was a brilliant idea. After the Council of Piacenza, in the summer of 1095, he was due to go to France; and there, he decided, in his own native land, he would make his great call to the faithful.

From the beginning of August to the end of October he toured the south and west of France. From Valence he went to Le Puy, on to Avignon and St-Gilles, then north to Lyons and into Burgundy. While at Le Puy he announced that a second great council would be held at Clermont in the Massif Central, beginning in the middle of November. As the tour progressed, strange rumours began to circulate – people had seen the *aurora borealis*, showers of stars and even comets. As yet no one knew exactly what was to come at the council; but throughout France that summer the mood of expectation grew and grew.

In the last week of October Urban revisited Cluny, to see once more the aged Abbot Hugh – he had been abbot since 1049 – and to gather more information on the Holy Land from Cluniac pilgrims. Then, after praying at the tomb of Saint Maiolus, the most holy of the abbots of Cluny, he went at last to Clermont; and on 18 November the council commenced.

Pope Urban certainly had a sense of the theatrical. For the first nine days the three hundred clerics debated various issues and gave formal decisions. The anathema was pronounced against simony, clerical marriage, and the retention of ecclesiastical benefits by lay people. The Truce of God was renewed and extended; and a high point was reached when the king, Philip I, was excommunicated for his adulterous marriage to the Countess of Anjou. But it was not until the last day, Tuesday 28 November, that Urban made his move.

By then the crowds in Clermont were so immense that there was no single building that could accommodate them all. The council moved from the cathedral to the church of Notre-Dame-du-Port on the city's eastern edge. Outside the church was a large open space, the Champet; and there the crowd gathered.

In the crowd there was a monk named Robert. A few years later, at the instigation of his abbot, he wrote down what he had seen and heard on that autumn day in Clermont. He was writing from memory, so his report of Urban's speech is probably not absolutely accurate; but in all the main points it agrees closely with the three other contemporary accounts. The pope, he says, addressed the crowd 'with a persuasive eloquence'. Urban made it clear that he was speaking not only to the assembled people, not only to France, but to all the Christian nations of the West. He spoke of their special sanctity, and of the terrible threat to their brothers and sisters in the East. His description of Saracen behaviour was calculated to arouse the disgust and anger of even the most unprincipled: 'They overturn and desecrate our altars; they circumcize Christians and pour the blood of the circumcized on the altars or in the fonts. They will take a Christian, cut open his stomach and tie his intestine to a stake; then stabbing at him with a spear, they will make him run, until he pulls out his own entrails and falls dead to the ground.'

There was more in the same tone, and Urban emphasized that these were not isolated incidents. Throughout the East, from Jerusalem to Byzantium, such things were happening, and no one seemed to care. He put before his audience the example of Charlemagne, and begged them to remember the virtues of their ancestors. He quoted the words of Christ: 'Whoever should abandon in my name his house or his brothers, his father or his mother, his wife or his children or his lands, will receive them again a hundredfold and will come to eternal life.' He implored the people to forget their quarrels – the royal and holy city of Jerusalem cried out for deliverance. 'Take the road to the Holy

Sepulchre,' he cried, 'and tear the land from the hands of these abominable people!'

He had barely finished when the crowd, as one person, shouted 'God wills it! God wills it!'

From Robert's account it is apparent that even the pope was taken aback by the strength and unity of the response. But he was a true orator, and he used the reply immediately. How could so many have spoken as one, he said, unless the Holy Ghost was present in all their hearts? And he called on all who were willing to take the cross to come forward at once and do so. But his agile mind could foresee a problem in the wild popular enthusiasm, and he hurriedly pointed out that only able-bodied men should volunteer. The old and the weak should refrain; women should not go without their husbands or brothers; priests should seek permission from their bishops, and lay people should seek the blessing of their priest.

Despite these restrictions the reaction to his words was far greater than even he had anticipated. A stock of cloth crosses had been prepared, to be sewn onto the clothes of volunteers, and before sunset the whole stock had been used. It seemed the speech had come as a revelation; word of it blazed through France, and everywhere people came forward to fight.

The success of Urban's appeal is an outstanding example of the power of coincidences in world history. Everything was right: the mood of the people, the conditions in which they lived, their needs and beliefs. Urban was the catalyst. In the course of that distant autumn afternoon history was changed.

After the initial exuberance, however, it became apparent that considerable organization would be necessary. The departure of the army was set for 15 August 1096, after the harvest. But, inspired and effervescent, there were many who had no wish to wait that long. The knights and lords who took the cross had to wait, if they were to order their affairs; but to the poor, the landless, the ignorant, a date nine months away was as far away as death – or further, for death might intervene at any moment in their insecure existence; and with death the chance of pilgrimage, and hence of salvation, would be gone for ever. And so when a man wearing a hermit's cape began to travel through Europe, preaching the crusade from a donkey's back and calling for immediate action, he found many thousands of followers. Worn down by the toil of generations, unable to change their lives, innumerable peasants in Europe sensed that if liberty and plenty existed in this world, it would surely be in another land – and Jerusalem, everyone knew, was set in a land flowing with milk and honey. All that the people lacked was a leader, and in Peter the Hermit they found one.

One of his followers – one of the very, very few who could have been literate – wrote of Peter: 'Whatever he said or did, it seemed like something half-divine.' It is not surprising; whenever liberty is promised and the promise is believed, he who promises always attracts a sort of worship. Peter, indeed, was a monk. He also rode a donkey, like Christ – although his literate follower, Guibert de Nogent, commented that Peter looked very much like the donkey and smelt considerably worse. In spite of these things, or because of them, this short, ugly, smelly visionary man came almost like a Messiah to all those who wanted a new life. They followed more impatiently than children.

Peter must have had great faith; if not, he must have been extremely stupid. Once, years before, he had attempted the pilgrimage to Jerusalem, and had been so abused by the Turks that he had turned back long before reaching the holy city. He had known the difficulties of the journey; perhaps he had forgotten, or perhaps he imagined that fifteen thousand could travel more easily than one. Whatever his reasons – if he had any – he kept his donkey facing east, and at the end of May 1096, when others at home were welcoming the new summer, the first of Peter's hordes arrived at the borders of Byzantium.

By then the folly of the expedition was apparent. Coming through Germany Peter's preaching had attracted many more followers; and while he had tarried, a part of his rabble had pressed ahead. Reaching Belgrade and finding there was no food available, these unwelcome, unexpected visitors had started to pillage the countryside. That was only a foretaste of things to come; this first group was small enough to send on under escort to Constantinople. But through May and early June Peter and his train – which now numbered at least twenty thousand – advanced like locusts over Hungary. By the end of June they had killed four thousand Hungarians, and Belgrade (then a border town of the Byzantine empire) had been sacked and burnt. Further into the empire, at Nish in present-day Yugoslavia, there was a pitched battle in which a quarter of Peter's company was killed; and yet on arrival in Sofia, where they were met by representatives of Alexius, they were made welcome. Their outrageous behaviour was forgiven; they were supplied with all their needs; and with guides and guards they moved swiftly on to Constantinople.

The emperor's mercy was politic rather than humane; by imposing some organization on the chaotic, unruly pilgrims, he could protect his territories best. He advised Peter not to cross the Hellespont before the arrival of the crusaders proper; but any hope of order was long gone. The enormous troop was little better than an army of brigands.

'Those Christians behaved abominably, sacking and burning the palaces of the city, stealing the lead from the roofs of the churches and selling it to the Greeks, so that the emperor was angry, and ordered them to cross the Hellespont.'

The writer of that terse comment was another pilgrim, probably from Apulia in southern Italy. His name is unknown, but he left a little book called *Gesta Francorum* – the Deeds of the Franks – describing, usually at first hand, the events of the first crusade. He was a professional soldier, though not a mercenary, and he regarded the People's Crusade with contempt.

'After they had crossed they did not cease from their misdeeds, and they burned and laid waste both houses and churches ... Peter the Hermit could not control such a mixed company of people, who would not obey him or listen to what he said.'

The People's Crusade was burning itself out; there was too much energy and too little direction, too much hope and too little knowledge. After crossing the Hellespont the peasant army lost all cohesion: some followers encamped at a place known as Kivetos or Civetot, on the south coast of the Gulf of Nicomedia; others raided the district of Nicea, killing anyone they could, including native Christians; a few thousand went beyond Nicea and captured a castle. They failed to notice that its water supply was outside the walls, and the castle was besieged by Turks. After a week, the peasants 'were so terribly afflicted by thirst that they bled their horses and asses and drank the blood; others let down belts and clothes into a sewer and squeezed the liquid into their mouths; others passed water into one another's cupped hands and drank; others dug up damp earth and lay down on their backs, piling the earth upon their chests.' By the eighth day they could bear it no longer, and surrendered. Some apostasized and were taken into slavery; the rest were killed. Working backwards, the Turks then successfully ambushed and slaughtered the group near Nicea, and at last burst upon the camp at Kivetos. A few of the Europeans survived, rescued by a Byzantine fleet. Alexius disarmed them and sent them home. They must have been glad to go.

Yet though they were brutal, the peasants were no worse than the average among their contemporaries; and there is a certain innocence in their simple enthusiasm that arouses compassion. Even the anonymous author of the *Gesta*, usually contemptuous of them, commented: 'These men were the first to endure martyrdom for the name of our Lord Jesus.' But faith, it was clear, was not enough.

From the first split in Germany to the final disaster at Kivetos, the People's Crusade had taken a mere six months. The knights and lords of the first crusade worked more slowly, and with more perseverance. From the shores of Europe to the walls of Jerusalem, their whole journey took almost three years.

They did not depart all together or all at once, but in four separate major armies. Urban, without consulting Alexius, had decreed that the first rendezvous should be at Constantinople; and when news of this and of the great response to the pope's call reached Alexius, he realized suddenly that a movement far greater than he had wished or anticipated had been unleashed. He had wanted a few thousand mercenaries; but great armies were coming, not led by knights but by nobles. All would need to be fed and accommodated, and once in the Holy Land would doubtless expect his support. He decided he would give it; but on certain conditions. In the meantime he prepared for the Crusaders' arrival.

Peter the Hermit and his motley assembly had taken Alexius by surprise. It was fortunate that the crusaders proper kept more closely to Urban's programme; had they all arrived so early, not even Constantinople could have supported them. The first group after Peter was a small army led by Hugh le Maisné. They came from France to Bari in southern Italy, and across the Adriatic to Dyrrachium – the present-day Durrës in Albania – and thence via

Thessalonika. They presented no problem to Alexius; Hugh was a younger son of ancient lineage and few means, and was delighted to be honoured by the emperor of Byzantium. But the others were not so easy; with them, Alexius needed all his powers of statesmanship.

Each of the four great Frankish armies had amongst its leaders men of distinctive character. Commanding the first army was Godfrey de Bouillon, Duke of Lower Lorraine, apparently the very image of the ideal knight of Christendom. He was tall, well-built, blond and bearded, a pious, near-ascetic man with simple tastes and unfailingly gracious behaviour. Legend has ascribed to him the character, as well as the appearance, of medieval Christian perfection; historical truth shows him to be rather less than ideal.

Godfrey was accompanied by his brother, Baldwin. When they left Europe in 1096, Godfrey was about thirty-six years old, Baldwin a little younger. Tall though Godfrey was, Baldwin was still taller and unlike his brother in almost every respect. Baldwin was dark-haired, clean-shaven and had a very pale skin; he was a tough, hard, cold man who revelled in the splendour of noble life and yet could easily endure the hardships of war.

The second army came under Bohemond, the Norman prince of Taranto in Italy. With him was his nephew, Tancred. Norman power had been established in Italy in 1040; Bohemond and Tancred both had the adventurous spirit of their forefathers, and a passionate desire for kingdoms of their own, or at least principalities greater than Atranto. Only thirteen years before the call to the Crusade, Bohemond had been fighting against Alexius in Greece and Macedonia; now uncle and nephew set forth as the emperor's allies, in hope of worldly wealth.

The third army had two leaders, one spiritual and the other secular. Both were mature men, highly respected by all the others. The spiritual leader was Adhemar, Bishop of Le Puy, about fifty years old; the secular, Raymond, Count of Toulouse and St-Gilles, who was almost sixty. Adhemar was the papal legate to the Crusade, Urban's official representative. Raymond's leadership was assumed rather than authorized: he had been the first nobleman to take the cross, as Adhemar had been the first volunteer of all, on that November afternoon in Clermont.

Finally, at the head of the fourth army, were Robert of

Normandy, son of William the Conqueror; Robert of Flanders, a warrior-pilgrim by inheritance and inclination; and Stephen of Blois, the Conqueror's son-in-law. The two Roberts remain enigmatic; but the character of Stephen, though he did not play a leading role in the later battles, can be clearly seen. He was a sympathetic and amiable man; he was very rich, owning considerable estates in France, and he enjoyed looking after them. In fact he had no desire to go crusading at all; but his wife, the daughter of the Conqueror, told him to go and would brook no argument. And so he went.

The armies travelled entirely separately. Godfrey and Baldwin took the northern overland route through Hungary, in the path of Peter the Hermit. Legend held that Charlemagne had used the same road. Leaving Lorraine in August 1096, a few weeks after Peter's arrival in Constantinople, they arrived in the Byzantine capital on 23 December. Bohemond and Tancred took the same passage as Hugh le Maisné, across the Adriatic and through Thessalonika, departing from Italy in October 1096 and arriving in Constantinople on 9 April 1097. Adhemar and Raymond left France about the same time, and went south-east down the Dalmatian coast to Dyrrachium; thereafter they followed Bohemond, and arrived shortly after him on 21 April. The fourth army, with the two Roberts and Stephen, also left France in October 1096, and going south through Italy, took the sea-route. Stephen was still half-minded to turn back to his comfortable French estates, and while some of the army went ahead, he rested for the winter in Italy. Eventually, possibly with the thought of his wife in mind, he decided he had better move on; but he managed to delay the actual departure from Europe a little longer by going to Brindisi. He left, at last, early in April 1097 and was in Constantinople a month later.

Medieval chroniclers often speak of hundreds of thousands, even millions of soldiers, when establishing the size of armies. However, one of the most eminent of modern historians, Steven Runciman, has given probable estimates of the numbers involved in the First Crusade, and though they are much less than the extravagant claims we are accustomed to hear, they are still impressive: a total of four thousand three hundred knights and thirty thousand infantry, not including the women and hangers-on. It may be a small army by modern standards, but the mere feat of its organization was, and is, a stupendous achievement.

It was as well for Alexius that the separate armies arrived at intervals. One by one he passed them over the Hellespont, and managed to keep the numbers in his territory within manageable limits. But it was not a simple task: Godfrey, showing himself somewhat less than a perfect Christian, had fought the emperor's troops during Holy Week; Bohemond behaved with suspiciously scrupulous correctness; Raymond repeatedly refused to take an oath of allegiance to the emperor; and the Europeans in general, overawed by the splendid, sophisticated society in which they found themselves, were ill at ease. Their awkwardness made them seem coarse and boorish, which increased the Byzantines' disdain and in turn made the Crusaders behave more badly.

The oath of allegiance was the condition under which Alexius offered his support in the Holy Land. By it he intended to regain control over Byzantine territories lost to Islam; and if the crusading nobles formed their own kingdoms or principalities, they would hold them as vassals of the emperor. The proposal caused difficulties, for while everyone knew that in practice such an oath was virtually meaningless, it would in theory give Alexius considerable powers over the western lords. Most of them took the oath as a formality; Bohemond, however, with his ingratiating punctiliousness, tried to use it as a lever to enhance his own status in the Crusade; Raymond felt it clashed with his loyalties in the West and could only be persuaded to take a qualified oath; and Tancred slipped through Constantinople at night, and took no oath at all.

By the time Stephen of Blois arrived, everyone else had moved on. Stephen took the oath as soon as he arrived, and was thrilled with the reception that Alexius gave him. Emboldened by distance, he wrote to his domineering wife, comparing Alexius to William the Conqueror – to the emperor's advantage: 'Your father, my love, made many great gifts, but he was almost nothing compared to this man.'

The Crusaders pressed on. A few survivors of Peter's rag-bag army, including Peter himself, joined them. At the same time as Stephen arrived in Constantinople the main force came to the walls of Nicea, and immediately laid siege to the town. A major battle took place in which the Turks, over-confident from their easy victories against the People's Crusade, were soundly defeated. The anonymous author of the *Gesta*, speaking for all the anonymous thousands of Crusaders, left a typically dry description of their success: the Turks, he wrote, 'came in high spirits, exulting in their certainty of victory, bringing with them ropes with which to lead us bound in Khorasan. They came along gleefully and began to descend a little way from the top of the mountain, but as many as came down had their heads cut off by our men, who threw the heads of the slain into the city by means of a sling, in order to cause more terror among the Turkish garrison.'

Yet the siege was still a long affair; it lasted seven weeks and three days. Stephen of Blois had time to catch up, arriving on 3 June; his arrival meant that the entire army was now together. Ever since Constantinople Stephen had begun to enjoy his enforced Crusade, and when Nicea surrendered on 19 June, he was as elated as anyone. If things continued in the same way, he would be back home sooner than he had expected – writing to his wife, he said: 'In five weeks' time we shall be at Jerusalem; unless we are held up at Antioch.'

They were. And even before they got there, the going was hard. The Turks, nonplussed by the loss of Nicea but still determined, forced a second battle, this time at Dorylaeum. Their battle cries were unnerving – 'All at once they began to howl and gabble and shout, saying with loud voices in their own language some devilish word which I did not understand ... there were innumerable Turks, howling and shouting like demons.' But the Crusaders encouraged themselves with a prayer which could well stand as the motto of all the mixed motives that had brought them so far: 'Stand fast all together, trusting in Christ and in the victory of the Holy Cross. Today, please God, we will all gain much booty.'

Victory at Dorylaeum went, in the end, to the Franks with much booty'; but by this time they had learned respect for the godless Turks. 'What man,' wrote *Gesta's* author, 'however experienced and learned, would dare to write of the skill and prowess and courage of the Turks? Nobody can deny that, if only they had stood firm in the faith of Christ, you could not find stronger or braver or more skilful soldiers. Yet by God's grace they were beaten by our men.'

After Dorylaeum the Anatolian desert had to be crossed –

'A land which was deserted, waterless and uninhabitable, from which we barely emerged or escaped alive, for we suffered greatly from hunger and thirst, and found nothing at all to eat except prickly plants which we gathered and rubbed between our hands.' Most of the horses died, and their riders had to walk, or ride oxen; and as the beasts of burden died, goats, dogs and sheep were made to carry loads and pull carts. After the desert there were a few days of respite; then came the obstacle of the Anti-Taurus mountains. It was the last trial before Antioch, and one of the hardest – 'a damnable mountain, which was so high and steep that none of our men dared to overtake another on the mountain path. Horses fell over the precipice, and one would drag the next down.' For the knights, toiling in armour up the treacherous paths it was especially difficult; many tried to sell their heavy armour, and finding no buyers, threw their arms away. But at last they struggled over 'that accursed mountain' and came to the plain of Antioch. It was 20 October 1097; the journey from Constantinople, by a roundabout route of some eight hundred miles, had taken six months.

The People's Crusade had been borne along by little more than faith and enthusiasm; and though the First Crusade was organized more thoroughly, with greater patience and foresight, it seems highly probable that if the Crusaders had clearly understood the task they set themselves, the response to Urban's call might have been far smaller. The Turks had proved to be greater warriors than expected; the Crusaders had a rapidly growing awareness of the ordeals to be faced, ordeals which had been increasing since Nicea, when the home-loving Stephen of Blois had voiced the hope that they would not be 'held up at Antioch'.

Everyone knew of Antioch: it was there that St Peter had founded his first bishopric. To the Crusaders that alone made it indisputably Christian property by right. But as they gathered on the plains before its walls, the city dwarfed their imagination. It covered three square miles; and behind the city, yet within its walls, rose the slopes of Mount Silpius, crowned with the citadel a thousand feet above the plain. The walls were 'very high and astonishingly broad, with four hundred and fifty towers'. As they gazed at those walls and towers, the Crusaders foresaw a long siege.

Not all the Christian armies were present at first. Before the crossing of the Anti-Taurus mountains both Baldwin and Tancred had set off with their respective forces south towards Cilicia, where they had both tried to establish private kingdoms. Neither was successful, and Tancred had continued around the Mediterranean coast, aiming for Antioch. Baldwin had rejoined the main army south of the Anti-Taurus range, and then on his own account had continued east to Edessa. There he succeeded, quite rapidly, in winning the personal rule he sought. On 10 March 1098 he became Prince of Edessa; and there he remained, for nearly two years. He had left Europe as a younger son without hope of real power at home; yet within his first year in Edessa he was the greatest of the Frankish princes in the East.

Meanwhile the siege of Antioch was going badly. It was not really a proper siege, because even when Tancred and his men were reunited with the main army, they could not possibly surround the city, and it was far too strong to take by storm. The Turks were able to keep regular supply-lines open, and made repeated raids on the Christian forces. But worse than any Turkish attacks were the hardships of the weather and of famine: a seventh of the Crusaders died of hunger outside Antioch.

The ordeal dragged on and on, and men began to desert. After ten weeks of siege, in early January 1098, Peter the Hermit vanished, only to be apprehended by Tancred's men and brought back. But Antioch seemed impregnable, and the siege interminable. At last, in March, the Franks actually managed to blockade the city, by building fortresses at key points around the walls and distributing their diminishing forces through them. For a while morale was raised by the thought that Antioch could be starved into submission; but then rumours began, saying that a huge combined Turkish army was gathering in the north. Many more Crusaders deserted in panic. Among them was 'that coward Stephen of Blois, count of Chartres, who pretended to be very ill'. In calling Stephen a coward the anonymous author of *Gesta Francorum* echoed the general opinion. But Stephen's cowardice, if such it was, is understandable; he had never wanted to join the Crusade in the first place, and had no wish for martyrdom. It seemed to him madness to stay, and simple common sense to withdraw, and perhaps fight again. Unhappily for him, hardly anyone agreed with him, least of all his termagant wife. When he finally arrived home, after a slow and probably apprehensive journey, she was so overcome with shame and fury that the unfortunate man was forced to set out again. With the alternatives of skirmishing with the Saracens or facing a running battle with his wife, Stephen chose the Saracens. To make matters worse, had he waited half a day more at Antioch Stephen could have joined in its conquest; for the morning after he left the city was taken, neither by force nor by blockade, but by treachery.

'The Franks made a deal with one of the men who were responsible for the towers. He was a cuirass-maker called Firuz whom they bribed with a fortune in money and lands. He worked in the tower that stood over the river-bed, where the river flowed out of the city into the valley. The Franks sealed their pact with the cuirass-maker, God damn him: and made their way to the watergate.' So wrote Ibn al-Athir, one of the most important historians of Islam. *Gesta's* author, who was in the first group of infiltrators, continues:

'The gate was shut, and some of us did not know where it was, for it was still dark. But by fumbling with our hands and poling about we found it, and all made a rush at it, so that we broke it down and entered'.

'Another gang of them,' writes Ibn al-Athir, 'climbed the tower with ropes.

'Nearly sixty of our men went up and occupied the towers which Firuz was guarding ... then an amazing number began to climb, and then ran quickly to the other towers. Whomsoever they found there they put to death at once.

'At dawn, when more than five hundred of them were in the city and the defenders were worn out after the night watch, they sounded their trumpets ...

'At this moment the shrieks of countless people arose – all the people in the city were screaming at once.

'Panic seized the ruler of the city, and he fled in terror ... If he had stood firm for an hour, the Franks would have been wiped out. They entered the city by the gates and sacked it, slaughtering all the Moslems they found there ...

'All this happened on the third of June. All the streets on every side were full of corpses, so that no one could endure to be there because of the stench, nor could anyone walk along the narrow paths of the city except over the corpses of the dead.'

No one had imagined they would be held up so long: the siege of the city, with its bloody climax, had taken eight months and a day.

The city's conquest was attended by visions and portentous events. A meteorite fell on the Turks; a spear-head, claimed to be the Holy Lance which pierced the side of Christ, was found buried in a cathedral; and in the final battle against the attempted relief of the city by Turkish forces, the Christians were aided by angels. St George and others appeared, clad – like the Templars a few years later – in white, bearing white banners and riding white horses. And while few people attached much credence even then to the Lance, everyone present was utterly convinced of the reality of the angelic knights – just as the soldiers of Mons were convinced, over nine centuries later, that angels had also saved them.

The rest of the journey to Jerusalem took just over a year. The Crusaders rested for five months in Antioch, gathering their strength; there was still a long fight ahead. Between Antioch and Jerusalem many more battles were fought, and the Crusaders were often close to starving; once at least they had to resort to cannibalism, eating their dead enemies. A pilgrim named Richard, in the army of Robert of Flanders, described how Peter the Hermit encouraged this, saying, 'Are there not corpses of Turks in plenty? Cooked and salted they will be good to eat.' Apparently they were, and they tasted rather like bacon.

The walls of Jerusalem were reached on 7 June 1099. Once more siege tactics came into operation. Less than a third of the original fighting force was still available – about twelve thousand infantry and thirteen hundred knights. But all by then were hardened fighters, and before them lay their goal, the Holy City; they could not be held back for long.

After a mere five weeks, on Friday 15 July, the walls were breached – tradition says it was at midday, the hour of the Crucifixion. The Crusaders wallowed in a hideous orgy of destruction – 'There was such a massacre,' *Gesta Francorum* tells us, 'that our men were wading up to their ankles in enemy blood.' Ibn al-Athir records more than seventy thousand Moslem dead. The city was looted, the Dome of the Rock pillaged; and then, 'rejoicing and weeping from excess of gladness', the Crusaders went to pray at the Holy Sepulchre.

Urban never knew of the unmitigated success of his monstrous brain-child; he died a fortnight after Jerusalem's fall, too soon for news to reach him. Adhemar, the papal legate, was also dead, killed, like many others at Antioch, not by Turks but by typhoid. The military leaders of the four armies had all survived. Baldwin, secure in his new-found greatness, was Prince of Edessa; Bohemond, left in charge of Antioch after considerable intrigue, became its prince; Tancred became Prince of Galilee. Raymond returned to Constantinople and the two Roberts to Europe; and Godfrey de Bouillon, Duke of Lower Lorraine, the tall, blond, bearded ascetic, was elected by popular vote to be Advocate of the Holy Sepulchre.

He refused the title of King of Jerusalem; it would not be right, he said, to wear a royal crown in the city where Christ had worn thorns. It was from such piety that his popularity sprang; but piety does not necessarily make a ruler strong. Godfrey was an ineffective leader; and, from the point of view of the welfare of the state, it was probably as well that he died within a year of receiving his title. But he had been almost universally liked and respected, and many mourned him.

Directly he heard the news of his brother's death Baldwin set out from Edessa. Politically he was the most far-sighted of the Frankish princes, and he wasted little time grieving for Godfrey; he came 'a little saddened by the death of his brother, but most happy to succeed to his heritage'. He, once a powerless younger son, had no scruples about the title of king; on 11 November 1100 he was crowned Baldwin I, King of Jerusalem. In him the Latin kingdom in the Holy Land found its true architect. When he took the new throne most of Palestine was under Latin control, with the principalities of Antioch, Galilee and Edessa; but the control was at best precarious. For the rest of his life, with extraordinary energy and vigour, Baldwin extended and consolidated the power he inherited. Sidon, Arsuf, Caesarea, Azotus, Acre – all fell to him. The ports were invaluable to the Christians; locked in their artificial states, far from their homelands, sea-routes afforded the safest means of communication with Europe. They were essential; there were not enough Franks in the Holy Land to defend all the territories they had conquered, and more men were needed continually. Pilgrims, bringing money and physical strength, came – many of them, but never enough. If they served in Baldwin's army, it was usually only for a season, for the majority did not want to settle in the East; thus there was never a reliable standing army, either for emergencies or for daily defence. But the sea-routes were expensive, and most pilgrims came overland, although the roads were far more dangerous than in the days when Islam held the Holy City. Everywhere there were Moslems who, living outside the Latin lands, regarded the Franks as sworn enemies of their religion, and who raided and marauded the invaders whenever possible. And so, 'because of these insults, and hearing of this brigandage, a few knights, filled with compassion and touched with the wish for a more perfect life, formed the plan to consecrate themselves especially to the defence of travellers, to the safety of the roads and the protection of the Holy Sepulchre'.

The knights were all Franks, veterans of the First Crusade. Baldwin died on 2 April 1118; perhaps it was his death that prompted their decision, for they joined together in the same year. Nearly half their lives had been spent in the East; it had become their home. Baldwin's chaplain, the historian Fulcher of Chartres, marvelled at the transformation.

'Consider and reflect,' he said, 'how we, who were westerners, have become orientals: those who were Italian or French have become Galileans or Palestinians; those who lived in Reims or Chartres are now citizens of Tyre or of Antioch. We have forgotten our birthplaces ... some are married, perhaps to a Syrian, an Armenian or even a Saracen who has received the grace of baptism, with children and even grandchildren ... one man cultivates his vines, another his fields; those who in their homelands were poor have been enriched by God. Why should they return to the West when the East is so favourable?'

The Crusaders had come to love their adopted land; they wanted and needed other westerners if they were to stay, for both their new country and their religion needed protection. But for others to come, the roads had to be made safe. Since 1048 there had existed in Jerusalem the Hospital, where sick or destitute pilgrims could find succour; but it was no one's duty to protect travelling pilgrims, either coming to Jerusalem or leaving it. The knights who joined together after Baldwin's death took on that duty.

The first of them was Hugh de Payens, a native of

Champagne. He was forty-eight, and had been east of Constantinople for twenty-two years. The group that formed around him was tiny, with probably no more than seven others at first; and even the names of some of those seven are uncertain. There was Geoffrey of St-Omer, a Flemish knight; Payen de Montdidier; Archambaud de St-Agnan; André de Montbard; Geoffrey Bisol, or Bisot; and finally, two men whose Christian names only are recorded: Rossal, or Roland, and Gondemare. Tradition says there were nine in this original brotherhood, but tradition does not give the name of the ninth.

Eight or nine men to police an empire: it was not many. But every one was a knight and a leader; and while the men of the Hospital were monks pure and simple, this handful of knights determined both to give themselves to Christ, *and to remain fighting men.*

The new king was Baldwin II, cousin of the first, and he saw the value of the little group immediately. They had taken the triple vows of poverty, chastity and obedience; they had sworn to defend the kingdom; they must be helped. Very soon the knights were given accommodation, in a building near the Dome of the Rock, on the supposed site of the Temple of Solomon. Already they had given themselves a name: the Poor Fellow-Soldiers of Jesus Christ. Its cumbersome humility is a fair indication of their simplicity, and their genuine piety. Before long, however, the ponderous title was altered, and they became the Knights of the Temple of Solomon – or, more simply: the Knights Templar. From blood and rage and piety, the Order of the Templars was born.

PART TWO

The Temple in Europe, 1128–1153

CHAPTER 2

STRANGERS AND PILGRIMS

France, 1128

> 'Hear; for I will speak of excellent things.'
> Proverbs VIII, 6

SOME TIME DURING 1126 – probably in the late summer or early autumn – a little monastery in northern France received two important guests. The outward appearance of the men who rode up to the monastery gate, and the monastery itself, would not have seemed at all distinguished. The men were bearded, clad in ordinary, very old clothes; the monastery had been established only eleven years before, and was a simple building of wood, in ground cleared from the virgin forest. But because of its abbot it was already known throughout Christendom; and so were its visitors. They were André de Montbard and his companion Gondemare, two of the founder-members of the Knights Templar. They had journeyed from the Holy Land back to their native country with the sole purpose of visiting this tiny monastery and meeting its celebrated abbot, for he, in the past few years, had become the most influential spiritual leader in the Christian world – and he happened to be André de Montbard's nephew. His name was Bernard of Clairvaux.

Bernard was a slightly-built man, with a sparse brown beard and the tonsure that marked his vocation. He was thirty-six then, but his body appeared as frail as an old man's, for he had a chronic gastric disorder that weakened him terribly; yet through the physical frailty there shone a glow of spiritual strength that affected all who came near him. He is one of the most remarkable men in the history of the Temple, a man who would have been extraordinary in any age.

He was one of seven children of a noble family from Fontaines, near Dijon. His father, Tescelin Sorel, Seigneur of Fontaines, was renowned for his gentleness and generosity, and his mother, Aleth, for her exceptional piety. But their fame was local; Bernard's was to be international. Before his birth his mother dreamed that she bore a barking dog within her, and a monk interpreting the dream said her child would be a healer, and a watch-dog of the Church. Whether or not the story is apocryphal, Bernard fulfilled it. At the age of twenty-one he decided to join the monastery of Citeaux; when he went there the following year he had persuaded twenty-nine others to go with him, including four of his five brothers. The fifth, who was too young, joined them later.

Life at Citeaux was so strictly austere that the monastery had all but ceased to function, so many of its monks had left to join less severe orders. Bernard and his group were prepared to accept the austerity; their arrival saved the monastery from extinction, and began the renaissance from which the present world-wide Cistercian Order sprang. Citeaux was so strengthened by the new group that a daughter-house was established a year later; another the year after, and a third the year after that. And Bernard, at twenty-five, was abbot of the third.

His monastery began in the utmost poverty. The Count of Champagne, Hugh, offered land for its site; and out of all the wide acres of the county, Bernard chose a dismal, thickly-wooded valley called the Vale of Absinth. There was nothing there save the forest and a river – Bernard and his monks cleared the land and built their dwellings entirely by themselves, living off berries, roots and leaves.

At first there was only a single building – church, refectory, kitchen and dormitory were all under one roof. The floor was earth; the windows were mere holes a few inches wide; the monks slept on leaves and straw. Bernard's own cell was no more than a cupboard under the stairs to the dormitory.

It is a wonder that the project worked; but it did, and magnificently. Praying as they worked, the monks were led in everything by the little abbot, and he in turn was led by his total surrender to God. His faith was simple, direct and uncompromising; and these qualities, tempered with love and compassion, made Bernard a man whom everyone could understand and few could resist. He was a visionary, and eloquent. From his sermons, letters, advice, praise and admonition, his reputation as a teacher and mentor spread rapidly – somewhat to his dismay, for he had little regard for himself. But if grace was God-given, Bernard believed it should be used for God's work, and he never shunned work. He scarcely slept at all, and ate the barest minimum; anything which, in his eyes, was less than complete worship, was a waste of time.

Such was the force of his faith that before ten years' abbacy had passed he had become the conscience of Christendom, resolving quarrels, reproving kings, advising all who asked and inspiring all who heard.

In the Holy Land, meanwhile, the Christian armies fought on, and the knights of the Temple grew famous. In 1120 Count Fulk of Anjou had joined them as an associate member; as such he was not committed to remaining with the Order all his life, but even after he had ceased active membership he gave the Temple an annual tribute of thirty pounds of silver. Several other French lords followed his example, and gifts came in from the East as well, from the patriarch of Jerusalem, the Syrian Church and the canons of the Holy Sepulchre. But though there were probably other associate members, the records show no further full members until 1126. In that year a most distinguished man joined the eight (or nine): Hugh, Count of Champagne – the man who had given Bernard the land for his monastery.

Bernard wrote to the count in his characteristic style, demonstrating at once his humanity and his spiritual values: 'If, for God's work, you have changed yourself from count to knight and from rich to poor, I congratulate you on your just advancement, and I glorify God in you – however, I swear it tries me sorely to be deprived of your delightful presence by God's mysterious ways; but at least we might see you from time to time, if it is possible. How can we forget the old friendship you have shown to our house? And with what joy we would have cared for you, body, soul and spirit, had you come to live with us! But since it is not so, we pray constantly for the absent one whom we cannot have amongst us.'

Count Hugh's arrival must have stirred many old memories in the knights of the Temple. He was a newcomer from the homeland they had left thirty years before; he was lord of Hugh de Payen's native country; and his friend, the great Abbot Bernard, was a nephew of one of the other knights. All at once two different requirements made it important that the Order should be officially recognized and sanctioned by the pope. Firstly, in the previous year, 1125, King Baldwin of Jerusalem had granted the title of Master of the Temple to Hugh de Payens; the Temple's material possessions were growing, and some reorganization was needed. Secondly, Baldwin had the opportunity to attack Damascus, and he needed more men. If the infant Order could gain Bernard's approval, papal recognition would surely follow; and with that nothing would be impossible. Baldwin wrote a carefully-worded letter to Bernard, and two knights were chosen to deliver it. The first choice was obvious: André de Montbard, Bernard's maternal uncle; and with him, as travelling companion, went Gondemare.

It must have been a strange experience for André when he and Gondemare rode up to the door of Clairvaux: despite their uncle-nephew relationship, André and Bernard were probably about the same age. They had almost certainly not seen each other for ten years, and in that time Bernard had become the most respected religious leader in the Christian world. Their conversation, when they met again as men, is not recorded, but it was certainly a joyous occasion. One may easily imagine them eagerly exchanging news of the family, of Count Hugh and of the new Order of the Temple. Bernard, like everyone else in Europe, had heard something of the holy knights; now he was to learn at first-hand of their deeds and hopes. And then, coming to the point of his journey, André presented Baldwin's letter.

'The brothers Templar, whom God has raised up for the defence of our province and to whom he has accorded special protection, desire to receive apostolic approval and also their own Rule of life ... Since we know well the weight of your intercession with God and also with His Vicar and with the other princes of Europe, we give into your care this two-fold mission, whose success will be very welcome to us. Let the constitution of the Templars be such as is suitable for men who live in the clash and tumult of war, and yet of a kind which will be acceptable to the Christian princes, of whom they have been the valuable auxiliaries. So far as in you lies and if God pleases, strive to bring this matter to a speedy and successful issue.'

Perhaps Hugh de Payens had never realized it, but uniting the virtues of worship and of war was, in the medieval world, an imaginative stroke of the highest rank. Bernard recognized it instantly. His combined military-religious inheritance, from his noble father and pious mother, sensed it: through the Templars, the boundaries of Christendom could be extended and strengthened – the fighting spirit of young Europeans could be expressed, and blessed. He gave his immediate approval, and promised to do all he could to help.

Considering the difficulties of long-distance communication, events moved swiftly. An appeal was made to the pope, Honorius II; he consented in principle and called for a council to debate the matter. While Bernard busied himself in Europe, the good news was sent to Jerusalem and Hugh, the Master himself, set out by sea to Italy. Several of the brethren accompanied him – different records give different numbers, five, six or even seven. Count Hugh did not go; indeed, he never returned to Europe at all. Certainly one full member at least would have stayed to manage the Temple's affairs in the Master's absence.

It would have been late in 1127 when Hugh and his brother knights landed in Italy. They were given an audience with the pope, and then, at the turn of the year, they went north to France; for the council was to be held at Troyes, only a short distance north-west of Clairvaux. And Hugh's home town of Payens – or Payns, as it is now – was only a few miles further away, on the left bank of the Seine, before its confluence with the Aube. At the age of twenty-six he had left the little town; when he returned he was fifty-eight.

It was a grand and holy assembly that gathered in the cathedral at Troyes on St Hilary's day that year, 13 January 1128 – a cold day, and colder still in the cathedral, especially for those lesser people who had to sit on the floor.

One of the more fortunate was a man named John Michael. Indeed, he counted himself most fortunate: not only could he sit on a bench rather than the chilly floor but he had a writing-desk there – for Bernard had chosen him to be the assembly's official scribe. Delighted with the honour, he began his record.

'I, John Michael,' he wrote, 'have been counted worthy to write by divine grace the present document at the order of the council and of Bernard, the venerable Abbot of Clairvaux, to whom this work was fittingly entrusted.'

The 'work' was the Rule of the Temple, the knights' new guide of conduct. It is long and detailed, with seventy-two articles covering every aspect of daily life. Such a work required knowledge both of spiritual life and life in the East, and no one man could concoct it; Bernard was its editor rather than its author. And yet he had barely been able to attend the council. Shortly before his health had been so bad that, being summoned to Troyes, he had replied: 'Your reason for invading my peace is on account of matters that are either easy or difficult. If easy, my assistance is not necessary. If difficult, I am not in a state to attend to them – at least, I cannot do anything that is impossible to other men.' Even saints can be irritable when they are ill; but he was persuaded to come at last and John Michael, with his parchment and quill, scratched down the names of those present.

Among the vague, anonymous crowd that filled the cathedral, so numerous that 'it would be difficult to tell of them all', the scribe saw famous men. There was Cardinal Matthew of Albano, the papal legate, presiding over the solemn occasion. Beside him were the archbishops of Reims and of Sens, and seated in a semicircle around these three were ten bishops and seven abbots. Two of the abbots, Bernard of Clairvaux and Stephen Harding of Citeaux, would later be recognized as saints; and though Cardinal Matthew presided in name, everyone knew that Bernard was the real leader of the council. Most of the councillors knew him personally, and the few who did not still admired and respected him.

There were secular lords present as well: 'others who were half-literate, but whom we bring as witnesses of this thing because they love the truth' – and because, if the new Order was recognized it was such men as they who would give it material support. The most important layman was Count Thybaud of Champagne, another friend of Bernard's. From the beginning he was well-disposed towards the Templars, for he had come into his title when his uncle Count Hugh had joined the Order. Hugh de Payens and his companions must have felt rough and uncultured in the presence of so many eminent men, and nervous at the thought of the important decision they awaited.

The Knights Templar were unlike any other knights the council members had ever seen. Instead of the gaudy magnificence of furs and silks beloved of ordinary knights, these men were dressed in old clothes, drab and tattered. There were no jewels, no gold, no intricate patterns on their weapons or shields: all were painted black. Instead of long, elegant hairstyles and trim beards, their hair was cut rigorously short, and their beards grew thick and bushy.

Glancing curiously at the improbable appearance of their supplicants, the councillors listened while Cardinal Matthew formally opened proceedings; and then at the cardinal's invitation, Hugh de Payens stood up to speak.

He spoke of the days long gone, when the Crusaders swept through the Holy Land and won Jerusalem from Islam; he spoke of the dangers the pilgrims faced, and the perpetual threats to the Latin states. He explained how his little group had been formed, and how the kings of Jerusalem had welcomed it; he described the way of life of his brotherhood, with its peculiar blend of prayer and battle. He did not make light of the difficulties; and yet, he said, the worst of it was that he and his brothers were fighting alone, unaided by the Christians of the West. Sometimes he seemed to hear Satan whispering, saying, 'Why do you labour in vain? Why do you expend so much effort to no purpose? Those men whom you serve acknowledge you as partners in labour but are unwilling to share in brotherhood. When do the benefactions of the faithful come to the Knights of the Temple? When are prayers said for the Templars by the faithful throughout the whole world?'

Finally he repeated the three desperate needs of the brotherhood, if it was to continue its work: the blessing and recognition of the Church, a Rule to govern their daily life, and practical aid in the form of money and men.

He need not have worried; for, with an appropriately sober enthusiasm, it was all accepted. Even without his impassioned plea Bernard's recommendation alone would have been sufficient for everyone – or almost everyone. In that group of honest men there was one whom nobody liked: Jean, Bishop of Orléans. John Michael, the scribe, contemptuously entitled him not 'episcopus' – bishop – but 'praesul' – a public dancer: and a fellow bishop once described him in writing as 'a succubus and a sodomite'. His private morals were a public scandal, so much so that his common nickname was 'Flora'; and the sole reason for his presence was that he was the king's favourite. He had no liking for Bernard, nor Bernard for him; but the king would have been offended by his exclusion; and though Bernard feared no man's anger he was a practical man, and had no wish to jeopardize the Templars' future.

Nor had the councillors any wish to be seen as instruments of Satan. Hugh had touched them on the quick, and they duly bestowed their blessing on him and his brotherhood; then carefully and conscientiously, they worked out the Rule of the Temple.

The document they produced was of a tortuously detailed complexity, as comprehensive as they could make it. The seventy-two articles of its original Latin version covered every-thing the councillors could think of, from general religious admonitions to the knights' daily diet. Its religious aspects were similar to those of any monastery, and were generally Benedictine in tone: the brothers were to pray together at appointed times each day, or, if they were absent from the house, to recite various numbers of paternosters. They should eat meat only three times a week; meals were to be held in silence, with a reading from the Scriptures, and silence was to be observed at night. The brothers were enjoined to care for any sick or elderly members of the Order, and to have mass said for the souls of their dead; and after the death of a brother they were to feed a pauper for forty days. They were to avoid contact with excommunicated people, although they could accept alms and other gifts from such people, and though trapping was allowed they were forbidden to hunt any creature except the lion. Hunting was too close to the life of an ordinary knight; the councillors guessed, probably correctly, that the thrill and abandon of the chase could awaken old sinful pleasures in the soldiers of Christ. But if hunting was bad, women were infinitely wrose. The shudder of horror (and possibly delight) is almost audible in the words of the Rule: 'The company of women is a perilous thing, for through them the ancient demon denied us the right to live in Paradise; and therefore women may not be received as sisters into the Order ... and we believe it is dangerous for any religious man to look too much at women's faces. And so none of you should presume to kiss a woman, neither widow, nor maiden, nor mother, nor sister, nor aunt, nor any other woman; therefore the knights of Christ must always flee from women's kisses.'

This was not quite so purely misogynist as it appears, for the brothers were also forbidden to act as godparents; the councillors' fear was that a longing for normal family life would be stirred in the knights by the relationship. Partly for the same reason it was forbidden for children either to enter the Order or to be promised to the Order, which was common practice in other religious houses; the Templars, from the beginning, were determined only to accept mature men who came forward of their own wish and conviction.

Their clothing, like everything else in their lives, was ordered by their Rule. No longer would they wear old, undistinguished, secondhand clothes; instead, as befitted warriors who had given up 'the delectable riches of the century' for a new life in God, the brother knights should dress uniformly in white, as an emblem of chastity and purity. 'But their robes must have no superfluity or pride about them, and no brother shall wear any fur, other than a sheepskin ... and so that the eyes of the gossiping envious should have nothing to criticize, the robes should be neither too short nor too long; and if any brother, through pride or bravado, should covet a better or more beautiful robe, let him be given the vilest of all.'

Their bedding, too, was designated: a straw mattress, a sheet and two blankets; they were to sleep wearing their cotton underclothes, gathered with a belt, and a light was to burn in the dormitory all night. The brothers could not have any personal property; everything was held in common. A gift to any one brother was a gift to all; not even a personal letter could be read privately, but was to be read aloud before the Master.

Everything in the Rule was intended to bring about, or if necessary to enforce, a communal way of life – an abrogation of the individual in favour of the corporate Order. The councillors saw personal pride as one of the root causes of jealousy and strife, and sought to prevent its appearance anywhere within the Order – even that inverted pride of talking about the extent of one's corruption before one's conversion. No pennants on lances, no jewels on armour, no pointed shoes, no excessive talking or laughter; instead, poverty, chastity and humility were demanded. But even above those three qualities – and they were a life-long commitment – the Rule demanded obedience.

'Every brother who is professed in the holy service should, through fear of the flames of Hell, give total obedience to the Master; for nothing is dearer to Jesus Christ than obedience, and if anything be commanded by the Master or by one to whom he has given this power, it should be done without demur as if it were a command from God ... for you must give up your own free will.'

Such renunciation probably comes easily to saints; but however strong their conviction, the Templars were not saints, and the more mundane councillors foresaw times when not even the threat of eternal burning, or the thought of Christ as a kind of spiritual dictator, would prevent the breaking of the Rule. And so a system of practical punishments was included, ranging from small penances, through humiliating acts such as eating one's food off the floor, and continuing as far as expulsion from the Order with or without perpetual imprisonment. Offences were taken seriously within the Order, from its beginning to its terrible end; at least one knight, imprisoned many years later for disobedience in the London Temple, was starved to death.

Thus the Rule of the Temple was established – rigorous, austere and apparently uncompromising. But at the end of the document is one little sentence: 'All the commandments which are said and written above are at the discretion and judgement of the Master.' In other words, nothing about the Rule was final; any article could be changed or deleted, and new articles could be added. When the council of Troyes ended, the councillors may well have gone away feeling they had done a good job, and that seventy-two regulations were quite enough for anyone. The Templars, however, thought otherwise. Although the original Rule contained several thoroughly military articles, such as the number of horses a knight should have, it was essentially a guide to religious duties. It gave little thought to the organization, administration or hierarchy that would be necessary; the initiation of new brothers took up a single paragraph; and nothing at all was said about the appointment of a new Master after Hugh's death. The Rule as it stood received papal approval; and then the Templars promptly set about adding to it. By the time they were satisfied with it, one hundred and thirty-nine years later, they had added more than six hundred further articles.

Much of this colossal list was of trivial importance, articles devised – sometimes in haste – to meet passing circumstances. But every one of them affected every Templar, and many were of the greatest importance. First among these was the question of hierarchy, and the delineation of each man's duties and responsibilities; for, though the principle underlying the Order – the idea of a non-mercenary permanent army – was alien to feudalism and pointed towards its end, the Order was organized on lines typical of the feudal society from which it sprang.

At its head was the Master; he was never known, during the lifetime of the Order, as 'Grand' Master: instead he was called the 'Master of the Temple in Jerusalem'. He was a very powerful man, but not a dictator, for while every brother was responsible to him, he in turn was responsible to the Order as a whole. His position, directly comparable to that of an abbot, gave him certain powers and privileges, but both were limited. He could distribute or dispose of some of the Order's possessions; he could give gifts in the Order's name; he could choose his horses and armour; and he was the guardian of a locked chest of jewels belonging to the Order. However, in all important decisions – for example, in giving or alienating one of the Order's properties, in planning a campaign or a special attack, in altering, adding to or cancelling any part of the Rule, in receiving a new brother, declaring war or concluding peace – in all such decisions, he was obliged to consult a chapter of knights; and though his voice might be influential, he had only one vote. His personal household, as the Order grew, contained eleven men: two companion knights, his advisers; a chaplain, a clerk, a cook, a blacksmith, an interpreter, a bodyguard, two footmen and a *sergent*. For ordinary use he had four horses; on campaign he had a round tent, larger than the others; and with him went the battle standard of the Order. The standard was a black cross on a white ground; this, the *gonfalon baucent*, has become a source of characteristic confusion amongst historians writing of the early Temple. *Beauséant*, meaning roughly 'of comely appearance', *beauceant* and *beaucent*, meaning nothing at all, are words often given as the standard's name. In fact *baucent*, as it appears in the Rule, is a very common word in medieval romances, and has two meanings: piebald, like a horse, and even more simply, a standard. Thus the name was not originally exclusive to the Templars; any army could and many armies did refer to their standard as baucent. Nor was the black cross and white ground the original Templar gonfalon; it was authorized in 1145, and by then Hugh de Payens was dead. But the double meaning, the standard which was also piebald, was peculiar to the Templars from the start, for the banner under which Hugh and his companions rode in those early days *was* black and white: in heraldic terms it was argent with a chief of sable – pure white, topped with a wide black band.

A few other Templars had the right to ride immediately beside the piebald standard: the Seneschal, the Marshal, the Commander of the City of Jerusalem and those of Tripoli and Antioch, and finally the provincial Masters in England, Portugal, Aragon, Hungary and France. These were all the most important officers of the Order.

The Seneschal was second-in-command to the Master. As well as the standard, he had a tent and a seal identical to the Master's, and acted for the Master in his absence. The Marshal was not only third-in-command but also supreme military commander, controlling the allocation of arms and horses, deciding tactics and strategy, and leading charges against the enemy. The Commander of the City of Jerusalem was responsible for the health and well-being of the brothers; he had a permanent escort of ten knights, and in the course of time, as Templar military activity grew, two further duties devolved to him: the primary duty of the protection of pilgrims, and the safeguarding and transport of one of Christendom's holiest relics, a piece of wood believed to be a fragment of the True Cross. Finally, the Commanders of the provinces of Tripoli and Antioch, and the provincial Masters: in their territories, these men were of authority equal to that of the Master, and relinquished it only if the Master himself was with them.

One other man may be ranked with these greater officers: the Draper. His duties were not military, but he was very important to the Order, for it was he who was responsible for everything concerning the brothers' clothing and bedding. His importance can be gauged from his right – identical to a commander's right – to have four horses and three tents for his household, which consisted of two squires, a bodyguard, and, naturally, a group of tailors.

All the properties belonging to the Order, whether they were fortresses or farms, were called 'houses'. Amongst the lesser officers, the two important groups were the commanders of the houses, responsible to their provincial commander; and the commanders of the knights, who acted as lieutenants to the Marshal.

And then came the knights. Without them the Order could not have existed; and though many of their Masters were men of distinction, whose lives and characters can be seen clearly, it is appropriate that the picture of the knight on horseback, clad in chain-mail and a white tunic, should remain as the characteristic image of the Templars; for it was the brother knights, with their warcry of '*Baucent!*', who were the vanguard and rearguard of every Templar force. Yet even they were not the most numerous group within the Order – they were drawn from the nobility, and were the spearhead and defence of the Order and of the Holy Land, but they needed a large support system to work effectively. This support was provided by the brother sergents. They were members of the rich bourgeoisie; their uniform was black or brown, and their duties ranged from cooking to fighting. They usually outnumbered the knights by about nine to one, and if the knights were the backbone of the Order, the sergents were the body. A sergent had only one horse, whereas a knight had three; but certain privileges were open to a sergent to which a knight could not aspire. For example, the commander of the port of Acre was always a sergent; the sergents were the bodyguards of the greater officers; the standardbearer too was a sergent.

At first the Order had no clergy of its own; its members were ministered to by priests and chaplains of the Church of Rome, who received board and lodging, but nothing more, and wore their normal habits. Before long, however, all that would change; and changing, too, was the process of initiation and acceptance into the Order. The original Rule skipped lightly over what was to become a central problem: qualifications for entry could scarcely have been less complicated.

'If any secular knight, or other man, wishes to leave the mass of perdition and to abandon this century, do not deny him entry. For thus said Saint Paul: "Approve the spirit if it comes from

God." When he is before the brothers, place the Rule before him, and if he wishes to obey its commands studiously, and the Master and brothers are happy to receive him, assemble the brothers in chapter and let him show his wish and his will before all.'

The councillors at Troyes were experienced churchmen, and must have felt that this was enough. Not the Templars, though; as military men they were less used to the concept of spiritual authority. They wanted to be correct, and they needed more detail. So they devised a long ceremony, and recorded it; it was calculated to deter anyone who was not absolutely committed. It began with the postulant standing before the assembled chapter of knights, listening to a speech curiously reminiscent of a wedding:

'Good brother knights, you see well that most of you have agreed to make [this man] a brother; if there is any one of you who knows any reason why he should not, in law, become a brother, let him say it, for it is better that such a thing should be said before rather than after this man has come among us.'

If nothing was said, the postulant was taken into an adjoining room and questioned by the oldest members of the Order. They asked him formally if he wished to join the brotherhood, and if he replied that he did, they showed him 'the charitable commandments and the great hardness of the house'. He had to understand clearly and agree that on entering the Order, he would 'willingly undergo everything for God and would be the servant and slave of the house for ever, for all the days of his life'. Then he was questioned on his status: was he married or engaged to be married? Had he ever made a vow or a promise to another Order? Had he any debts he could not pay? (If so, it was an absolute bar to entry.) Was he healthy? Had he any hidden illness? Was he any man's serf?

If the elders were satisfied with his answers, they recommended the postulant to the chapter, to whom the postulant's answers were repeated. The Master, or the officer in charge, then asked the chapter if they wished, in the name of God, that the man should join, and they replied: 'In the name of God, let him do so.' Only then was the postulant brought in again. Kneeling, with his hands in an attitude of prayer, he made his formal request:

'Sire, I have come before God, before you and the brothers,

and I beg and require you in the name of God and of Our Lady to accord to me your company and the benefits of the house, as one who will henceforth always be its servant and slave.'

Then came the Master's exhortation to the postulant:

'Good brother, you are asking a great thing, for you see only the outer shell of our religion; you see that we have good horses, good harnesses, good food and drink and clothes, and it may seem to you that you will be at ease here. But you do not know the strong commandments which are within; for it is a difficult thing that you, who are lord of yourself, should make yourself the servant of another. You will hardly do anything that you wish: if you want to be in Europe, you may be sent beyond the seas; if you wish to be in Acre, you may be sent to Tripoli, or Antioch, or Armenia. If you wish to sleep, you may be awakened, and if you are wakeful you may be ordered to lie down. Good sweet brother, can you suffer well all these hardships?'

'Yes,' the postulant should answer, 'I will suffer all that is pleasing to God.'

'Good brother,' the Master would reply, 'in our company you must not seek lordship or riches, nor honour, nor bodily ease. You must seek three things: to renounce and reject the sins of this world; to do the service of Our Lord; and to be poor and penitent. Will you promise to God and Our Lady that henceforth, all the days of your life, you will obey the Master of the Temple and any commander placed above you? That you will live in chastity, without personal property? That you will uphold the good customs of our house? That you will help, in so far as you are able, to conquer the Holy Land of Jerusalem? That you will never leave this Order, neither through strength nor weakness, neither in worse times nor better?'

If the postulant was still determined to join, and if the chapter still agreed, the Master then pronounced the words of acceptance:

'In the name of God, of Our Lady, of Saint Peter and of our father the pope, we accord to you, to your father, your mother and all those of your lineage whom you wish, the benefits of the house, as they have been from its beginning and will be until its end. And you, you accord to us all the benefits which you have and will have; and we promise you bread, and water, and hardship, and work, and the poor robe of the house.'

CHAPTER 3

HUGH

Europe and the Holy Land, 1128–1136

'A dream comes through the multitude
of business ...'
Ecclesiastes V, 3

I N THE LATIN STATES of the Holy Land, 1127 had been a fairly
uneventful year. Baldwin II, King of Jerusalem, had only
made one minor campaign, and that not until August. His
relationship with the patriarch of Jerusalem, Gombard, was
good; between them the two men managed the Holy City easily,
and beyond the Christian frontiers, in Ascalon, Damascus, Homs,
Aleppo and Mosul, the Moslems were quiet. Baldwin had been
able to reduce his personal responsibilities, too: the year before,
he had renounced the regency of Antioch when Bohemond II
came of age. The new prince had arrived by sea from Italy in
October 1126; he was tall, handsome, blond, and eighteen years
old. He was also a cousin of the king of Sicily and a grandson of
the king of France, and as soon as he arrived in Antioch he had
married Baldwin's second daughter, Alice. Baldwin was delighted; apart from anything else, Alice was a wilful and
troublesome girl, and Antioch was three hundred miles from
Jerusalem.

With the unaccustomed peace of 1127 – peace in his home,
peace in the city, peace in the country – Baldwin was able to
meditate on the future. The knights of the Temple were
promising people, experienced, trustworthy and obedient. There

was no one else like them in the entire Holy Land. If they were more numerous, his cherished projects – the conquests of Damascus and Ascalon – might become possible. Bernard of Clairvaux had appeared well-disposed towards the knights; the time seemed right for the next move. Thus, when Hugh de Payens and his brethren left for Europe that autumn, they left from a background of comparative stability. But about the time that they were standing before the council of Troyes, things began to change in Jerusalem. The patriarch Gombard died, and was replaced by Stephen, abbot of a monastery in Chartres, and, as it happened, a relative of Baldwin's. But the relationship counted for little with Stephen, who had definite ideas about his position in Jerusalem. Where Gombard had been easy-going and amenable, Stephen was intransigent: he felt that the Holy City should be the suzerainty of the patriarch, not the king. The delicate balance of peace was upset, and before long a feud began to develop between the two men. Baldwin was determined to retain his power; he realized that there was good reason why a man of God should govern the city of God, but Jerusalem had become as much a temporal state as a spiritual one. He was a political man; and so while Stephen argued, Baldwin planned.

Kingship in Jerusalem was, strictly speaking, elective: the king was chosen by the knights and barons, a man first among equals rather than a monarch. The system had one great advantage – freely chosen, the king would be freely served. Potentially, however, it was a hazardous process; if the electors could not agree, the king would be weak and the kingdom at risk. Baldwin was convinced that a hereditary monarchy would be more politically stable. There were already precedents in Christian Jerusalem – Godfrey de Bouillon, its first ruler, had been elected, but Baldwin I was his brother, and Baldwin II was cousin to both.

Unfortunately he had one major handicap, if he wanted to found a dynasty: all his children were girls. Alice, the second, was married; the two youngest were still children; but Melissande, the eldest, was a beautiful young woman. Baldwin decided it was time she was given a husband, and in the wake of the Templars a second delegation was sent to France.

By then the council of Troyes was over. Having won spiritual approval, the little band of Templars had started the second stage of their work, and were looking for material help. It was not slow in coming.

In fact the first donation was made before the council ever began: late in 1127, Count Thybaud of Champagne presented the Order with a property at Barbonne-Fayel, fifty-five kilometres north-west of Troyes. It contained a farm which still exists, and is still called *La Commanderie*.

At least three further properties were given at the time of the council. Hugh de Payens set the example by donating his own land in Payens; the two councillors who followed suit gave land and buildings at Puisieux and Laon, respectively north-west and north-east of Paris.

The knights parted company then, travelling with the blessings of the pope and St Bernard to gather aid throughout France. Some notes remain of Hugh's tour; they are sketchy and have been the subject of occasional scholarly wrangling, but taking the most reliable, an outline of the journey can be traced.

It seems that he rode west to begin with, for in April and May 1128 he was a guest of one of his old comrades-in-arms, Fulk, the Count of Anjou, who had joined the Order as an associate member in 1120. Fulk's court, like many medieval courts, was mobile, and in those two months was gathered in Tours and Le Mans. From there Hugh went north towards the Channel, passing through lands belonging to King Henry I of England. In Normandy, Hugh and Henry met, and according to the Anglo-Saxon Chronicle, 'The king received him with great honour and gave him great treasures, consisting of gold and silver; and then he sent him to England and there he was received by all good men and they all gave him treasure – and in Scotland also – and sent by him to Jerusalem great property entirely in gold and silver ....'

There are no further details of Hugh's Channel crossing, or of his British tour, but he certainly found support in Britain – the Chronicle says that 'He summoned people out to Jerusalem, and there went with him and after him so large a number as never had done since the days of Pope Urban' – and it is probable that the original London Temple in Chancery Lane was founded then. The British tour was long; it seems to have occupied Hugh throughout June, July and August of 1128. In September he was back over the Channel, this time in Flanders, at the family home of his brother Templar, Geoffrey de St-Omer. Geoffrey had already given his own property there to the Order, including a large house in Ypres, and in the name of the Order had received from Count William of Flanders the *Relief des Flandres* – a considerable gift, being the legal dues payable to the Count on the exchange or sale of property in his county. Unfortunately the count had died shortly after making the gift, but his successor renewed it on 13 September, with Hugh as a signatory; and two days later, on 15 September, Geoffrey's father gave the Order the *Relief* of his land in St-Omer.

After that, Hugh's trail vanishes, but he was certainly still busy. Four other properties at least are believed to date from 1128: Coulommiers, east of Paris – another gift of Count Thybaud of Champagne; Ensigné and Challans, respectively east and north-west of La Rochelle; and Val-de-la-Haye, north-west of Rouen. Val-de-la-Haye is of particular interest, for it is reputed to have been donated by Henry I of England; and in its church was a stained-glass window depicting a Templar at prayer. This window was subsequently moved, firstly to St-Denis and then to Élancourt, twenty-three kilometres south-east of Paris, where it still exists.

Hugh appears next back at Troyes, a year after the council's meeting there. And in the months between his visit to Flanders and his return to Troyes, an event had taken place which must have given him great joy, both personally and in his role as Master of the Temple. Baldwin's second delegation, requesting a suitable son-in-law from the king of France, had accomplished its mission, and the recommended suitor was none other than Fulk of Anjou.

He was eminently suitable. He knew the Holy Land and the Templars already; he was a mature man, an experienced warrior, very rich and very well connected – his son was the son-in-law of Henry I. The fact that he was rather short, not particularly handsome, and red-headed seemed irrelevant; Baldwin accepted him on Melissande's behalf, and Fulk accepted Melissande.

He left France, apparently with Hugh, in the spring of 1129. By then the Templars had established a good strong foothold in Europe – not only in France, England and Scotland, but in Portugal as well, where Queen Theresa had given them the castle and benefits of Soure, on the River Mondego. That been one of the earliest gifts, on 19 March 1128. In just over a year, a basic network of houses and castles had been created over most of western Europe, and an unknown number of men had pledged themselves to the Order. Many went with Hugh and Fulk, direct to the Holy Land and the wars with the Saracens, but some had to stay to administer the new properties, to gather their crops and their tithes, to continue the promotion of the Order in Europe, and, above all, to send further support to Jerusalem. These were Christendom's quiet heroes, for if the Templars became Jerusalem's main defenders, the knights in turn relied mainly on their European members to supply them with their best horses, their best armour, their best men and much of their money. The servants of the Temple in Europe, men who never held a sword in a holy war and who never saw a Saracen in their lives, became the quartermasters of the Crusades, and should not be forgotten. Already, in 1129, they were legion, scattered across western Europe from Portugal to Scotland; and already the Order of the Temple was changing. From the tiny brotherhood of nine it had mushroomed into a miniature empire, its capital in Jerusalem, its colonies in Europe; and the seedling properties, sown broadcast in the old world, had to be united and organized. Over them all, one man was set up as Master of the Temple in France. It was Payen de Montdidier, one of the founder members of the Order. Suddenly, the organization proper was beginning.

After his prodigious successes at home, Hugh left Europe for the last time. De Montdidier remained in France, where he presumably spent the rest of his life in the infant administration, receiving gifts for the group, training new brothers in their duties, and at least once visiting England. He was there in 1139 or so, when he received a tribute of 40 *solidi* from William, Earl of Warenne, and land at Hook Norton in Oxfordshire from its lord, Robert d'Oilli. Hugh de Payens and Fulk, accompanied by their secular followers and the new brethren, sailed for Acre, arriving there in May 1129. They proceeded to Jerusalem, where, at the end of May, Fulk and Melissande were married. By general agreement Fulk was the best possible choice, a man under whom the crusading barons would willingly serve. Apparently the only person who disagreed was Melissande, who also appears to have been the only person not consulted; but Baldwin, pleased by the numbers of new Templars, his new son-in-law, and all the other reinforcements, cheerfully ignored his daughter and settled down with Fulk to discuss the conquest of Damascus.

The resulting battle, in October, was a sound defeat for the Franks. Any battle, even today, is to some extent a matter of chance; in the twelfth century, without a standing army shaped by drill and discipline, it was far more so. Indeed, the decision to give battle was almost as important as the battle itself; for once battle was joined, it was largely out of the commander's direct control, since it was almost impossible for him to rearrange his forces. Unless the attacking army had the advantage of surprise, the fight depended mostly on the morale, courage, skill and luck of the individual warriors; and Baldwin's presence was no surprise at all to the Damascenes. The most orderly part of the whole fiasco was the retreat back to Banyas. Perhaps Baldwin had hoped in the beginning that the Templars would provide the necessary core of discipline. There is no record of the Templars' performance at Damascus, though they were certainly there; but if Baldwin placed his hope in them, it was unrealistic to do so. For all the knowledge and ability of Hugh and the other founders of the Order, the concept of organized, united battle was still alien to the new brethren. They were trained as European knights; they were not a fighting team yet. Moreover, they were in a strange country, fighting on unfamiliar land, in a climate and conditions that were still new to them; the new Templars wished to cut Saracen throats as soon as possible, but Damascus was too soon.

But despite Damascus, the Templars impressed their compatriots in the Holy Land. One early historian, Jacques de Vitry, described how they were always ready and armed 'at whatever time of the day or night they may be called, either to fight or to accompany travellers; and when they pursue the enemy, they do not ask "How many are they?", but only, "Where are they?" '

Such reports found their way back to Europe, carried by pilgrims and secular knights. They caught the imagination of the people, adding tremendously to the success of the Templars who had remained in Europe; and in 1130 a conference took place in Toulouse with the express purpose of conferring gifts upon the Order of the Temple. The manuscript remains in Toulouse today, a long document with the names of forty-five donors listed on it. Their gifts ranged from small amounts of money – 'a penny now and sixpence when I die' – to gold, and the benefits of churches; and in between are some particularly practical and vivid donations: one man's best horse and armour, another's horse and armour 'when I die, if I have them, and if I do not, then twenty pieces of gold'; one woman's best coverlet, and from many women an annual gift of a shirt and a pair of breeches, and their best cloaks when they died.

Nor was this all the Templars received. The brethren in Europe had asked; the people in Europe gave and gave. In England there were properties in Buckinghamshire, Lincolnshire, Hertfordshire and Essex; in France, land and buildings in Dôle, Baudiment, Carlat, Soissons, Laon, Nice, Foix, Richereches and La Rochelle; in Germany, the castle of Supplingebourg; in Catalonia, the castles of Graneña and Barbera; and in Aragon and Navarre, the twin kingdoms, the Templars were named as inheritors of a third of the entire realm.

As well as this everywhere men flocked to join the Order. It is inconceivable today that a monastic Order could attract such a widespread, popular response; but the reasons for its attraction then are clear. Sometimes they were private and particular, as in the instance of the knight whose wife and three children had all died in quick succession, or the knight whose wife was stricken with leprosy after bearing him a daughter, and had to live apart from him for ever. Sometimes it was men who were bored with self-indulgence and the slavery to liberty, the constant need to think of the morrow; to those, as to many others then and now, personal free will was not the greatest freedom but the heaviest responsibility. But in general, the unique attraction of the Templars was their combination of war and worship, the two passions of the age. The Church's influence in society was far greater than it is today; only a very exceptional person could go against the teaching of the Church without feeling he was genuinely placing his soul at risk. Of course, many people did defy their priest or their bishop, and slipped into drunkenness, gambling, adultery; but when they did so, it was with a bad conscience. For there was a distinction between the Church's effect on a man's conscious mind and his unconscious heart, between his duty and his desires; the Church told people what they ought to do, and it was often very different from what they wanted to do. Secular knights found the dichotomy the most difficult to resolve; almost their entire way of life was suspect in the Church's eyes.

To all these people – men who had lost their land or their families, or who wished for a worthy aim in life, or who wanted to do their Christian duty without renouncing their martial skills – the Templars offered an ideal opportunity. There were many monastic Orders which offered salvation through payer, meditation or charitable acts; but at that time only the Templars promised eternal life through fighting.

And to those who could not fight – women, the old, the infirm, and all who for one reason or another could not leave their homes – salvation could come through the Temple as well. Time and again gifts were given 'for the remission of my sins', 'for the health of my soul', 'for the redemption of my soul and my brother's'; and even the dead could be included: 'I, and my brother, and our sisters, and their husbands, give this to the Poor Knights of the Temple of Solomon for the remission of all our sins and those of all our parents . . .' When the Templars admitted a new brother and claimed all his property, they drove a hard bargain; but the benefits were immense.

To some of those who otherwise were eligible, the life of a Templar may have seemed too austere, for in its discipline, its self-abnegation and its totally ordered nature, it was undeniably hard. But there were divisions for these people as well: they could either be associate brothers like Fulk of Anjou, or they could join for a specified period. Many of these brothers were family men who had no wish to leave their families for ever; others were men whose children were grown up. However many ties a man had with worldly life, a way could be found into part of the brotherhood. Hugh de Payens himself had been married – it is one of the few details known of his life. His wife had died, though it is not known when; perhaps it was her death that prompted him to go crusading. They had a son, who became the abbot of St Colomb at Sens, and was, like his father, a member of the middle-rank nobility. This nobility was the last, though not the least, of the reasons for the Order's popularity, for people could be just as snobbish then as now. Hugh's credibility was rooted almost as much in his social rank as in St Bernard's recommendation; and when an idea is socially acceptable, spiritually admirable and inwardly desirable, there is no limit to its possible success.

The stream became a torrent. It is said that Hugh took three hundred new brothers back to the Holy Land with him, and more men, more money, more horses and more armour followed him continually. The more the better, as far as Baldwin was concerned; the defence of the Holy Land would need all that Europe offered. In Jerusalem in 1130 the peace of 1127 was long forgotten; Stephen the patriarch refused to compromise, and in the north the Moslems had found a new leader. His name was Zengi; he had come to power quietly when he was made governor of Aleppo on 28 June 1128. But despite his quiet beginning, he was determined to drive the Frankish invaders from the Holy Land, and by 1130 had become master of northern Syria.

In February 1130 the young prince Bohemond II of Antioch, Baldwin's son-in-law through his second daughter Alice, was killed in battle at the age of twenty-two. He left a daughter but no son, and Alice, the self-willed, ambitious, argumentative Alice, instantly declared herself regent – and offered allegiance to Zengi. It was treason of every sort: betrayal of her religion, her culture, her society, and her king, who was also her father. There is a certain grandness in the gesture; but it could not succeed. Baldwin and Fulk went in haste to Antioch, where Alice barred the gates before them; but the barons of the city took the king's side, as every element of their natures made them bound to do. Alice was fortunate; her fate was in Baldwin's hands but she was his daughter, and she was not executed but banished.

So once again Baldwin was Regent of Antioch, a post he would gladly have avoided. However, he had one release that year: Stephen the patriarch died, some said of poison. It may well have been so; Stephen, at any rate, had no illusions about the king's feelings for him, for when Baldwin visited him to enquire about his health, Stephen answered: 'Sire, I am faring as you desire.'

In Europe too the Church was unhealthy. During the night of 13 February 1130 Pope Honorius died; and according to the Anglo-Saxon Chronicle 'there now grew up such heresy as there had never been before. May Christ establish counsel for his wretched people!' Schism in the Church, two claimants for the papal throne; for the sprawling Christian empire, in its efforts to be united, it was the worst thing that could have happened.

However, its immediate effects on eastern Christendom were muted; there were too many other, more pressing problems to cope with. For Baldwin in particular, Europe was a long way off and a long time ago; if Christians in the West could not keep their own house in order, it was not his business, provided they continued to send support. By then he was getting old – he was about sixty when he had been crowned in 1118 – and he was tired of strife. He wanted only to ensure peace in his realm after his death, and in the summer of 1131, when he felt he was dying, he gathered his nobles together and proposed that Fulk and Melissande be joint sovereigns. The lords and knights willingly accepted; then the new Patriarch, William – unlike Stephen, a peaceable man – made Baldwin a monk and a canon of the Holy Sepulchre. Almost immediately afterwards, the king died. It was Friday, 21 August 1131.

Fulk and Melissande were crowned together three weeks later, on 14 September. They had a son, named Baldwin after his grandfather, and were both very popular. In so far as these things may be, it seemed an ideal marriage. But Fulk's reign began with trouble: Alice. On her father's death she reasserted her position as Regent of Antioch, and this time the issue was less clear-cut. The lords of the northern Holy Land had taken no oath of allegiance to Fulk; no more had she. Moreover, there were many precedents in Europe for a queen to act as regent for her child, and the question of Jerusalem's automatic overlordship of Antioch was open. Fulk managed to quell the rebellion, with some difficulty; he claimed the regency, Alice retreated, and power was delegated to the Constable of Antioch. The solution was neither satisfactory nor final, and it revealed a weakness in Fulk's character: he lacked Baldwin's ruthlessness. He liked to be liked, and in the military Holy Land such a need was a weakness, especially in a king.

Like a reflection of the temporal trouble in the East, the papal schism in Europe was still unresolved. But in the West, an arbiter was found, one man whom all would respect and whose decision could be final: Bernard of Clairvaux was asked to judge. One man, one little, frail, extraordinary man: he held all Christendom, east and west, in his palm, and became the international apostle of unity.

Both the rival popes had some claims to the papacy. The first, who had taken the name of Innocent II, had been recommended to the cardinals by the dying Pope Honorius, and had been accepted by four; the second, who called himself Anacletus II, had only been accepted by two. It had been known for a long time before Honorius's death that Anacletus wanted to be pope; he was a rich, ambitious Roman, influential in parts of the city through his money and social standing. Many people accused him of cupidity, sacrilege, simony and perjury; the accusations were widespread, and the characteristics were obviously not appropriate for a pope. But those who feared Anacletus also feared his influence, and tried to forestall his election by a totally uncanonical subterfuge. The election of a new pope could not take place until three days after the old pope's death; Innocent's supporters elected him while Honorius was still alive. Anacletus was not in the least put off by this, however; he went ahead with his own election, and then, to make his point clear, decided to launch a civil war in Rome. He attacked the building in which Innocent was staying, but was beaten off; then with his supporters he took over the Basilica of St Peter by force. He stole the treasures of the Basilica, including the golden crucifix, and after repeating the operation in various other churches, was able to buy the support of most of the rest of Rome.

A few days later, in different parts of the city, both popes were consecrated. Neither would relinquish his position to the other, and Innocent, finding Rome unsafe, fled to France. There he met both Louis VI – Louis the Fat – and Henry of England, and appealed to them for help. After some time, Louis decided to support Innocent, and called Bernard from Clairvaux to assist. But none of them, neither the fat king, nor the aspiring pope, nor the future saint, could have foreseen the consequences of their action; for it opened the way towards the greatest single prize the Templars ever won.

In 1130, almost as soon as the schism had begun, Anacletus had written a letter to an unknown person claiming that 'the whole Eastern Church, the Churches of Jerusalem, Antioch and Constantinople are with us, visit us, and maintain friendly relations with us'; and in 1132, shortly after Bernard was called in, Innocent wrote to King Louis and said: 'We have received letters of obedience and submission from our brother, William, patriarch of Jerusalem.' In fact the Christians in the East were not very interested in the problem, and Fulk probably least of all: a terrible domestic crisis had forced itself upon him.

Melissande was about half his age, and beautiful; and despite Fulk's popularity with the nobles of Jerusalem, she cared little for him, short and plain and red-headed as he was. But there was one for whom she did care; her cousin, Hugh of Le Puiset, lord of Jaffa. He had grown up in Baldwin's court, and was about the same age as Melissande. Like Melissande, he had married; like Melissande, his spouse was considerably older; and after their marriages, the two young people continued to be as close to each other as ever before. Scandalous gossip spread; Fulk, who loved his wife dearly, grew jealous; the court was divided into two factions, those for the king and those for the count; and then Hugh was accused of treason. It was said he had plotted against the king's life. He did not appear on the day of his trial, and was judged guilty. Melissande and the Patriarch appealed for clemency from the king who, always seeking to please his wife, contented himself with exiling Hugh for three years. But just before Hugh was due to go into exile, he was stabbed and almost killed. Immediately and obviously, everyone suspected Fulk. The attacker was caught; he confessed that the attack was his own idea, and he was sentenced to death by dismemberment. He repeated his confession, clearing the king, after both his legs and both his arms had been cut off. However, Hugh died not long afterwards; and though it was not his fault, Melissande never forgave Fulk.

The records of the Templars are almost silent for those years, but some things may be deduced from what remains. Hugh de Payens, the Master of the Temple, had maintained a correspondence with Bernard of Clairvaux. One of Bernard's letters to him still exists. It was written about the same time as Bernard's involvement in the papal schism – the little monk must have been extremely busy. It is a long letter, addressed to Hugh de Payens, but intended to be open to everyone. It is known as *De Laude Novae Militae* – 'In praise of the new knighthood'.

'Once, twice and thrice, my dearest Hugh,' said St Bernard,

'you have asked me to write a note of encouragement for you and your brothers, and, since I am forbidden a lance, to wield my pen against hostile tyrants; and you have assured me that I would be very useful to you ... I have waited a certain time before replying to you, not because I do not appreciate your request, but so that I may be better able to satisfy it. Truly I have made you wait long enough.'

The letter more than justified the long wait: it was thirteen chapters of praise for the Templars, mixed with acid criticism of secular knights.

'A new knighthood has appeared in the land of the Incarnation, a knighthood which fights a double battle, against adversaries of flesh and blood and against the spirit of evil. I do not think it a marvellous thing that these knights resist physical enemies with physical force, because that, I know, is not rare. But they take up arms with forces of the spirit against vices and demons, and that I call not only marvellous, but worthy of all the praise given to men of God ... the knight who protects his soul with the armour of faith, as he covers his body with a coat of mail, is truly without fear and above reproach. Doubly armed, he fears neither men nor demons.'

Amongst all those who knew of the Templars, there were some who could not reconcile the ideas of a religious man and war; in canonical law and common feeling the two were incompatible. Killing, even in battle, was surely homicide; but Bernard, with diplomatic sophistry, distinguished between the homicide of a secular knight and what he termed the malicide of a holy knight, who had to kill men to kill evil. To see the enemy as the incarnation of evil – it was the forerunner of all military propaganda since, and it was as effective in Bernard's century as it has been in ours.

Bernard's contempt for ordinary knights knew no bounds; they were as frivolous and vain as the Templars were serious and praiseworthy.

'You encumber your horses with silk, and you cover your armour with indescribable frippery. You paint your lances, your shields and your saddles. The bits of your bridles and your stirrups are encrusted with gold and silver and precious stones. With pomp you decorate yourselves for death, and you ride only to ruin ... Are these trinkets the trappings of a knight or the tawdry ornaments of women? Or perhaps you think that your enemy's weapons will be turned aside by gold? That gems will be spared? That silk cannot be pierced? There are three essential things for a knight in battle: he must be alert to his defence, quick to his saddle and prompt in his attack. But *you* – you, on the contrary, like women, have your hair so long you cannot see; your clothes are so long they brush your feet; you hide your delicate, tender hands in enormous sleeves – and then, dressed up like this, you go and fight for the most vain and ridiculous things!'

Vanity succeeds only when it is taken seriously. Bernard's view of secular knights was as clear, as innocent and as embarrassing as that of the child who saw through the Emperor's 'new clothes'. The contrast with the Templars could hardly have been more vivid; the last barriers were swept aside, and everywhere people clamoured to help the Holy Knights.

The Latin states of the East were still in turmoil; every man was needed. Fulk travelled almost constantly, quelling rebellion, defending cities, occasionally capturing a new piece of territory. Out of the early years of his reign, only one – 1134 – was even comparatively peaceful. But in 1136, one perennial problem was finally solved: the business of Alice and Antioch; and the solution came through a delightful piece of intrigue.

Fulk, of course, had been forced to take over the regency of Antioch after Alice's second rebellion. He had delegated authority to another man, and this representative had died. His successor was a particularly unpleasant man, Bishop Radulph of Mamistra who, like Alice, wanted as much personal power as possible. He opened negotiations with the exiled Alice; Alice asked Melissande to intervene with Fulk on her behalf; and Fulk, still eager to please his wife, permitted Alice to return to Antioch. Once there she rapidly disposed of Radulph and then, to consolidate the power which was so nearly hers, decided to marry her daughter Constance to the son of the Byzantine emperor. The Frankish knights and barons were horrified at the thought, and sent a desperate message to Fulk, telling him to find Constance another husband as fast as possible. Suddenly Fulk saw a way to rid himself of the termagant Alice for ever, and with all haste summoned a French nobleman, Raymond of Poitiers, to the Holy Land. He was working against time, for Constantinople was much closer than Europe, and the Byzantine emperor was interested in Alice's suggestion. But Raymond, travelling quickly, arrived in Antioch in April 1136 and, on arrival, following Fulk's instructions, sent word to Alice that he had come to seek her hand in marriage. It was perfectly plausible: he was a nobleman, and thirty-seven years old; Alice was about twenty-nine; and little Constance was only nine. Alice was thrilled – she remained in her palace and prepared herself to receive the distinguished suitor. And here one must feel some compassion for her, for she was utterly duped. While she was making herself ready her daughter was removed from the palace, taken to Raymond, and the man and the little girl were married.

There was absolutely nothing that Alice could do. Raymond, as Constance's husband, had legal precedence over Alice; as a nobleman and a warrior, he immediately gained the support of the barons of the city; and he was loyal to Fulk. Powerless and enraged, Alice left Antioch; and she never returned.

Against this background, of papal schism in Europe, of civil strife in the Holy Land, of war, intrigue, praise and deception, the Knights Templar continued their work, and watched their Order grow. And then, on 24 May 1136, Hugh de Payens died. He was about sixty-six, for those days quite an old man; and in his long life, he had achieved something very rare: he had had a dream, and he had lived to see it fulfilled. He was an unusual, a fortunate, and – we may hope – a happy man.

CHAPTER 4

OMNE DATUM OPTIMU

France and the Holy Land, 1139–115᾽

'Behold, I set before you this day
a blessing and a curse.'
Deuteronomy XI, 26

THE SELF-STYLED POPE, Anacletus II, was excommunicated in 1135 at the Council of Pisa, by Innocent II and fifty-six bishops from France and Italy, including St Bernard. Bernard had given Innocent his complete support, and though it had taken him more than two years, he seemed to have resolved the schism. He had done it almost single-handed, and during those two years he had grown more influential every day; the Council of Pisa was the zenith of his career. He was a constant friend of the Templars, and was still active on their behalf. As his open letter to Hugh circulated through Europe, the shower of gifts continued: the Order found particular favour in Spain, Portugal, Languedoc and England, where the newly-crowned King Stephen gave his land at Cowley, near Oxford, as the first in a long series of gifts. And during its eight-day course, between 30 May and 6 June, the Pisan council achieved its second objective: with Bernard's guidance and Innocent's approval, the Rule of the Temple was amended and extended, in Innocent's first official involvement with the Order.

It was inevitable that, before long, Innocent should take the Templars to his heart; Bernard's enthusiastic help to both would have been sufficient bond. But from the turmoil of his election, Innocent had learnt one thing: the Church needed temporal muscles to support its spiritual body. Another split like the one just past could be disastrous; there might not be another saint to stitch the wound together. Besides that, there were Christians east and west complaining that Holy Mother Church did not do enough to protect her children in the East. With the deaths of Hugh de Payens and the old king of Jerusalem, Baldwin II, the first generation of Crusaders had come to an end; the first fervour had gone, and Fulk's difficulties demanded organized aid.

The new Master of the Temple was another Frenchman, Robert de Craon, also known as Robert the Burgundian. It may be that he was the mysterious, unnamed ninth founder-member, or else that he joined the group very soon after its formation, for a charter dated 1125 from Nazareth is witnessed by 'Robert the Templar'; but it is impossible to be certain.

In its formative years, the Temple could not help but reflect the characters of its Masters, and under Robert it changed dramatically. Hugh left an Order with international fame and considerable wealth; under Robert it grew to become a body with political power throughout the Old World. Like Hugh, Robert was a nobleman, but he was of a greater lineage – there were kings of France among his ancestors, and tradition names Anselm, Archbishop of Canterbury, as his brother-in-law.

Hugh had had a moral conviction and serenity almost as shattering as Bernard's; Robert, by contrast, although a pious man, was a diplomat, a man who knew men and who manipulated them for the ends he believed to be right. He had two elder brothers, and for the younger son of a nobleman the only way then to maintain a life concomitant with his social rank was to make a good marriage. Robert had tried that, with some success – he had a son, named Anselm after the famous archbishop, who eventually became bishop of London. And when Robert's wife died, the existence of the Templars offered a new alternative.

He was probably about thirty-seven when he went to the Holy Land, for Pope Urban had preached the First Crusade in Robert's home district, and Robert, as a boy, had heard him. The nobleman and the military seemed made for each other: soon after his arrival in the Holy Land, Robert was Seneschal of the Temple, second-in-command to Hugh, and in that capacity he returned to Europe for the year 1132, mustering support and accepting gifts. Then followed another five years in the Holy Land; and when he came back to the West again, in 1138, he was

Master of the Temple. The anti-pope Anacletus died on 25 January 1138; 'the broken branch, the rotten limb, has been cut off,' wrote St Bernard. 'He, that wicked one I mean who made Israel to sin, has been swallowed up by death and has gone down into the belly of hell.' Anacletus had never accepted Innocent as pope, and had held sway over Rome until his death. But at last Innocent was able to enter the city, and there he and Robert met.

The Templars owned a house in Rome where Robert would have stayed; however, the meetings of pope and Master probably took place in the Lateran. Robert had already shown his ability as an administrator; in his talks with Innocent, he displayed his skill in persuasion. As Innocent knew well, Robert's brotherhood bore a special duty; Robert argued that in order to fulfill this duty, the Templars needed special rights. The Christian East was not self-sufficient; almost everything it needed had to be imported from the West. Pilgrimage had become a profitable business in the ports of Italy; the stream of worshippers was unending, and while the Templars did their utmost, they were stretched to their limits, constrained by lack of money, the duty of paying tithes and their subjection to the king and patriarch of Jerusalem. When king and patriarch disagreed, the Templars' loyalty was torn; and despite the bounteous gifts they had received throughout Christendom, tithes and local taxes on their scattered properties made many more of a burden than a blessing. The Order's responsibilities had grown immeasurably since they first vowed to keep the roads to Jerusalem safe for pilgrims – there were more roads, and many more pilgrims; there was the administration of all their far-flung houses and castles and farms; and above all there was the defence of the Holy Kingdom. And while their first and last loyalty was to Christians and to the Church, the brethren needed greater freedom of action.

The exact dates of these meetings are not known, but Innocent certainly did not take long to agree. He recognized his opportunity, and before the year was finished he had decided his grand strategy. A ready-made and utterly loyal army was offered to him; in one infallible move, by demonstrating beyond doubt the Church's willingness to succour its children, he could silence its critics and secure its temporal defence.

The move that he made had no precedent, and remains

without parallel in the entire history of the Church. It was
announced on 29 March 1139.

'Bishop Innocent, to our dear son Robert, Master of the holy
knights of the Temple which is in Jerusalem, and to his
successors and brothers both present and future for ever: *Omne
datum optimum ...*'

Every best gift – the high-sounding phrase could have been
nothing but rhetoric; but Innocent meant exactly what he said.
Firstly he gave the Templars the right to appoint their own
chaplains, who would be responsible to the Master and not to any
local bishop; and he gave them the right to build their own
churches. These two clauses alone might have seemed sufficiently
revolutionary, for hitherto the Temple had been dependent on
bishops to provide both chaplains and churches; yet there was
more to follow. The defenders of the Church should be
supported by the Church; therefore, every clergyman in
Christendom was expressly forbidden to claim tithes from the
Templars – but the Templars could claim tithes from others. And
then, in a last commanding flourish, Innocent freed the Templars
from all authority, except his own. Their temporal administrators
were to be responsible only to the Order, and not to any prince or
king or emperor; nor could any bishop, archbishop or patriarch
claim their spiritual allegiance. That was the prerogative of the
pope alone. No one was permitted to extract an oath or demand
homage from a Templar; nor could any person, lay or eccles-
iastic, presume to change the statutes of the Templars' rule. Their
law was their own, to be altered only by the Master and a general
chapter of knights.

Twenty-one years after its foundation, the Order of the
Temple had come of age. Innocent gave the Templars the keys to
the Church, the keys to the kingdom; and had it been possible, he
might have given them the keys to Heaven itself.

Total earthly freedom, total independence – every best gift.
St Bernard, as the Templars' former spiritual patron, must have
rejoiced at the news. Indeed, it is possible that he had some direct
influence on Innocent's decision to give the Templars their
unique world-status, for he was in Rome during the summer of
1138, and stayed at the Templars' house there. There is a story
that when he departed, he left behind him – perhaps by accident,
perhaps on purpose – one of his linen tunics, and that a sick

Templar was cured simply by touching the garment. Whether or not the story is true, he was certainly in Rome then, and undoubtedly would have met Innocent again. They lacked only the fat king of France, Louis VI, to make up the original triumvirate that had cleared the ground for the Templars' freedom; but by then Louis the Fat was a year dead.

His successor was Louis VII, known as 'the Young' – the new king was only sixteen when he came to the throne. This Louis was a youth of exceptional piety, but he had a certain worldliness. On hearing of Innocent's 'gift' to the Templars, he passed a decree limiting any other gifts: his subjects could donate whatsoever they wished to the Order with the exceptions of castles and towns, and with the proviso that their donations did not infringe the rights of the Crown in any way. This was quick and astute action, fairly rare for Louis the Young – presumably he acted on his ministers' advice.

His reaction was typical of those who had suddenly lost authority over the Templars. The question of freedom from tithes grew into a running battle that stretched over many decades, east and west; and in the East in particular, the historian William, Archbishop of Tyre, commented that 'It was the Patriarch of Jerusalem who upheld both the institution of the Order and its first benefits.' It seemed extraordinary, even scandalous, that he should then be deprived of any rights over the Order.

Robert does not appear to have let such criticism worry him unduly. In the eyes of common people, the Templars' new-found liberty made them even more attractive, if that were possible, and Robert exploited the mood by arranging for a translation of the Rule from its nearly incomprehensible Latin to ordinary French.

And here something happened which has surprised and mystified people ever since. The translation of such a Rule, one might well suppose, would be a straightforward affair, and mistakes would not be likely to occur; but there are two differences between the Latin and the French Rules – differences of fundamental importance to the Order's life. The first and lesser one concerns the term of probation for a new brother. In the original Rule, a new brother was deemed a novice for a period decided 'by the reflection and prudence of the Master, according to the honesty of the life of he who wishes to enter' – a simple condition, common to any religious order. Yet in the French Rule this clause is entirely deleted. It would be tempting to ascribe this to a copyist's mistake, if it were not for the next, and far greater, change.

The most powerful spiritual weapon of the pope was excommunication, by which a living man was prevented from entering a church, from participating in Mass and even, in theory, from having any contact with ordinary Christians. Of course, to many of those who were excommunicated, the first two prohibitions made little difference, and the third was flouted; but the interdict extended beyond death, and cut a man's soul off from God. To believers, excommunication was a fearful threat and a terrible punishment; and a person who had contact with an excommunicate became excommunicate himself. Because of this, the Latin Rule of the Temple prevented contact between Templars and excommunicates, saying, 'In those places where you know non-excommunicated knights are gathered, there we say you must go.' But the French Rule turned this logical statute upsidedown, and having done so, strengthened the inversion: 'In those places where you know *excommunicated* knights to be assembled, there we *command* you to go; *if there are any of them who wish to join the Order, you should not consider the temporal profit as much as the eternal safety of their souls.*'

Even that, it might be said, was merely another error on the part of an inattentive copyist; and if it was a simple case of the omission of a word, even such a crucial word as 'non-' in 'non-excommunicated', the argument could be plausible. But it loses weight quickly: the order to go amongst excommunicates is worded differently and is more strongly expressed than the previous ban; and in the next clause it goes yet further. The Latin text states that the brothers should 'take great care and prevent any brother from being with a man who is publicly excom-municate'; the French changes this completely, and says, 'In no other way should the brothers of the Temple have contact with a manifestly excommunicate man.'

It is this last alteration, with its tone of limited but specific encouragement, that gives the feeling of authenticity – the feeling that the Rule was changed deliberately.

Of course there was nothing to prevent the Rule being changed, even to such a radical extent; but in all other respects the French Rule corresponds with the Latin, and the question remains: why did Robert decide to make this particular, far-reaching change, and why did the brethren agree? Had St Bernard or Innocent known of the change, they could not have approved; but by then the Rule had become secret, to be read only to a new member on his entry to the Order. The best answer – the simplest, and one characteristic of Robert – lies in the independence he had won for his Order. By extending their brotherhood to those the Church rejected, the Templars underlined their independence of the ordinary clergy, and opened their ranks to a multitude of potential recruits, some of whom might be very rich. Another possible answer is that the change was due to an exaggerated sense of Christian charity on the part of the Templars – that they wished to save the souls of those Christians otherwise barred from Christ.

But somehow neither of those explanations, nor any other that has been suggested, is completely satisfactory. The brethren themselves did not always adhere to their new Rule; they seemed to remember it when it suited them, and forget it when it did not. The question is open. But whatever the answer, the Templars soon made use of the change: in 1143 Geoffrey de Mandeville, Count of Essex, died excommunicate – and was buried by the Templars in consecrated ground, and clad in the Order's white robe.

Innocent died that same year, to be replaced by Celestine II, who favoured the Templars no less than he. For all Bernard's work, the schism was not yet completely resolved; Anacletus had been replaced by the anti-pope Victor. Victor was not a shadow of the man Anacletus had been, though, and within a few months he submitted personally to Bernard. Nevertheless the continuing state of tension persuaded Celestine to issue a Bull entitled *Milites Templi*, an almost exact repeat of Innocent's extraordinary *Omne Datum Optimum*. Celestine did not have time to do much else – he died the next year, and was replaced by Lucius II, who issued another repeat, also called *Milites Templi*, and then died the year after.

Following the pattern, the next pope, Eugenius III, issued a fourth repetition, this time called *Militia Dei*. But he, at any rate, was of a hardier constitution, which was just as well; a weak man might have been killed by the shock of his inheritance. For on

Christmas Eve 1144, Edessa, the Christian stronghold on the north-eastern frontier of the Holy Land, had been recaptured by the Moslems.

It was the first important loss of the Christians in the East, and to Christendom as a whole the defeat was a tremendous psychological blow. Since the first Baldwin had taken it in 1098 on his way to the throne of Jerusalem, Edessa had remained secure, a delusive symbol of a Frankish eternity, distant and invincible. The loss of the city blasted western Christians out of their complacency. They looked to their souls and disliked what they saw; and for guidance they turned to their incarnate conscience, Bernard of Clairvaux.

The answer was obvious: a new Crusade. Louis, the young king, had already begun to work out a plan; Eugenius, the pope, had already approved it in principle. But the people of France hesitated until they heard their saint. At Vézelay, midway between Dijon and Paris, on Easter Sunday, 31 March 1146, he spoke.

There had not been a scene like it since the days of Pope Urban. Like Urban, Bernard had to preach from a platform out-of-doors; no building could contain the throng. And as with Urban, the response was staggering: so many volunteers came forward, the material for crosses ran out and Bernard had to tear up his own outer clothes to make more. Then afterwards, like Peter the Hermit, 'The abbot, who bore a hardy spirit in his frail and almost lifeless body, hastened about, preaching everywhere, and soon the number of those bearing crosses had increased immeasurably.'

The comment is from an eye-witness of the ceremony at Vézelay, a monk named Odo de Deuil, King Louis' new chaplain. Odo was, in many ways, a remarkable man. Contemporary descriptions of him do not seem especially helpful at first, listing conventional virtues that were admired at the time – liberality, dignity, courtesy, seriousness, intellectuality, clemency. However, a look at his life shows that this description, rather than being a simple stereotype of an honoured man, was probably accurate. The abbot of his monastery was Suger, whose status can be measured by St Bernard's proposal, and Louis' acceptance of him, as Regent of France during the king's absence on the Crusade. And from there, Odo can be measured; for Suger trained him to succeed to the abbacy, and proposed him to Louis as the King's private chaplain for the crusade. Louis soon referred to Odo publicly as his friend and mentor. But the clearest illustration of Odo's character is the work that he left – a description of the Second Crusade, from its hopeful beginning to its tragic end.

Before the Crusade began, Odo read accounts of the first expedition, in order to assess the difficulties and dangers that lay before Crusaders; and then, when the whole disastrous operation was over, he wrote his own account – 'for never will there fail to be pilgrims to the Holy Sepulchre; and they will, I hope, be the more cautious because of our experiences'. Hardly anyone else wrote about the Second Crusade at all, preferring to forget it all as soon as possible; and Odo was alone in writing a narrative which is vivid, entertaining, artistic and informative.

At Vézélay in 1146, it had been agreed that the new Crusaders should leave France one year later. They gathered punctually in Paris at the abode of St Denis; Louis, Bernard and Pope Eugenius were present, accompanied by three hundred Knights Templar, 'all clothed in their white robes'. It was a ceremony pregnant with symbolism: Suger, as abbot, presented Louis with the *Oriflamme*, a scarlet banner decorated with golden flames and mounted on a golden lance – the battle-banner of St Denis; and Eugenius granted a new right to the Templars. Henceforward they, and they alone, could wear a red cross on the left breast and the shoulder of their mantles so that everyone might see in them a double emblem – the white of purity and the red of martyrdom.

No one knows exactly how many men left Europe that year. Bernard wrote, 'Cities and towns were empty. Scarcely is it possible now to find one man among seven women; to such an extent that everywhere there are widows whose husbands are still alive.' The opinion of the women was expressed by one of the men who did not go – a troubadour named Marcabrun, in one of whose songs a woman weeps for her lost lover:

> Curs'd be King Louis that did send
> To bid all men Christ's tomb defend –
> Whereby my breast with grief is filled.

One thing is certain: more men went than were wanted. Eugenius, like Odo, had learnt something from history, and had understood the difficulty of a multi-national Crusade. The Templars, the pope's own army, were predominantly Frenchmen; Louis was the very password of piety; and Eugenius felt that this should be a French Crusade. Temporal rivalries could obstruct spiritual goals all too easily. Unfortunately Bernard, forgetting international jealousies, more or less forced the Germans to go as well. Conrad III, the King and uncrowned Emperor of the Germans, did not want to go at all; but Bernard, with his fine rhetoric, said to him: 'Man, what have I not done for you? What ought I to have done for you that I have left undone?' And Conrad, seeing in Bernard the image of Christ in judgement, agreed to go. It would have been better if he had not.

The Crusaders set off in 1147, following the route of the First Crusade, overland through Hungary towards Constantinople, with the Germans leading the way; and Constantinople, the fabulous focus of the Byzantine empire, became their abiding hazard. Odo put it succinctly: 'Constantinople is arrogant in her wealth, treacherous in her practices, corrupt in her faith; just as she fears everyone on account of her wealth, she is dreaded by everyone because of her treachery and faithlessness.' The judgement may seem harsh, and to do the Greeks justice it should be noted that the Germans, preceding the French contingent, misbehaved themselves terribly, so that by the time the Frenchmen arrived – and remembering the problems the First Crusade had caused her – Constantinople expected the worst. However, it is too easy to look back over the centuries and present a dry analysis of cause and effect; current events, especially of a military or religious nature, are suffused with emotion, and for contemporary opinion to be understood, they should be seen with that perspective. So it was not without cause that Odo quoted Virgil and said, 'I fear the Greeks, even when they bear gifts.'

From the start, Louis was intensely embarrassed by the Byzantine diplomats, whose words were so flattering 'as to disgrace not only an emperor, but even a buffoon'. But flattery, it seemed, came easily to them – 'French flatterers,' said Odo, 'even if they wish, cannot equal the Greeks.' Nominally, the Germans, Greeks and French had the same faith, and so held the Crusade as a common cause. In practice, each nation kept its own material interests at heart and jockeyed for position throughout the

Crusade. For Odo, then, 'the Greeks lightly swore whatever they thought would please us, but they neither kept faith with us nor maintained respect for themselves. In general they really have the opinion that anything which is done for the holy empire cannot be considered perjury.'

But in the opinion of the French and Germans, the Greeks were perjurers and worse. They provided guides for both armies; and in each case it appeared to the foreigners that the guides were traitors who led them into the hands of the Moslems. The Germans, in the vanguard, were surprised and slaughtered by the Turks, and the French were led into places 'still stained with the blood of the Germans', where they too were attacked and defeated.

Mistrust and deceit led to catastrophe. The majority of these Second Crusaders never saw the Holy Land. 'Alas,' wrote Odo, 'what a pitiable fortune that the fierce Saxons, Batavians and other Germans perished so miserably because of the treachery of the indolent Greeks! And with the fall of the Franks, the two-fold grief is unbearable; both nations will always have something to bewail if the sons of these men do not avenge their fathers' death.' The Greeks were culpable, it is true, but they were also scapegoats for the Crusaders' misfortunes and lack of good judgement. Nevertheless, French and Germans alike did, in time, wreak an awful revenge on Constantinople; and out of all the disasters of the Second Crusade, the Knights Templar were the only ones to emerge with honour.

The Templar contingent was led not by Robert the Burgundian, but by Everard de Barres, then Master of the Temple in France. In Constantinople, de Barres showed some diplomatic skill in talks with the emperor; but the real value of the Templars and their discipline was not demonstrated until some time after Constantinople, when the crusading army was attempting to cross a mountain, and was surrounded by Moslems.

'The Templars and Lord Everard de Barres, who should be revered for his piety and who furnished the army an honourable example, saved their own possessions wisely and alertly and protected those of other people as courageously as possible. Now the king liked the example they set and was glad to imitate it ... therefore it was decided that during this dangerous period all should establish fraternity with the Templars, rich and poor taking oath that they would not flee the field and that they would obey in every respect the officers assigned them by the Templars.'

The Templars' orders to the Crusaders were simple and basic; their simplicity shows how chaotic the army was before.

'Because the Turks were quick to flee, our men were commanded to endure, until they received an order, the attacks of the enemies; and to withdraw forthwith when they were recalled, even though they should be making a stand as originally commanded. When they had learned this, they were also taught the order of march, so that a person in front would not rush to the rear and the guards on the flanks would not fall into disorder. Moreover those whom nature or fortune had made foot-soldiers (for, because they had lost or sold their equipment, many nobles were marching among the crowd in a manner unusual for them) were drawn up at the very rear in order to oppose with their bows the enemies.'

Odo's detailed description of these elementary arrangements betrays his surprise at them, and reveals the extent of the Crusaders' previous disarray and lack of discipline. Nevertheless, even such minimal organization prevailed, for the time being, against the Turkish mountain guerillas; the Crusaders worked their way down to level ground, where 'upon reaching the mud flats many Turks found death and a grave in a place suited to their filthy natures. While our wrathful attack and lengthy pursuit destroyed those fugitives, everybody's hunger was slight and his day was brighter.'

Yet the Crusaders' new-found ability to fight together was a short-lived advantage – the Turks used a scorched-earth policy, and 'by gathering the flocks and cattle from everywhere and allowing them to graze ahead of us, they destroyed the produce which they could not burn.' Without food, horses and men in the Christian army soon began to starve; the horses were eaten; clothing, arms, tents were abandoned.

There were four more battles, all of them won under the Templars' leadership; and the Templars, by a ruse, managed to forestall the end for a while. Though they themselves were well-nigh starving, they had kept their horses, and by presenting a brave front, convinced the Turks that the army was still strong. But it was only a shell, and could not withstand much longer the duplicity of the Greeks and the harrying of the Turks.

Arriving at Adalia, on the north-east Mediterranean coast, Louis was persuaded to go on by sea. Odo went with him. A great part of the army died of illness, starvation or attack in and around the port; of those who survived, a very large proportion gave up, and turned for home. Only a few straggled on, overland to Antioch.

The young king remained in the Holy Land for fifteen months, until the early summer of 1149. Odo, whose work is as much a eulogy of the king as a history of the Crusade, makes no mention of that period, and another contemporary chronicler says, dismissively, 'He was not able to do anything useful, anything worthy of mention, or actually, anything worthy of France.'

He had even run out of money and, in the first recorded instance of a role which was to become of prime importance to the Order, had had to borrow from the Templars. One of his vassal lords took on 30,000 sous of the debt; for the rest, Louis wrote to his Regent, Suger, with a curious mixture of diffidence and authority.

'I do not see how we could have lasted a moment in this country,' he said, 'without the help which they have continued to give us to the present; this is why I beg you to give them further emblems of acknowledgement, and to show them how much I am attached to them. I feel it necessary to warn you that they have just lent me a very considerable sum, which should be paid as soon as possible, both to keep my word and to prevent suffering to them. Therefore you should take care to deliver to them without delay two thousand silver marks. ...'

The overland journey from Europe had taken Louis a year; his return by sea took about seven weeks. King Conrad of Germany had preceded him; so too had news of the series of defeats. When Louis and his retinue landed in Italy, they immediately began a campaign of propaganda against the Byzantines, blaming most of the failure on their supposed treachery. Instantly another Crusade was called for, this time against the Byzantines. St Bernard, astonished and horrified at Louis' total failure, adopted the new idea eagerly. Considering that the Greeks were a part of Christendom, whatever their failings, this was a rather unsaintly act, to say the least. One cannot help feeling that, despite Bernard's railing at the Crusaders' sinful natures and their consequent punishment by God, he took the defeat personally. And although the Byzantine explanation was widely accepted, popular opinion was disinclined to credit the explanation of popular sin. To strive so energetically in the wake of disaster seemed to smack of guilt, or at least of fault, and Bernard's prestige was very severely damaged. Though, too, Louis and Suger agreed with Bernard, Eugenius was very reluctant to try again; in his opinion, mixing French and Germans had put the expedition at risk from the start. Finally, any new attempt would have to have German support, in spite of the international problems; and Conrad utterly refused any further involvement, even after Bernard had subjected him personally to another powerful tirade.

Following the chain of shocks that had characterized the Second Crusade came one final one, comparatively slight in public eyes, but enormous to the Templars. Robert the Burgundian, the Master of the Temple, had died on 13 January 1149, and had been replaced by the French provincial Master, Everard de Barres. But despite his example during the Second Crusade, leadership of the Order was too great a task for him. After only three years as Master, he resigned. De Barres gave little explanation, beyond expressing a wish to devote himself exclusively to the peaceful worship and contemplation of God; but the brethren – presumably recognizing that an unwilling Master could not be a useful one – did not stand in his way. He was obliged to join another Order; and he became a monk of Clairvaux, under Bernard, remaining there until his death, twenty-four years later, in 1176.

A new Master, Bernard de Trémélai, was duly elected; and about the same time news came to St Bernard that may have brought him a kind of comfort: his uncle, André de Montbard, was appointed Seneschal of the Temple. Uncle and nephew continued to correspond in terms of great affection, and Bernard frequently entreated André to visit Europe again. Bernard's last letter to André, written in the spring of 1153, is especially touching. By then the abbot was about sixty-three, and his chronic physical frailty was beginning to tell.

'The letters you have just sent me found me lying in my bed,' he wrote. 'I received them with outstretched hands; I have read and reread them avidly, but I wish even more strongly to see you. I find the same wish in your letters, but also your fears for the land that Our Lord honoured with His presence and consecrated with His blood. Misfortune on our princes ...

'But let us mount above the sun, and may our conversation continue in the heavens. There, my Andrew, will be the fruits of your labours, and there your reward ... You wish to see me, but you say that it depends on me, for you write awaiting my decision. And what can I say to you? I long to see you, but I fear that you will not come; and thus suspended between yes and no, I am dragged from one side to the other, and do not wish to choose. But I bow mostly before what you say of the great sorrows of the Holy Land, and it seems to me its condition would be made worse by your absence. So I dare not call you back – but how much I would love to see you before I die! You will judge better than I ... and it may be that your journey would not be useless, for, through the grace of God, there could be knights who would wish to follow you, for you are renowned and loved everywhere. But this I say to you: if you do come, do not delay, lest you find me here no more; for I am already very weak, and do not expect to stay long on this earth.'

André could not return; and Bernard, old, ill, disappointed and lonely, died in his own humble monastery with his monks around him. It was 9 a.m., 20 August 1153.

Two other people in the story died that same year: the pope, Eugenius, and the fourth Master of the Temple, Bernard de Trémélai. He was killed fighting at Ascalon in late July. It is probable that André had not even received St Bernard's last letter by then; but he must have thought often of his nephew, and of that day twenty-seven years earlier when the two of them had met at Clairvaux. So much had happened in that short time; and André was no longer a supplicant knight, seeking holy approval for his brethren. Now, more blessed than bishops, more powerful than princes, he was fifth Master of the Temple.

The Kingdom Beyond the Sea: Outremer, 1131–1303

PART THREE
The Kingdom Beyond the Sea:
Outremer (1174–1193)

CHAPTER 5

LIVING WATERS

The Holy Land, 1131–1168

'A fountain of gardens, a well of living
waters, and streams from Lebanon . . .'
Song of Solomon

THE HOLY LAND has a grand name, but geographically it is tiny. Today one can fly over the entire length and breadth of the Crusader states in an hour or two. Its most common name in Europe was *Outremer* – simply the French words for 'beyond the sea', capturing in a breath the qualities of distance, strangeness, sanctity and vicious glory that characterized the Templars as much as the sacred soil which they defended. To the inhabitants of the Holy Land, of course, 'beyond the sea' meant Europe; but in this book – looking south, with European eyes – Outremer is that collection of kingdoms and principalities which the Crusaders founded and the Templars policed. The old kingdom of Jerusalem, the principality of Antioch and the two counties – Tripoli and Edessa – were arranged roughly in the shape of a T. At the height of the Latin dominion in the East, the four states together measured six hundred miles or so south to north, and about three hundred west to east – a long narrow strip, from the eastern horn of the Red Sea and along the eastern Mediterranean coast, crossed by a top-heavy bar from Seleucia, north of Cyprus, to Edessa. Tripoli was the smallest of the states: even when the Crusaders were at the peak of their power, its greatest length was eighty-five miles, and its greatest width only forty. On its southern frontier with Jerusalem, this diminished to a mere coastal corridor: between

Beirut and the actual city of Tripoli, the Frankish occupation went only twenty miles inland.

An empire, and a holy one; but, in modern terms, it was miniature – a total area of little more than eleven thousand square miles. Nevertheless, it was often too much for the invading Franks to defend. On a map it may be spanned with a finger; from the air it may be scanned in an hour. But on the ground, when the fastest transport was by horse and the surest communication was by pigeon, those eleven thousand square miles would stretch out and threaten; for the Franks were surrounded by enemies.

Fear was their constant companion. The caves that pocked the landscape could hide a fatal ambush; a mountain could conceal an army; and it was impossible to patrol all the long, straggling frontiers. Their mood can be understood better still when one knows that the resident European population of the combined Latin states never exceeded twenty thousand; and of course, not all of those were fighting men. In the entire kingdom of Jerusalem there were less than a thousand secular knights and barons, and just over five thousand sergents, the fully-armed infantry. In addition there may have been another thousand European Christian civilians, and a few hundred clergymen; and these figures were mirrored in the combined totals of the other three states. In the cities and throughout the country, the Europeans were vastly outnumbered by the native Christian population, those who had been there before the First Crusade and who would remain when the land had been purged of Europeans. But although the native Christians paid taxes to and were supposed to fight for the Franks, they were not to be relied on; all too often the Franks appeared to them not as brother Christians but as oppressive invaders. It was easy for them to betray the Franks to the Moslems, and on many occasions they did. However, the Latin states had two other fighting arms – the half-caste mercenary turcopoles who, again, could be as unreliable as any other mercenaries; and the military Orders. And it was expected that they, at least, could be relied on utterly.

The Templars were the first. From their beginning they had been explicitly military; and not long after their recognition at Troyes, they were joined by a second Order, the Hospitallers. The Hospital of St John was founded in Jerusalem in 1048, and for about a century remained exactly that: a hospital, for the succour and welfare of pilgrims. But seeing the phenomenal popularity of the Templars, the Hospital was reorganized on military lines in imitation, and – which is more astonishing – soon began to attract as much support as the Order of the Temple. Despite the Templars' success, there was still room for competition.

The two Orders were usually able to provide anything from six hundred to a thousand knights, divided more or less equally; and that figure, set against the population figures above, shows their importance in civil and military life more clearly than anything else. They could represent as much as six per cent of the resident Frankish population; and they were the *only* standing army.

Given that, it is unfortunate to have to admit that the first recorded military engagement which the Templars undertook by themselves was actually a defeat. It took place in 1138, near a town called Teqoa, only nine miles south of Jerusalem. The town had been captured by Moslems; its proximity to the Holy City shows how weak the Christian defences were, and how vulnerable anything but a walled city or fortress could be. Hearing the news, a detachment of Templars rode out, with the second Master, Robert the Burgundian, leading them. But despite his diplomatic and administrative abilities, Robert, on that occasion at least, appeared less capable as a commander in the field. Archbishop William of Tyre, the historian, held a permanent grudge against the Templars, and against Robert in particular, because of the ecclesiastical privileges granted in *Omne Datum Optimum*. He never missed a chance to criticize the Order, and saw Teqoa as a just revenge. Robert and the brethren, he says, recaptured the town easily; but they 'made the mistake of not pursuing the Moslems as they fled'. The Templars remained in the town; the Moslems regrouped outside and counter-attacked; and William noted, with gloomy satisfaction, 'the whole space from Hebron to Teqoa [ten miles] was strewn with Templar corpses'.

William was probably exaggerating; but even if his description was the literal truth, Teqoa should be seen in perspective – it was one small battle among scores of small ones and a good many large ones; one fairly minor defeat among a quantity of major defeats, and major victories. And infinitely worse than Teqoa were three new, very powerful threats to Christian security in the Holy Land.

The first threat was direct: Zengi, the new Moslem leader. By 1130 he had all of northern Syria at his command. In 1131 he attacked Baghdad twice, and, being defeated each time, turned his attention to the West. Men of his command attacked Antioch in 1133; in 1135 he himself entered the principality, after attempting Damascus; in 1138 he approached Damascus again, but was fobbed off with the gift of the equally Moslem city of Homs; and in 1139 he besieged and captured Baalbek. In between times he had harried the Christian frontier fortresses, and had become an experienced menace, a force to be reckoned with.

The second was more subtle, and far more sinister: the Assassins, under their legendary master, the Old Man of the Mountains. Curiously, the Assassins were, in some ways, a Moslem parallel of the Templars, for they too were an order of holy warriors. But they did not fight openly in the field, and their fighting creed was not the simple opposition of Christian and Moslem, cross and crescent. Their inspiration was Arabic Islam rather than Turkish Islam, Shiism rather than Sunnism. In other words, they believed that spiritual leadership of the Islamic world should have been through the immediate descendants of the Prophet Mohammed, not through the Caliphs of Baghdad; and consequently, they saw most of the Moslems around them, as well as the Christians, as enemies.

With so many enemies, it might be supposed that they were not a great threat; but they were clandestine killers, masters of the craft of ruthless and efficient murder. Their obedience to the Old Man, their master, was unquestioning, and their courage was augmented by hashish. It was this which gave them their name, which correctly is *Hashishiyun*. The word was corrupted by the Franks into 'assassin', and ever since it has retained its meaning – a political murderer. And it was precisely this factor, their complex political motivation, which made them dreaded by Moslems and Christians alike; for they could not be recognized, they could kill whom they chose, and – if it suited them – they would make an alliance with either side.

The final threat was the most corrosive, and contributed most to the final downfall of the Latin states in the East: the alliance of the Franks and the Byzantines broke down. The emperor promised support to the Franks on condition that they would restore to him any land they conquered which had previously been taken from him by Moslems. One of these territories was the principality of Antioch, which the Franks had sat on firmly ever since they took it in 1098; and by 1137 the Byzantines had decided, equally firmly, that they wanted Antioch back. The emperor John Comnenus crossed the Hellespont with a large army, and laid siege to the city.

So Christians besieged a Christian city. It was the fatal irony of Outremer. The new King Fulk gave no support to Prince Raymond of Antioch, despite the part the prince had played in removing the irksome Alice; and in 1138 Raymond gave homage to John Comnenus, and the Byzantine flag flew over Antioch.

Yet the irony was compounded further; the politics had yet another twist. For when John Comnenus besieged Antioch, the Moslems of Damascus, still resolutely independent of Zengi, attacked Tripoli. They were beaten off; and then two years later, in 1139, the Damascenes and King Fulk became allies against Zengi. And Fulk was given back Banyas, into the bargain.

That, then, was the picture of Outremer in the first generation of Frankish rule: a complex and almost unbelievable web of enmities and alliances, where one side could side with the other against its own brothers in faith, and where boundaries fluctuated constantly as towns, cities and fortresses were lost and regained. And it was a picture which remained true for most of the two hundred years of Outremer's existence: small wonder, then, that once the Holy Land appeared safely Christian, the Christians of the West found it easier to ignore those distant, complicated events, and preferred to think of their own problems. But Zengi, the ambitious, belligerent enemy of Christendom, was ready to remind them.

> Where is the crown with which you were graced,
> And your splendid diadem?
> Where are the ornaments of the Queen,
> The royal prince's wife,
> And the splendours of the wedding palace,
> And the tasselled tissues of gold?
> Why is the husband absent from the wedding chamber,

And his friends from the church?
What has become of his companions?
They sing no longer the Songs of David.

1144: Edessa was gone, conquered by Zengi, amid scenes of
bloodshed and terror. Five thousand people suffocated in the
panic-stricken crowds; many thousands more were slaughtered;
and a priest of Edessa wept.

> All that has suddenly been taken from you,
> All that has vanished and has been eclipsed;
> It was nothing but dreams and phantoms
> That awakening has dispersed.

Moslems saw Zengi as the instrument of a merciful God, and said
the desert flowered where he passed by. Christians called him 'the
receptacle of the Devil, and the artisan of evil'. But each side
agreed that he had chosen his moment well, for the year before,
both his major opponents – King Fulk and John Comnenus –
had died, both, coincidentally, in hunting accidents. Without
John, the Antiochenes and Byzantines had come to blows again:
no threat to Zengi from the west. Without Fulk, the
Frankish–Damascene alliance had ended: no threat from the
south. Edessa marked the real beginning of the Moslem counter-
offensive; and in the years which followed, as the Latin states
fought daily for their very existence, the Templars came to the
fore.

People in despair will cling to any hope, however nebulous.
When news of Edessa arrived in the West, it was accompanied by
the rumour of a Christian king in the East, who was fighting the
Saracens and winning. He was called John – Prester John. Many
people then, and many others over a century later, believed in
him utterly, and pinned their hopes of success on him. And after
the ensuing expedition of the Second Crusade, when the
Templars were taken as the exemplar and commanders of the
royal army, many people swore that a knight clad all in white
appeared from nowhere to help them at their times of greatest
trouble, only to vanish, when all were safe, as mysteriously as he
had come. The Templars already bore an air of some mystery
about them – their Rule was now secret, and no brother was
permitted to reveal it to anyone; and their chapters, or general

meetings, were conducted in the utmost secrecy, behind locked and guarded doors and shuttered windows. Anything forbidden is both attractive and frightening, and some people, linking the Order's silence with the tale of the strange white knight, found the Templars yet more intriguing and enticing. The attraction is obvious: an elite band, its base in the holiest part of Christendom, with international connections, international riches, a secret internal organization, and freedom from all the customary temporal and spiritual ties. They could be seen in every way as a very prestigious group indeed.

But others interpreted the same elements differently; secrecy, wealth, freedom and power made the Order an object of suspicion and apprehension. The Templars' advocates could extol their austerity, their dedication and their unity. Their critics could point to the paradoxes: knights who took the Templar vow of poverty joined the richest brotherhood in the world; the vow of obedience meant that a man need no longer obey his king; the vow to defend Christendom meant that a man could ignore his archbishop. To their advocates, the chain of Templar castles in the Holy Land was the Christians' first defence, and their properties in Europe were a logical system of support. The critics saw these as a potential threat, firstly to the security of the Holy Land itself, since the Templars were not bound to stand by either the king or the patriarch; and secondly to the security of almost every country in Europe, where the brotherhood was the only regular disciplined army.

Neither view was completely right; but neither was completely wrong. Throughout the first forty-five years of the Order's existence, there is no direct evidence that the Templars ever abused their rights, and there is repeated circumstantial evidence in their favour: for example, the letters of Louis VII to Suger, and this comment in an early charter:

'We do not believe that the faithful can forget what consolation and assistance the Templars have afforded to the residents, the pilgrims, the poor and all those who wished to visit the Sepulchre of the Lord.'

Yet to do the Templars' critics justice, the direct and indirect records of that same period do not testify to outstanding military brilliance. By 1153, to be sure, the brethren owned castles from Gaza to Armenia; but at least once – at Teqoa – they had been defeated, and in two other more important battles their conduct had appeared to be less than honourable. These were the battles of Damascus, in 1148, and Ascalon, in 1153.

Damascus – proudly independent of other Moslems and the Franks, it had tantalized both sides for decades. Time and again Zengi had tried to conquer it, and it was outside the walls of Damascus that he died in 1146, murdered in his sleep by a European eunuch slave. Then, when Louis VII and Conrad of Germany trailed into the Holy Land with the remnants of the Second Crusade, the Franks decided to take their turn. The capture of Damascus, known from the Bible in every part of Christendom, would have been more than compensation for the loss of Edessa: it would have made the disasters through Byzantium seem worthwhile. But, for reasons which seemed as inexplicable then as they do now, the city was not won, and many put the blame on the Templars.

It is easy to understand why Franks and Moslems alike referred to Damascus as 'the Pearl of the Desert'. Visually it was stunning, and today, in an aerial approach to the city, three colours hold dramatic dominion – the white of the buildings, brilliant in the sunshine; the green oasis, the 'gardens' around the city; and the dusky yellow of the all-encompassing desert. It is emerald and pearl, set in gold.

Certainly, like any city, Damascus has its foul and filthy parts, its high-rise blocks, its tenth-rate architecture; but these desecrations do not damage the overall impression, that this city is something immensely valuable; and eight centuries ago, when the crusading armies of the west were still struggling to establish themselves fully in the East, its effect on those who saw it, and even on those who merely heard of it, must have been hypnotic. In the unrelenting hardness of the Franks' precarious lives, the dream of Damascus took root and flourished easily.

The nature of that dream, and the facts and legends on which it fed, are simply told: Damascus is genuinely unique. To most of the Crusaders, the lands of the eastern Mediterranean were especially favoured, for it was there that all the events of biblical days had taken place; but even compared to Jerusalem, Damascus was believed to be particularly blessed. It is the oldest continuously inhabited city of the globe – it existed a millenium before Abraham was born. Yet its value to the Franks was more than that of mere antiquity, or even of strategic use. Frankish possession of the city would drive a physical wedge between Moslems of north and south, more strongly than any Franco-Damascene alliance, and this counted. But what probably counted more with the common soldiers and pilgrims was that near Damascus was Abel's tomb; in another direction but equally close was a convent with an icon said to be a likeness of the Virgin and Child, painted by St Luke, and the first one of its kind; south of the city was the tomb of St George; in the city itself was the tomb of John the Baptist; and the whole site was the site of the Garden of Eden. It was from the clay of the river Barada, on which Damascus stands, that Adam was made – at any rate, the Moslems proudly maintained this was so, and the Franks eagerly accepted the information.

There were oddities, and errors too, surrounding these pieces of received knowledge. Abel's tomb is some twenty feet long, and so narrow as to be out of any human proportion; but the Lebanon guards a similar grave, in which Seth, Adam's third son, is said to lie, while Nimrod sleeps in a sepulchre near Hermon – a sepulchre thirty feet long; and according to Genesis, 'there were giants in the earth in those days'. The painted Virgin of Seidnaya (which means two things, 'Our Lady' and 'a hunting place') was, and is, believed to weep. The Templars accepted this belief, and with the mixture of faith and astute publicity typical of their early days, they bottled some of the tears and sent them back to Europe.

If every place that claims to have John the Baptist's head is to be believed, he must have had three or four heads at least. Similarly, rival bids for honour suggest that several Gardens of Eden existed; but perhaps the error of greatest pathos is the one concerning the tomb of St George. The idea that the patron saint of England was buried here must have thrilled and fascinated many of the Europeans; but he is not. The George buried near Damascus was not a Roman officer, but an Abyssinian porter, executed for his part in St Paul's escape from the city.

In a sense, though, the errors and the oddities are not important. What is important is that these things about the Holy Land in general and Damascus in particular were commonly held to be true. Without such beliefs, the Crusades would not have been attempted, and the Templars would not have existed. And in this secular century, looking back to those people, it is necessary to remember that when they saw Jerusalem – or Antioch – or Damascus, they did not just see walls and towers and buildings; they did not just think of territorial conquest. They saw places which brought their bibles to life. Names familiar and revered from earliest childhood were no longer only words spoken by their parents or their priests, they were solid, three-dimensional realities, and their conquest was an act of worship.

Worship walks in Damascus, now as then – worship of Allah, of Jehovah, of Christ and of commerce. It is the basic activity of the city; in one form or another, it goes on all the time, and usually with a great deal of noise and colour attached. The muezzin's cries ring out five times a day, calling the faithful to prayer – and since the sing-song wail nowadays often comes from a tape-recorder, it can be very loud indeed. It needs to be, if it is to be heard over the bells that peal in joy, or toll in sad deliberation; over the rumble of cars and lorries; over the discontented growls of camels, the sharp tinkle of bicycle bells, the pleading of beggars, the shouts of merchants, the constant hum of conversation and the staccato rattle of tric-trac in the cafés. It is a bustling, cheerful, lively, cosmopolitan confusion; and if, in that, Damascus is becoming similar to many of the world's other great cities, there are still things which make it unlike any other. There is the street called Straight, which is; it is covered with an arched roof along its whole undeviating length, and the sunlight streams through windows, making bright bars of the swirling dust; and – something which is neither error nor oddity – it is the site of St Paul's baptism. For those inclined to historical pilgrimages, there is Saladin's tomb, a cleanly simple building containing a grotesquely inappropriate nineteenth-century German sarcophagus; the tomb of Nur-ed-Din, and the tomb of Baibars, both of whom appear later in this tale; the tomb of – one must admit: there are a great number of tombs in this city.

There are also places, and people, of great living beauty here. The people are everywhere, nuns, priests, muezzins, children, sherbet sellers – most of them immensely hospitable, and ready to chat, especially about politics; they have a disarming manner of reviling everyone's politics (and their political memories are very long), while simultaneously protesting an obviously genuine liking for all the individuals who make, run and suffer the policies. First among the places of beauty must be the Great Ommayad Mosque, whose site has been sacred for three thousand years, and whose walls incorporate elements of Greek, Christian, Roman, and pre-Roman Aramean shrines. In its present form it was laid out in the very early eighth century; the equivalent of seven years' worth of the entire town's income was spent on its construction, and it was lit by six hundred lamps suspended on chains of solid gold. Those, and many other gold trimmings, have long vanished in fires and battles – and they would have gone even earlier if the Crusaders had won through. Nevertheless it remains a place of outstanding visual beauty, and deep tranquility, with its cloistral and majestic colonnades, its tiled floors and its walls of mosaic. These are unusual in Islam, for they are representational, depicting rivers, houses and orchards in some unknown, idyllic time and place. Some say that the pictures record Damascus as it once was – the gardens of paradise, the setting of virginal innocence, and that the Crusaders' defeat in 1148 sprang from their unworthiness for such a prize.

For the Franks, the road that led to that dismal failure began in Antioch in the spring of 1148, when Louis VII and his wife Eleanor of Aquitaine were there. Eleanor's reputation has always been low, for her character was out of tune with the virtues which were valued at the time and the qualities demanded of a queen. Louis was serious and pious, to the point of being ponderous; Eleanor was lively and light-hearted, witty and elegant. Churchmen and politicians in her husband's court were frequently scandalized by her flirtatious behaviour; less solemn men were delighted. One of these was Raymond, Prince of Antioch, and, as it happened, Eleanor's uncle. His child-wife Constance was still only twenty, but they had already been married for eleven years, and not long after Eleanor's arrival in Antioch, it seemed clear to everyone that Raymond and his niece had a more than usually affectionate relationship. Louis' honour was offended and, taking Eleanor with him by force, he led his army on to Jerusalem.

On 24 June, a council of war took place in the Holy City. The emperor Conrad, Louis, the Masters of the Temple and the Hospital, and Fulk's son and successor Baldwin III were there. Somehow they came to the decision that Damascus should be their goal – even though it was the only Moslem city with the slightest degree of friendship for the Franks. The army – the biggest the Franks ever assembled – set out in mid-July, via Banyas. They arrived at Damascus on 24 July and pitched camp south of the city, in an area of gardens and orchards. It was a perfect base, and at first the attack was promising. Within two days the Damascenes were barricading their streets while the Franks beat on the city walls. Then on 27 July, the entire Christian army struck camp and moved to the eastern side of the city. Superficially the reason was the advance of Moslem re-inforcements; but the ordinary soldiers were suspicious, for their commanders had taken them from the best to the worst possible base – it was exposed and waterless, and faced the strongest part of the city walls. Immediately they had moved the Franks found themselves on the defensive. The Moslem reinforcements were close at hand; the Franks could expect none. With no water, no food and no natural defence they could do nothing, and the next day they began to retreat.

Moslem archers pursued and harried them, and this time the plain was, literally, covered with bodies of horses and men, corpses that lay and rotted unburied for months, 'stinking so powerfully,' said Ibn al-Qalaisi, 'that the birds almost fell out of the sky . . . for which let God be praised and blessed!'

This was not simply defeat, it was disaster: the enormous army had been routed in five days, and the myth of Frankish invincibility had vanished completely. Naturally, everyone looked for a reason and a scapegoat. To the common soldiers, and to the civilians who had stayed at home, the reason seemed beyond doubt: it *must* have been treachery. The only question then was the identity of the traitor.

There were almost as many alternatives as there were commanders. Louis and Conrad bitterly blamed all the Palestinian barons, as did many of the soldiers, saying the barons had been jealous of the French and German success in the early part of the battle. The barons in turn blamed the two kings, saying they did not understand the political situation in the Holy Land; that one Moslem was not necessarily like another; and that the friendly Damascenes should never have been attacked at all. Others suggested maliciously that Louis had only wanted to prove himself to Eleanor by making the attack, and that he then lost heart.

But the most common story was that the Moslems had offered a colossal bribe to one or more of the influential commanders – either the Palestinian barons, or else the Templars.

The barons may indeed have been bribed; no one could say for certain, and no one can say. And whether or not one is willing to accept it, it remains possible that the Templars, aware of the political implications of losing the one Franco-Moslem alliance, may have put their Order first, and may have been guilty of corruption. Despite the Templars' high ideals, the accusation becomes more plausible in the light of their actions at Ascalon, only five years later.

At this point, however, two new characters enter the tale, a Moslem and a Frank – Nur ed-Din, Zengi's son and successor; and Reynald de Chatillon. Nur ed-Din was actually Zengi's second son, and on Zengi's death the Franks had hoped that the two brothers would fight between themselves. But they divided their father's lands peacefully; the elder took Iraq and Nur ed-Din took Syria. From there he went on to surpass his father: his had been the army that had reinforced Damascus, and he was the threat that the Damascenes used to maintain their tenuous treaty with the Franks.

Reynald de Chatillon was also a younger son, but less fortunate in his family. He came from Chatillon-sur-Loing, about a hundred miles south of Paris, and was a member of the minor nobility. It was a story typical of many of the Crusaders: he could not expect any worthwhile inheritance in France, and left, probably in Louis VII's army, to seek his fortune in the Holy Land.

But apart from the circumstances of his departure, he was not in the least typical of the majority of Crusaders. The religious motive played no part at all for him; he was a fortune-hunter pure and simple, and in the Holy Land he won, and lost, several fortunes, all with the ease of the born brigand.

In recorded history he first appears in Antioch, infamous Antioch, in 1151. Prince Raymond of Antioch was two years dead by then, killed in battle against Nur ed-Din, who had sent the Prince's skull, encased in silver, to the Sunnite Caliph of

Baghdad. Constance had then shown she had something of her mother Alice's spirit, and, determinedly refusing all her suitors, governed Antioch herself. She had probably met Reynald already, and it is clear that, when it suited him, Reynald could be charming; for early in 1153, Constance decided to marry him, although he was little more than a penniless soldier of fortune. The marriage required the king's consent, and Reynald set off at once to get it. Baldwin was busy besieging Ascalon, and he and Reynald met there. They had a brief interview, during which Reynald impressed the king with his vigour. The suitor seemed likely to defend Antioch well, and the king was preoccupied; he gave his consent, Reynald hurried back to Antioch, and the marriage took place at once.

And then Reynald began to show his true character. Already he had been criticized, for the Antiochenes were shocked that Constance should have chosen a husband of such lowly status. 'Many people wondered at this,' wrote William of Tyre, 'and there was great talk throughout the country; but despite it all, Reynald was Prince of Antioch.' As prince, he would brook no criticism from those he believed inferior, and when he discovered that the old patriarch of the city was one of his sternest critics, he kidnapped the old man, stripped him naked, beat him, then tied him up, smeared his head with honey and left him for a whole day on a hot roof-top, tormented with flies and wasps. However, like any other bully, Reynald paid attention to his superiors, and on receiving a severe reprimand from Baldwin, he reacted in equally characteristic style: the patriarch was released and led on horseback in honour around Antioch, with Reynald himself leading the horse on foot.

But this man, so thoroughly unattractive in some ways, was also a warrior of the utmost daring; and as such, he eventually won considerable popularity among the Franks. Yet the only people whom he respected were the Templars, and it is not greatly to their credit that they accepted this. Later, they went so far as to make a formal alliance with him – an alliance whose ultimate consequence was the opposite of all the Temple stood for: the disintegration and defeat of Outremer. That, though, was a long way off, and in 1153 it could not have been sensed or foreseen. While Reynald tortured the old patriarch, the siege of

Ascalon was in full swing, and the Templars were in the vanguard.

The Moslems called Ascalon 'the Virgin of the Desert', for it alone had held out inviolate since the days of the First Crusade. At the beginning of the year Baldwin decided to change that, and proposed the project to the knights of Jerusalem. It was accepted immediately and commanders all swore on the True Cross that they would not give up until the conquest was achieved. They had a long wait.

The city was laid out in a vast semi-circle, its straight side on the sea and its arc massively fortified. The Christians managed to blockade it, including the seaward side, but the city was so well stocked and the walls were so strong that the blockade made little difference for months. Pilgrims at Easter reinforced the Christians, but this was balanced in June when an Egyptian fleet broke through the sea blockade with supplies. The besieging Christians were considerably disconcerted, and agreed on an extra effort. Hitherto their main weapons had been catapults, ballistas and battering rams. The catapults hurled entire rocks; the ballistas flung gigantic spears, seven feet long and headed with iron tips four inches and more across. Now it was decided to build a siege tower that could overtop the walls – not exactly original, but frequently effective.

The finished construction was immense, and very impressive – or very frightening, depending on one's point of view. It was hung about with osiers and cables to protect it from rocks – for the Moslems had catapults too – and with fresh skins to absorb the impact of spears and arrows. Before it there was a 'tortoise', a mobile tunnel of wooden beams and planks. Protected under this, men smoothed the way for the great tower. A platform of moveable planks lay under the tower's wheels, and like some terrible monster, the whole machine inched slowly forward until it stood before the very walls. The Moslems hurled everything they could at it; the Franks hurled everything they could back; and neither made any impression on the other.

Then suddenly, and in a quite unexpected manner, the tower's attack succeeded. It was late July, and night-time. The Moslems sent out a small group under cover of darkness to set fire to the tower. It blazed up rapidly, making the night lurid with flames and sparks; the Christians could not extinguish it. But as they despairingly watched it burn, the wind changed – the flames blew against the city walls, already weakened by the rams, and in the small hours of the morning a part of the wall collapsed.

The Templars were in charge of that particular section, and the Master, Bernard de Trémélai, led an assault through the breach. Thirty-nine of the brethren accompanied him. At first the Ascalonites assumed these were merely the vanguard for the rest of the army, and were about to surrender; but when no more Christians appeared, they surrounded the Templars, and slew them all. The breach was quickly blocked; and next day, forty Templar corpses dangled from the Moslem battlements.

Nevertheless, the siege was bound to succeed eventually. Three weeks more brought the Moslems to the brink of starvation, for no more supply-ships had come through; and on 19 August, the city surrendered. The inhabitants were allowed safe passage to Egypt, with their moveable goods; when they got there, most of them were robbed and killed by fellow-Moslem Bedouins.

At Ascalon, the mosques were turned into churches; the Christians settled in; and talk spread about the Templars. The reason there had been no support for the thirty-nine dead brothers and the Master was known, and undisputed by those brothers that survived: Bernard de Trémélai had ordered a group of Templars to hold the breach *on the outside*, and to prevent other Christians from entering. Why he had done so was another question; the survivors could not or would not explain, and he, being dead, could not be asked. The most charitable said the Templars had wanted to have the honour of conquering the city; many others said they had coveted the first-comer's share of the booty. Whichever was correct, the city would have fallen three weeks earlier if the Templars had behaved less impetuously.

The stories of corruption in the defeat at Damascus had had a final twist, typical of the sarcastic humour of soldiers who feel their commanders have betrayed them: it was said that the money the Moslems were reputed to have paid had all turned out to be counterfeit. No such joke lightened the feeling at Ascalon: de Trémélai and his brothers had been selfish, dishonourable and stupid.

The honeymoon between the Templars and the rest of

Christendom was long over. That indefinable point had been passed earlier by some people than by others; but now everyone outside the brotherhood assessed the Order on practice, not promise, and everything the brethren did became open to two views.

Like a game of chess, the gains and losses continued. The Moslem prince of Damascus was impressed by the conquest of Ascalon, and began to pay Baldwin an annual tribute. To the ordinary Damascenes, however, alliance was one thing, tribute quite another, and in 1154 the gates of Damascus were opened to Nur ed-Din. Without even fighting, he had fulfilled his father's dream, and won the Pearl of the Desert.

At the same time another inter-Moslem power struggle was going on in Cairo: a courtier named Nasr murdered the Caliph, but failed to assume the throne and fled across the Sinai Desert. He was aiming to make a great circle south of the Frankish territories, towards refuge in Damascus; but as he passed by Montreal, seventy-five miles south of the Dead Sea, he was ambushed and captured by Templars. He instantly expressed a strong wish to become a Christian, and was instructed in the faith for four days; then an embassy arrived from the dead Caliph's sisters in Cairo, offering a ransom of sixty thousand dinars for the murderer. The Templars handed him over at once and took the money; he was taken back, chained, to Cairo, where the Caliph's four widows mutilated him before he was hanged.

The Templars' critics pounced on the incident. A repentant infidel, another soul for the Kingdom of God, had been sent to his death for mere money. Comparisons were made between the Templars and Judas Iscariot. But, as had become usual, there was another interpretation: Nasr's acceptance of Christianity could not have been more than a way to save his life, and money was more useful in the fight for the Kingdom of God on earth than the addition of one dubious convert.

Roughly the same argument applied on another occasion, only the year after. Reynald de Chatillon had been exercising himself in Antioch again.

One technicality had been overlooked in the marriage of Constance and Reynald: the allegiance owed by Antioch to the Byzantine emperor. Constance should have asked the emperor as well as King Baldwin before she married Reynald; she had not done so, and he was offended. He was also worried that the new prince might try to regain Antioch's freedom from Byzantium, and to pre-empt this he devised an unusual offer. Despite his irregular marriage, Reynald would be recognized as Prince of Antioch if he agreed to fight for the emperor against the Armenians. And if he fought successfully, the emperor promised a cash reward as well.

Of course Reynald accepted the deal – money, fighting, and imperial support; he could not have resisted it. He won his battles against the Armenians, and asked for his money. It was not forthcoming; the emperor wanted a few more victories first. But Reynald could play that game too, and presented the country he had conquered to the Templars. The brethren accepted the offer, occupied Alexandretta and rebuilt the twin castles of Gastun and Baghras, overlooking the Syrian Gates. Reynald's reputation did not stand in their way.

But the picture should be balanced: it is too easy, at this distance in time, for a distorted image to build up. It should be remembered that the incidents above were exceptional events, highlights that stood out in people's minds against the Order's mundane duties of policing the highways and protecting pilgrims. There were other highlights too, of a more honourable sort; here are two examples, from actions at Antioch and Jerusalem. André de Montbard described the first one in a poignant letter of supplication to the then Master, Everard de Barres, after he returned to France, but before he retired from the Order.

'Since we were deprived of your dear presence, we have had the misfortune to lose, in a combat, the Prince of Antioch (Raymond, whose skull was set in silver) and all his nobility. A second accident succeeded that first: the Parthians have just invaded the county of Antioch, and since none dared resist them they have fortified and garrisoned the place. . . . As soon as we heard of the disaster, we assembled, and with the King of Jerusalem, resolved to go to the aid of the stricken province. We could not furnish more than a hundred and twenty knights, and a thousand servants and mercenaries, and to equip the latter, we had to borrow seven thousand besants at Acre and a thousand at Jerusalem. . . . And we had hardly arrived in the neighbourhood of Antioch when Nur ed-Din on one side and the Parthians on the other laid siege to us and confined us within the walls of the city.

'Never has your presence been more necessary to your brothers; and however Providence may dispose of us, do not hesitate to start your journey back. We know that God can as easily deliver us from our enemies as He can change an idolator into a true worshipper, and we put all our trust in Him. But do not be surprised at the small number of brothers we send to you; we would rather, on your order, assemble and keep here all our men who are on your side of the sea; for the majority of those whom we brought to the aid of Antioch are dead . . . Our situation is such that we do not have colours to paint it, or words to express it.'

The desperate appeal is no coward's cry; de Montbard and his brothers had done all they could, and wrote in full expectation that de Barres, as Master, would hold to his vows. That he did not, but left the Order to join the Cistercians at Clairvaux, illustrates the dilemma that a study of the Templars presents. Their contemporaries must have found the same problem, that one can never wholly condemn nor wholly praise the Knights of the Order of the Temple. If, individually and together, they often fell short of their ideals and their vows, they were usually far more faithful to their united purpose than any other group of military men. St Bernard had spoken of them as doubly armed; they could equally be seen as doubly burdened, forever trying to balance monastic morality with pragmatic politics. It is not surprising that they did not always live up to their own stern ideal; what is surprising is how often, indeed how generally, they came close to it.

The action at Jerusalem, another image of honour, took place in 1152, when de Trémélai was Master. King Baldwin and he, with their respective forces, had been conducting a reasonably successful campaign against Nur ed-Din, de Trémélai at Nablus and Baldwin at Tripoli. Jerusalem was thus without its two main leaders. Knowing this, a Moslem army advanced by forced marches rapidly towards the city, and pitched camp on the Mount of Olives. They had intended to launch a surprise attack, but they were seen; the Templars who had remained in Jerusalem were alerted, and they, accompanied by knights of the Hospital and a mob of civilians, attacked the Moslems under cover of darkness. The surprise was turned entirely around; the Moslem army, jolted out of sleep, broke, fled and dispersed, only to be trapped on the banks of the Jordan. Five thouand died, so the reports say, killed, or drowned in the river.

It was after this attack, averted and turned to victory, that Baldwin decided to try for Ascalon. There, de Trémélai met his death, and André de Montbard, St Bernard's uncle, was elected Master of the Temple – the greatest honour of his life, and the heaviest responsibility. But he did not have long to enjoy the one or endure the other: he died less than three years later, on 17 January 1156 – the last, as far as is known, of that original band of eight or nine.

The sixth Master of the Temple was Bertrand de Blanquefort, a member of the Blanquefort family of Bordeaux. He was Master for thirteen years, but for two of them he was quite unable to administer the Order at all – for on Thursday, 19 June 1157, he was captured in battle and taken in chains to Damascus.

It happened outside Banyas. Nur ed-Din, now the confident ruler of Damascus, was reaching out again; Banyas was besieged. Baldwin and de Blanquefort came quickly to its rescue – too quickly, for they had no time to assess the Moslem force. Ibn al-Qalanisi reported.

'When the Franks approached, our men came out upon them from the rear like lions on their prey, and there followed an orgy of slaughter, capture and looting. Few of the Franks escaped. On the following Monday the prisoners and the heads of those killed arrived in Damascus . . .'

Among the prisoners were de Blanquefort and eighty-seven of his brothers – he at least was spared the gruesome end, decapitation or scalping, normally given to captives of the Moslems. Some three hundred other Templars had been killed in the battle.

'The prisoners, with their equipment and a selection of horses, were paraded around the city, and the spectacle caused great joy . . . a huge crowd of citizens, old men, young men, women and children came out to see the glorious victory granted by God.'

One of the Templars' maxims was never to retreat unless the odds were greater than three to one. Three hundred dead and eighty-eight in captivity – the Order had almost been destroyed. But the next year those who had survived salvaged their honour in what was effectively a return match; and that time the thirty remaining knights defeated a force of two hundred Moslems.

Reynald de Chatillon, the brigand of Antioch, was busy as well, but on strictly selfish errands. With funds extorted from the tortured patriarch, he had raped the isle of Cyprus. There is no other word for his action: his attack had no motive but greed and lust for the beautiful and defenceless. The island was peaceful and prosperous, and basked in the rule of the Byzantine emperor's nephew – a connection which may have been enough to incite Reynald's vindictive, revengeful nature. Crops were destroyed, sheep and cattle stolen; the old people and children were killed; churches, shops, houses and convents were pillaged and burnt; the women were abducted to Antioch, the men were imprisoned for future ransom, and the priests were sent to Byzantium – after each one's nose had been cut off.

Reynald's actions were all backed by his confident belief that no one could do anything about them. Baldwin had tried too late to warn the Cypriots of the assault; and after it was over he could do little more, for Reynald was too valuable. But, partly to show his opinion of the affair, he did marry the emperor's niece; and Reynald had underestimated the emperor. As his father John Comnenus had done in 1138, Manuel entered Antioch in 1159, and utterly humiliated Reynald. The imperial army was so vast, Reynald could not resist. He was led barefoot to the emperor's tent; before it he lay prostrate in the dust, 'and,' said William of Tyre, 'he wept and cried for so long that everyone was nauseated.' Crocodiles, it is said, do the same.

Manuel, as emperor, could have deposed Reynald. His main reason for not doing so was that it would have been too complicated. Antioch as a submissive vassal state added a certain prestige to his empire; as a direct responsibility, it would have taken his money and men. He was a politician through and through, always willing to balance allies against enemies if it helped his own cause; and so, after accepting Reynald's homage, he made a truce – with Nur ed-Din.

The Franks in the Holy Land were infuriated; but it did have one immediate good consequence for them, for six thousand Christian prisoners were released from Moslem captivity, including Bertrand de Blanquefort. If none of the other five thousand nine hundred and ninety-nine had learned anything of the Saracens from their time in Saracen jails, he had, and he soon began to put it into use.

Reynald de Chatillon, quite unrepentant, continued marauding wherever he could; but his value as an asset diminished accordingly, and when, in 1160, he made one raid too many, nobody came to help him. Overblown with self-confidence, he took on Nur ed-Din's brother, was surrounded, captured and imprisoned – not for two years, like de Blanquefort, but fifteen. One of his last acts before that had been to confirm a sale of property to the Templars; but they, like all others, seemed happy to see him go.

For the Holy Knights, peace was as far away as ever, only to be achieved on the edge of a sword. War was always with them, and a simple life on Earth was prohibited by their special blend of politics and faith. The cause was not just their immediate enemies, the Moslems; events in far-off Europe still affected them deeply. In 1152 Frederick Barbarossa had been crowned Emperor of the Germans, and the papal schism had broken out afresh. Frederick supported a candidate named Octavian, the Templars another named Alexander. Alexander won, and in 1162 reissued *Omne Datum Optimum*, strengthening yet again its extraordinary privileges, to the extent of actually taxing the Holy See and the entire Church in support of the Order. But the springs of Europe were running dry; so many knights died in the Holy Land, the supply of recruits was diminishing. Martyrdom was losing its attraction. No longer could both Orders hope for sufficient aid for each. Rivalries cut in every direction: between the pope and Barbarossa, the Templars and Hospitallers, the patriarch and king, the Church of East and West. The two Military Orders had even met in open fights together, jealously guarding their mutually exclusive property and prestige.

There was, however, one lighter side; Templars and Hospitallers were as one in their detestation of the patriarch of Jerusalem, and they both went to comical lengths to show it. William of Tyre found their behaviour shocking, but not even he could remove its absurdity. He describes how the Hospitallers built towers opposite the Church of the Holy Sepulchre, towers 'higher and more gorgeous than those of the church consecrated with the blood of Our Lord and Saviour', and containing very loud bells.

'When the Patriarch wished to speak to the people and mounted into his pulpit, the brethren at once sounded their bells with so much activity and at such length that the Patriarch lacked the strength to raise his voice sufficiently and therefore, in spite of all his efforts, the people could not hear him.'

And while the patriarch tried to preach, and the bells clanged around him, there was a constant thudding at the door as well – because the Templars were using it for archery practice.

Such moments were needed from time to time, to break the dreadful rhythm of strife and tension. For despite their super-human ideals, the Templars were very human; and the story demonstrates another human failing: the arrogance, which, by invisible degrees, had become part of their way of life, and which, in 1168, suddenly became visible to all.

King Baldwin's wife Theodora, the niece of the Byzantine Emperor, was only thirteen when she married. In 1162, when she was just sixteen, she was widowed, for on 10 February, Baldwin III died, killed by his doctor's would-be cures. The couple had no children, and the throne of Jerusalem passed to Baldwin's younger brother, Amalric. By then, Egypt had been recognized by Frank and Moslem alike as being the key to power in the Holy Land: its possession by the Franks would split Islam's geographical strength, perhaps for ever; its unification with the Sunnite Caliph of Baghdad would fatally surround the Franks. Amalric was no coward; in 1163 and 1167 he launched attacks on Egypt, both of which were driven off. The second, however, was resolved with a treaty of benefit to both sides, and there the matter might have rested for a few years at least. But the temptation of Egypt, the Nile's fertile flood-lands, the country's natural resources and its strategic importance, was too great. In 1168 Amalric proposed a third assault; and the Templars refused their support.

CHAPTER 6

THE IDEAL SARACEN

Egypt and the Holy Land, 1169–1187

'I will give children to be their princes,
and babes shall rule over them.'
Isaiah III, 4.

AMALRIC'S INVASION OF EGYPT in 1168 was in direct contravention of his treaty of the year before, and when the Templars refused to accompany him, their critics and enemies made much of it. They were jealous, some said, because the project originated with the Master of the Hospital. Others were infuriated that the Order, founded for the defence of the Holy Land, should not aid its king, and complained that in their independence the Templars were falling prey to pride. De Blanquefort, the Master, replied that he and his brethren – and the king – were bound by the treaty. The retort came back that a treaty with an infidel was not binding; the Knights retaliated by quoting St Jerome, who said, 'It matters not to whom, but by whom, we swear.'

Treason, or honourable behaviour: the answer still depends on one's point of view. Thomas Fuller, an English historian writing in the seventeenth century, described the affair and said, 'When a crown is the prize of the game, we must not expect fair play of the gamesters'; but William of Tyre, generally one of the Templars' strongest critics, admitted that they had behaved with honour. Amalric was certainly treacherous, and his treachery benefited no one but the Moslems. The Frankish attack was beaten off, by joint Egyptian and Syrian forces, and the grateful Egyptian caliph made the chief Syrian officer his vizier. The new vizier died two years later, and was replaced by his nephew, an obscure young Moslem whose sense of honour and religion would put the Christians to shame. The young man's name was Saladin.

By 1169 the Christian conquest of Jerusalem, seventy years before, was no longer a cause for Christian rejoicing, it was merely a historical fact. Seventy years; three generations; more than enough time for the heady exhilaration of those first days to have dimmed into something less than a memory. Anyone who had taken part in the battles and adventures at the beginning of the century was long dead. To people in Europe the Holy City was Christian, and that was that. It had been so since their grandfathers' time, and would probably remain so; after all, it was God's city, and they were God's only true worshippers. Even the shock when Edessa fell had worn off – partly because people did not like to talk about the botched and bungled Second Crusade; partly because they had accepted the new status quo, since the Holy City itself was safe; but mostly because, to Europeans, preoccupied with their own problems, it was all so far away.

To many of the Franks in the Holy Land as well, the old dream was tarnished. Jerusalem the Golden was made of stone and brick and mud like any other city. To be sure it was holy, and they would defend it for that – but more importantly, it was their home. Thousands of Christians of Frankish stock living in the Holy Land had never seen Europe; they never would, and they never especially wanted to. It too was far away, and was cold and dark and wet. And they had difficulties as great as any in Europe, for theirs was not the thrill of conquest, but the daily problem of protecting their homes in an unfriendly land.

In some ways these men, the grandsons of the first Crusaders, had the hardest lot of any Franks in the East. When they fought, it was not for the glory of the Church of Rome, nor even necessarily for the kingdom of God on earth; it was for the defence of the only place they knew as home.

Jerusalem as a distant dream could easily have an aura of sanctity. As a place to live in, from day to day and year to year, it only retained its holiness to those who were committed to God, the clergy and the men of the Military Orders. For them, place-names in the gospels were living realities. Reading each day in their bibles the names of towns, rivers, mountains and valleys which they saw around them, life had point and purpose above the daily round. Christ's eyes had seen the same sights; His feet had touched the same soil. To men such as these, living in the lands of the scriptures could be a source of strength and inspiration.

And the Templars had a second source of strength: stability and order. With the dual discipline of monks and warriors, their lives were rigorously organized; every moment of the day contained a duty accountable to others.

In summer, a day in the life of a Templar began at four in the morning. In winter, it began at six, but apart from that, and variations in food and clothing and church ceremonies according to the season, each day ran roughly like this: with a bell, one member of the household would awaken all the others; to dress, they would simply slip their robes of white, brown or black over the underclothes they had slept in. They were not expected to wash, and they had no breakfast. They would go directly from their dormitories to the chapel for matins, where they went through the prayers for the hours of prime, terce and sext – morning, mid-morning and mid-day – at the same time. Thus the monastic duties of the morning were concentrated together; being monks, they would not neglect the hours, but being warriors with a care for their bodies as well as their souls, they could not always be in chapel. After mass, they dispersed to their various tasks; the knights' duty was to check their horses, harnesses, arms and armour, to correct anything that might be wrong with these, and then to proceed with their constant training, using their standard weapons – the iron-headed lance, the mace, the sword, dagger and shield.

The first meal of the day was late in the morning, or at noon; knights and sergents ate first, followed by the servant brothers. Mercenaries were last. Each man brought his bowl, cup, spoon and knife to table; only the Master, or the commander of the house, drank from a glass, both as an honour and as a precaution against poison. Sitting on benches at their long, plain wooden tables, the brothers would not speak during the meal; the only voice was that of a brother priest reading from the bible. Requests were made with signs; the knights, if they chose, could exchange their food for the servants', but they were not encouraged to abstain from eating altogether – they always had to be fit for battle, for which the cry could come at any moment. Apart from that, there was only one circumstance in which a brother could leave the table without permission, and that was if he had a nose-bleed. An odd exception; they must have been common events to have been written into the Rule.

There are other curious exceptions as well. The brothers had to be in chapel during the afternoon to hear the offices of none and vespers which, as in the morning, were run together. But some were allowed to stay away: brother baker, 'if he has his hands in the dough'; brother blacksmith, 'if he has iron hot in the fire'; a brother squire, 'if he is paring or shoeing the horses' hoofs' – and 'any brother who is washing his hair'. But all the brethren had to recite the paternoster, be it to the rhythm of a hammer or the sluice of water. Altogether they would each recite one hundred and forty-eight paternosters each day – fourteen for each hour, eighteen for vespers, thirty for the living and thirty for the dead. It must have been very difficult to keep count.

The repetition would be almost constant; yet even if it became mechanical, it would form a tranquilizing, meditative background to all their thoughts and actions.

They would eat again in the evening; if, as happened three times a week, they were given meat, there would be two or even three different sorts, as well as wine and water to drink; and then the day would end as it had begun, with prayers together and a general blessing.

This, then, was their basic prescribed daily ritual, and if that had been all, it would have had little to distinguish it from the calm and peaceful routine of a well-ordered monastery. Amongst all the activity, indeed – all the activity one can imagine associated with horses, with men in constant training for war, and with the work of any contained and rather primitive community – the characteristic atmosphere of any Templar house would have been one of calm. But this tranquility in bustling activity did not come by accident; it was the fruit of conscious ordination and well-organized administration.

All the brethren were instructed to behave graciously at all times to each other, as was fitting for servants of Christ. Loud laughter was to be avoided; conversation was to be minimal, and conducted in soft voices. Against this somewhat effeminate ideal, however, there was a specific injunction that voluntary servants of the Order should not be beaten by the knights, which suggests a certain latitude in the knightly conception of gentleness.

From the beginning, the administration of the Order was feudal, and at first it must have been fairly lax – a loose, but never happy-go-lucky organization. Even before the first generation of brothers were dead, though, this had been tightened up very considerably; and despite the comparative lack of direct evidence, internal evidence of the various records gives something of a picture of Templar bureaucracy.

It was a bureaucratic organization, that much is apparent. Everything in the Templar empire was strictly centred on Jerusalem; and everything in the Temple of Jerusalem was focussed on the Master, at least in theory, if not in actual practice. Clearly it would have been impossible for the one man to have audited the accounts, for example, of every Templar house, from Ireland to Oultrejourdain (the south-eastern section of the kingdom of Jerusalem), from Portugal to Hungary; but he was the pinnacle of a pyramid with a very wide base, and the whole federative structure looked up to him. He could, if he chose, inspect any part of any one of the local organizations; and by the same token, if any brother, however, humble, had a complaint or felt he had been dealt with unjustly at local level, that brother could bring his case before the Master himself.

Appropriately for an Order in which obedience was paramount, infringements of the Rule were punished strictly, but, it appears, impartially. Cases were heard and judgements given in the weekly chapter; the general chapter was a grander, less frequent affair, in which powerful members of the Order would convene to discuss internal and external politics. Although humbler, the regular weekly chapters were no less formally arranged.

They would normally take place on a Sunday, after mass, either in the chapel or the main hall of the house, and they were held in every house where four or more brothers resided. All brothers, servants, sergents and knights took part. Entering the meeting, they would genuflect before the altar, recite a paternoster, and before sitting down would remove their hats – of red or white felt – and their coifs. (At this point the Rule gives the charming detail that bald brothers were allowed to keep their coifs on.) The Master, commander or senior brother present would then begin proceedings with a sermon, full of moral and spiritual injunctions; and then the floor was open to confessions. These were not confessions of spiritual misdeeds, which would require priestly absolution, but of breaches of discipline. However, the two were so closely linked that many brethren, especially the simpler ones, failed to see the distinction – a failure in understanding shared by many outsiders, and which in later years would do the Order much harm.

Voluntary confessions were dealt with more leniently than those following accusations; and while any brother was able to bring another's fault into the open, if the accusation proved wrong or malicious, the accuser was required to apologize publicly and to submit himself to the justice of the house.

After admitting his misdeed, the defaulter had to leave the assembly, while his case was debated in secret. Many years later this secrecy, like the confusion over confession, pardon and absolution, was used as a weapon to accuse and chastize the entire Order, but its original purpose was simple and logical: punishment came not from an individual brother, which could lead to ill-feeling between brethren, but from the Order as a whole.

It is particularly interesting, in the light of the accusations which were used to bring the Order to its end, to examine the actions which the brethren themselves counted as crimes. At the lower end of the scale were such offences as the loss or destruction of anything belonging to the Order. Typical offences recorded in this section are the loss of a hammer in a river, by a brother who threw it at a bird, and the breaking of a tray of glasses by another who, having dropped one glass, threw down the entire tray in anger. Accidental or deliberate minor misdeeds like these would entail punishments varying from a one-day weekly fast on bread and water for a year, through scourging on the bare back, to the penance of a year's degradation, in which the guilty brother lost the right to wear his distinctive mantle, and was obliged to eat off the floor with the dogs – which he was not permitted to chase away. Of necessity this category of offence was vague, depending on what might happen from week to week; the brethren in the chapter could not merely look up the appropriate punishment in a book, but had to use their discretion. It was the serious crimes which were precisely annotated, and for which punishment was standard.

Ten major offences merited expulsion from the Order. They were simony, larceny, sodomy, heresy, conspiracy, treason, the murder of a Christian, revealing the secrets of the chapter, retreating from fewer than three enemies, and leaving the house by any means other than the gate. Any brother found guilty of one of these offences was required to come before the entire chapter, wearing only his breeches and a belt around his neck. He would then be whipped, either with a flail or with his belt, and 'given permission to save himself' – which meant he was thrown out, and obliged to join another, stricter Order. He could not, however, join the Hospitallers – they and the Templars agreed early on that they would not accept each others' expelled brethren.

Every one of these offences compromised the internal or external security of the Order; this was why they were punished so severely – so that all the world could see the purging of infamous behaviour from the ranks of the Temple. And yet, despite the fact that the Templars themselves did not tolerate such things, accusations of five of these exact crimes – simony, sodomy, heresy, conspiracy and treason – formed the basis for the Temple's cataclysmic downfall.

In reality, of course, they were very rare occurrences; sodomy, for example, is only recorded once in the Temple's entire two-hundred-year history. The deliberations of the weekly chapter would usually be over a few trivial misdemeanours. Proceedings would then be wound up with a valedictory blessing from the senior brother present, in which he would remind the others that unconfessed misconduct had not been pardoned. For the rest,

'I give you what pardon I may, in the name of God, and of Our Lady, and of St Peter, and of St Paul, and of yourselves who have given me the power.'

But the last Master, Jacques de Molay, changed that; his chapters would end with the words, 'I pardon you the faults which, through shame of the flesh or fear of the justice of the house, you have not confessed.'

The difference, though well-meant, was profound. It is possible that the brethren of his generation interpreted this to

mean all sins, and not mere breaches of discipline, were absolved.
Deeds their forebears would have eschewed may then have
become common.

In the early days, however, and for most of the Order's
history, the Rule, though hard, was the Rule, and was to be
obeyed. And it was this very strictness, allied with the spiritual
inspiration they found in their surroundings, that gave the
Templar brothers their special sense of purpose and stability.
Even elderly Templars, and the sick or wounded, were able to
keep this comfort. Special consideration was given them; they
were cared for with great gentleness, and considerable wisdom.
Victims of that most dreaded disease, leprosy, had to leave the
Order and join a special group, the Order of St Lazarus, but even
they were treated with compassion; and – most enlightened of all
– the Order treated epileptics not as people possessed by demons,
but as ill people where illness could be controlled.

Apart from the Hospitallers, no one else in Outremer had the
security and direction of a closely-regulated way of life. The
ordinary Franks no longer had the single, uniting ambitions of
their forebears, or their simple objectives; those were achieved,
and in their stead they had all the rivalries, jealousies, enmities
and alliances that characterize any disunited group. And the
Templars, proud and confident in their organization, impatient
and contemptuous of the secular life it contrasted with, contributed to the disarray elsewhere.

Yet at this time the Christians in the Holy Land could not
afford disunity; their grandfathers had profited from Moslem
divisions, but there had never been any real Christian conquest of
the East. Although cities and castles had been taken, nothing had
ever really been secured; Christian safety rested less on Christian
might than on Moslem weakness.

It could not last. Sooner or later, the Islamic countries that
surrounded the Franks were bound to come together.
De Blanquefort, with the piercing military sense that could make
the Templar Masters sound like prophets, had once said that his
greatest fear was that a single Moslem prince would 'reunite the
two most powerful realms, Cairo and Damascus, and abolish the
very name of Christian'. For decades the Franks had depended on
the mutual enmity of Shiite Egypt and Sunnite Syria, and had
played diplomatic games with the states in between, knowing

that if it was essential, the Christians of both Byzantium and Europe would probably rally to their aid. And for decades the mixture had worked; but in the last third of the twelfth century, the young Syrian vizier of Egypt destroyed the balance for ever.

Saladin was one of those rare people whose qualities commanded the respect of his friends and his enemies. Almost everyone who encountered him said the same: apart from his gifts as a leader, he was just, he was pious, he was moderate; he was generally merciful, he was extremely courageous, he was always faithful to his word. They were all the qualities of the perfect Moslem, the ideal Saracen; they were ideal Christian qualities too, but no leader in the Christian camp shared them, not even among the Templars. Even if any Christian had displayed those qualities, it would not have lessened Saladin's determination, as a devout Moslem, to reclaim Jerusalem and get rid of the infidels – especially the Templars whom, as men of honour, he trusted, but whom, as warriors of another religion, he hated deeply.

But Saladin had not always been so ambitious. Despite the apocryphal tales of youthful exploits at hunting, as a young man he appears to have been studious, conservative, unobtrusive and rather priggish. He was born in 1137 or '38 – the year 532 of the Mohammedan era – in the fortress of Tekrit, on the banks of the river Tigris, north-east of Baghdad. As a child he lived first at Baalbek; he was in Damascus when Nur ed-Din took it over in 1154, and stayed there as a member of the court for another nine years. Then, in 1163, Amalric of Jerusalem had launched his first attack on Egypt. Saladin's uncle voiced the general opinion concerning the country – it was 'a country without *men*, and with a precarious and contemptible government'. But it also had virtually unlimited resources, and both Amalric and Nur ed-Din recognized it as the key to power. Nur ed-Din attacked it the year after Amalric; Amalric responded with another attack in 1167; and Saladin made his legendary entry into Franco-Moslem history. In his first independent command, he withstood a siege of seventy-five days in Alexandria, surrounded by joint Frankish and Egyptian forces, until a Syrian army rescued him. While his men were evacuated, he was held hostage in Amalric's camp; and there, it is said, he was given Christian knighthood.

There is no certain proof of this story, but true or not, it does demonstrate the respect the Franks and the Templars eventually held for Saladin. One of the greatest reasons for this respect was his complete integrity; he never broke a treaty. In the feudal Latin states, such behaviour was theoretically the norm; in practice it was almost unheard of. It was one rule that even the Templars broke; and as much as anything else, it was this lack of trustworthiness that caused the downfall of Outremer.

Bertrand de Blanquefort died on 2 January 1169. His successor was Philip de Milly of Nablus, a nobleman of Frankish stock, but born in the Holy Land: the first Master to be a native Palestinian. In his secular life he had been a powerful lord, holding the fiefs of Oultrejourdain, which included the mighty castles of Kerak and Montreal. And he was chosen by the Templars because of his secular status, for he never had any religious vocation – he entered the Order on 13 August 1169, and was Master within a week. Under him the Templars had one notable victory: in December 1170, Saladin, testing his new-found power in Egypt, crossed the border and invested the fortress of Daron, the Franks' most southerly stronghold on the Mediterranean coast. It was a weak castle, and was on the verge of surrender when Amalric and the Templars rescued it. The Order needed a victory like that, for their behaviour over Egypt still rankled, and in Armenia, far to the north, an apostate Templar was actually leading Moslem raids on Frankish territory. However, de Milly did not stay long: less than two years after his election, he resigned the post of Master and became Amalric's permanent ambassador to Constantinople. Of his two reasons for leaving, only one was convincing: he felt he could serve the Holy Land better in his new role. His other reason was one which no true Templar would ever have countenanced: discouragement, for the flood of support from Europe had dried to a mere trickle.

In the year 1170, the Holy Land was struck by a series of devastating earthquakes that toppled towns and castles no man could destroy – the Chronicle of Pisa for 1172 tells us that six thousand people were killed. Those inclined to read such things as portents expected imminent disaster, but there was no apparent immediate sequel apart from the almost incidental election of a new Master of the Temple. If the prophets could have looked a little further, though, this election would have seemed disastrous enough.

Odo de St Amand was the name of the eighth Master. He had held courtly ranks, as Marshal of Jerusalem and Cupbearer to the King, but despite this, he showed himself as Master to be a loyal Templar and nothing other, defending the rights of the Order against all comers. William of Tyre recovered from his momentary weakness and sailed into the attack with full force: St Amand, he said, 'was a man with the blast of fury in his nostrils, neither fearing God nor respecting men'; and even allowing for William's colossal bias, St Amand's actions seem to bear this out. He made no compromises to patriarch or king, but stuck rigorously to the absolute letter of Templar privileges. Technically this was an unassailable attitude; in practice, compromise made relationships easier. The Templars' rights had been won through diplomacy; to insist on those rights seemed arrogant.

There was no direct clash until 1172, but then it came with a vengeance. An embassy came to King Amalric, from – of all people – the Assassins. These militant Shiites were alarmed by Saladin's rise in Egypt, for, although the country was still nominally ruled by the Shiite Caliph, Saladin himself was Sunnite, and as vizier he held the real power. And so the Assassins sought an alliance with Amalric, Shiites and Christians against Sunnites; and the ambassadors indicated that if the alliance was successful, the Old Man of the Mountains and all his men would adopt Christianity. That was unlikely, but Amalric did not care; the Assassins would be formidable allies. They only stipulated one condition: that a tribute imposed on some of their territory by the Templars should be lifted. A negligible price; Amalric agreed, promising the Templars that he would make good the loss. It was then that he discovered that a reputation for breaking promises can be a serious handicap.

As the Assassin ambassadors were returning to their mountain castle Alamut – the Eagle's Nest – they were ambushed and killed by a single Templar knight, in a style worthy of their own. All that is known of the killer is that he was called Walter de Mesnil, and he had only one eye. It is not known whether or not Odo de St Amand ordered the killing; but once it was done, he backed Walter at once. Amalric was infuriated, and demanded that Walter be tried as a common murderer; St Amand refused to hand him over, pointing out, as he had often done before, that

he Order was responsible only to the pope, who would judge the
:ase – if it ever got that far. As far as the Templars were
:oncerned, Amalric's promise to repay their lost tribute was so
much empty air; the Order preferred hard cash to a dubious
alliance.

On Amalric's third invasion of Egypt, the brethren had
shown they would not fight against their will; by killing the
ambassadors, they interfered directly with Amalric's government. The king stopped talking. At the head of a group of
soldiers, he rode to Sidon, where Walter was being held in
supposed safety, burst into the Templars' house and personally
arrested the one-eyed knight. Walter was carried off to prison,
and nothing more was heard of him.

Nonetheless, the projected alliance of Franks and Assassins
came to nought, and the Templars held fast to their tribute. They
ignored the king when they chose and followed their own
counsel. Amalric grew steadily more enraged, and when, in a
minor battle in 1174, twelve Templar knights surrendered an
untenable fortress to Moslems, the king 'trussed them up at once'
– meaning he hanged them. And he tried to do more: with
William of Tyre he began drafting a letter to the pope, detailing
his grievances, and requesting the dissolution of the Order. But
the letter was never sent, nor even finished, because on 11 July
1174, Amalric 'ended his life of a bloody flux' – or more
prosaically, a combination of typhus and dysentery.

Less than two months before, death had taken Nur ed-Din
from the Moslems; the cause was a quinsy; and two months after
Amalric, the Shiite Caliph of Cairo died. The new Syrian Sultan
was a boy of eleven; the new king of Jerusalem was thirteen; and
the new King of Egypt was Saladin, thirty-seven years old and
eager for success.

Saladin brought Egypt back to the orthodox Sunnite fold,
smoothly and quietly, without any objection from the Egyptian
people. Politically it was less easy for him in Egypt, and in 1175
he agreed to two years' truce with Jerusalem, while he set his new
kingdom in order. And though they would have attacked if they
could, the Franks counted themselves fortunate in the truce; for
their king, the thirteen-year-old Baldwin IV, was not only a
minor – he was a leper.

So, at any rate, say the contemporary accounts. Baldwin IV

was fatally ill, there is no doubt. His disease had not been noticed until he was about ten, when his tutor – William of Tyre, the archbishop and historian – was watching him playing with some friends. The boys were having a trial of endurance digging their fingernails into each others' arms; the young prince was the only one not to wince at all, and William discovered that the boy could not feel pain. They called it leprosy; but no one, not even the heir to the throne, would have been allowed an ordinary life if he were leprous. It was, says Fuller, 'the leprosy called elephantiasis noisome to the patient, but not infectious to the company' – yet deadly, nevertheless; and around the Holy Land Saladin was drawing a noose that was equally deadly. Damascus had opened its gates to him in November 1174, and, in Fuller's words,
'Jerusalem was a poor weatherbeaten kingdom, bleak and open to the storm of enemies on all sides, having no covert or shelter of any good friend near it, lying in the lion's mouth betwixt his upper and nether jaw; Damascus on the north, and Egypt on the south; two potent Turkish kingdoms, united under a puissant prince, Saladin. . . . Our western princes were prodigal of their pity, but niggardly of their help. The heat of the war in Palestine had cooled their desires to go thither.'

Not all the Moslem states submitted so easily to Egypt, though, and those that did not were helped, when possible, by the Franks. Aleppo was one, rescued from Saladin's siege by a Frankish army at the beginning of February 1175. Aleppo actually held a large number of Christian prisoners from previous battles; when the siege was lifted, the Aleppans released them all in gratitude to their saviours. Among the freed men was that archetypal robber baron, Reynald de Chatillon – older, but not a bit wiser, and not the least dismayed by his fifteen years' incarceration.

And now the tables of the war were completely turned; in Moslem and Frank, the spirits of their grandfathers were blown away like the desert sands, and the old formula that had led the Christians to Jerusalem – Moslem anarchy against Frankish monarchy – was exactly reversed. The jaws of the lion closed slowly around the Holy Kingdom, and within the kingdom rivalries spread like the disease in Baldwin's body. King and kingdom were killing themselves.

The rivalries of those eleven years, 1175 to 1186, were as complex as any theatrical tragedy. Like such a plot, the different levels of the plot unfolded stage by stage, worked together and culminated in disaster.

Reynald de Chatillon, Raymond of Tripoli, the Templars, the Hospitallers and Baldwin the leper king – these were the first main characters. Since Baldwin was a minor, he needed a regent until he came of age at sixteen; the regent was Raymond of Tripoli. Supported by the native barons and the Hospitallers, he tried to establish peaceful relations with the Moslems around them; a continuation of the war was too heavily loaded against the Christians. But the Templars and Reynald were committed to war – the Templars in their role of knights of God, Reynald by his former assumption of princely power and by the bandit's brain. Released from prison, he had found himself landless, an unemployed warrior prince, for his old fief of Antioch had been ceded in his absence to his step-son, and his wife Constance was dead. So, very soon after his release, he had married the heiress of Oultrejourdain and set himself up as lord of the two castles of Kerak and Montreal – once the property of Philip de Milly, seventh Master of the Temple, and still, as the south-eastern defence of the Holy Kingdom, one of the most strategically important areas of all.

But the distance between Europe and Outremer – which had once been as cogent an attraction to the oppressed and dispossessed as the holiness of crusading had been to the pious – was becoming a false friend to the new generation of Franks in the Holy Land. If there is terror in going out to invade a foreign land, there is excitement too, and the possibility for rich and poor of finding a new and better life on earth. But that excitement, and that possibility, have a limited existence. When the land has been carved up, there are no more estates to win, no more kingdoms to create; and a poor man can only exchange one master for another. And when aggression must turn to defence, the thrill of war evaporates; and only the terror remains. Moreover, those men who continued, in the late twelfth century, to come out from Europe, filled with whatever mixture of piety, vainglory and greed, found in the East a people whom they only half recognized as kin. The bonds of language were there, and a superficial veneer of common culture; but little more. Westerners came out looking for a world which the Franks of the East knew no longer existed. Devout Europeans could not comprehend that simply in order to survive, treaties with the infidel were essential; and the hopeful and avaricious were similarly disappointed when they found that they had been called only to defend other men's land, without great material reward for themselves. So the reinforcements from the West dwindled, and dwindled more; and those small numbers who did arrive, ignorant of the delicacy of the political situation, all, for their own reasons – the love of God or the love of loot – joined the perilous, warlike combination of Reynald and the Templars.

The opposition between the two Christian camps, the one wishing for peace and the other uncompromisingly militant, was embittered by personal feuds. Reynald's new wife had been married before; her first husband had been murdered, and she was convinced that the Regent, Raymond of Tripoli, was to blame. The Seneschal of the Temple, Gerard de Ridefort, also had a personal grudge against Raymond. He had come to the east as an ordinary knight with the Second Crusade, and had attached himself to Raymond's court. Raymond had promised him the hand of the first eligible heiress, but the first one turned out to be too eligible – her name was Lucia of Botrun, and when an Italian merchant offered Raymond the girl's weight in gold for her hand in marriage, Raymond conveniently forgot his promise. In disgust, Gerard joined the Templars, without speaking of, or forgetting, his disappointment and anger. Silently and privately, he began to plot revenge.

But in spite of this split in the state of Jerusalem, things seemed to go well at first. In 1177, Baldwin the leper was sixteen, and was counted an adult. Raymond stepped down from the regency; Baldwin assumed full power, and soon showed that he made up for any disability with sheer nerve. The truce with Egypt ended; almost at once the crippled king was faced with an invasion as Saladin and his army crossed the Mediterranean coastal border. St Amand massed all the Templar knights at Gaza, which seemed the obvious objective; but Saladin bypassed it completely, pushing on north, and Baldwin, with only five hundred knights, set out to confront him. They met at Ascalon, where the great Egyptian army encompassed the Frankish force and held it helpless in the town. Leaving Baldwin and the five hundred surrounded, Saladin went yet further north. Suddenly his true objective was clear: Jerusalem itself, open and undefended.

It seemed that all the Saracens had to do was walk in and take over. But then Baldwin showed what he could do: with desperate bravery he called St Amand from Gaza, led his five hundred in a charge through the enemy lines, rendezvoused with the Templars and rode north at full speed to circle round Saladin.

The Saracens, too confident, had slackened discipline. On 25 November, they were crossing a ravine at a place called Montgisard – only forty-five miles north-west of Jerusalem – when Baldwin attacked, approaching utterly unexpectedly from the north. There were twenty-six thousand Saracen horsemen, only a few hundred Christians; but the Saracens were routed. Most were killed; Saladin himself only escaped because he rode a racing camel. The young king, with his hands bandaged, rode in the forefront of the Christian charge – with St George beside him, people said, and the True Cross shining as brightly as the sun. Whether or not that was so, it was an almost incredible victory, an echo of the days of the First Crusade. But it was also the last time such a great Moslem army was beaten by such a small force, and in the long run it did no more than stave off final defeat. With more support from the West, things might have turned out differently. The Franks had some reason to hope for support, for in that very year Henry II of England and Louis VII of France agreed to go crusading together, and the pope sent an envoy in search of Prester John; but Louis and Henry soon scrapped their idea, and although the papal envoy got as far as Abyssinia, Prester John was never found.

Once upon a time there had been room for curiosity, interest and even friendship between the Franks and the Moslems. A generation earlier, such a friendship had sprung up between the Templars and a Moslem diplomat, Prince Usama of Shaizar. He lived mainly in Cairo and Damascus, but he made frequent trips in the earlier part of the century to Jerusalem, observing and noting the Frankish way of life with an interest that ignored politics. He despised Frankish medical treatment; he admired the system of justice instituted by King Amalric; he was astonished at the Franks' apparent lack of marital jealousy; and he liked and respected the Templars.

'When I was in Jerusalem,' Usama wrote, 'I used to go to the al-Aqsa Mosque [the Dome of the Rock], beside which is a small oratory which the Franks have made into a church. Whenever I went into the mosque, which was in the hands of Templars who were friends of mine, they would put the little oratory at my disposal, so that I could say my prayers there. One day I had gone in, said the *Allahu akbar* and risen to begin my prayers, when a Frank threw himself on me from behind, lifted me up and turned me so that I was facing east. "That's the way to pray!", he said. Some Templars at once intervened, seized the man and took him out of my way. But the moment they stopped watching him he seized me again and forced me to face east, repeating that this was the way to pray. Again the Templars intervened and took him away. They apologized to me and said: "He is a foreigner who has just arrived today, and he has never seen anyone pray facing any other direction than east." "I have finished my prayers," I said, and left, stupefied by the fanatic.'

By the second generation, Christians from the west were foreigners, to Franks and Moslems alike; but by the third generation, no one had time for tolerance any more. To the Moslems under Saladin, the war had become the *jihad*, the holy war; to the Franks it had become a daily fight for survival. However, they had cried wolf once too often; the 'foreigners' they had sometimes disdained had stopped coming, though the need was greater than ever before.

Whatever their Christian critics had said, the Templars had kept faith in their treaties with Moslems. Now even that trust could not be afforded. On the banks of the upper Jordan, at the ford where Jacob wrestled with the angel, they began to build a castle. It was in the centre of an area of no-man's-land where fortification was specifically excluded by treaty; St Amand, still sticking to the letter of the rules, said that the treaty was between Saladin and King Baldwin, and that therefore the Templars could do as they liked. Saladin offered Baldwin first 60,000, then 100,000 gold pieces, to stop the construction, but the Templars could not be prevented. Baldwin joined in the sophistry: while the Templars built, he laid a defensive ring around them, claiming that the defence and the construction were two entirely separate operations. Building commenced in October 1178; by April 1179 the castle was finished. It was named Chastelet, and garrison of fifteen hundred mercenaries and sixty Templar nights, including the Seneschal, was installed. The defensive ring retired, and at once Saladin laid siege to the new castle. He was repulsed, and spent the next few weeks raiding in the district; and then on 10 June, he revenged his defeat at Montgisard. The Franks were passing through Marj Ayun, the Valley of Springs, by the upper Jordan – Baldwin (carried in a litter), Raymond, St Amand, the Templars, the royal army: they were all there. Their passage disturbed the flocks grazing in the valley, and from an observation post high on a hill, Saladin watched. His attack was as much a surprise as Baldwin's had been at Montgisard, and his success was as great. The king and Raymond escaped; the Christian army was scattered; and St Amand was captured. And it was the Templars' fault. Not even they denied it, for they had joined battle on first sight of the Moslem army, before the royal army was ready, and they had been flung back on their fellow Christians by the Moslem counter-attack. Rashness, bravado, defeat; the king, and the kingdom's first lord, barely saved; their Master in captivity – the Templars had a lot to answer for at Marj Ayun.

Moving south, Saladin came once again to Chastelet, the castle at Jacob's Ford. For five days, from 24 to 29 August, he besieged it, sending sappers to mine the walls; and this time he succeeded. The walls, thrown up in such haste but a few months before, collapsed, and at the end nothing was left: not a man, not a stone: every man in the garrison was killed, and the castle razed to the ground, only ten months after building had begun.

With no possibility of peace or trust, a secular knight captured in battle could still hope to be spared for ransom. A Templar gave no quarter, and expected none; and in obedience to his Rule, he refused to be ransomed for anything more than his belt and his sword. So it was with St Amand, and he died after a year in a dungeon in Damascus, too proud, it was said, to consider a ransom.

Whether through pride or simply a too-literal understanding of the written word, St Amand had been troublesome to the kingdom – to what extent may be judged by the reprimand sent to him by Pope Alexander III in 1179:

'We learn that the brethren of the Temple . . . exceed the privileges which have been granted to them by the Holy See and presume to do many things which cause scandal among the people of God and grievous ill to souls. . . . We do therefore forbid them to receive churches and tithes from the hands of laymen without the consent of their bishops; they are to avoid those who are excommunicated and laid under interdict by name; in such churches as do not belong to them of right, they are to leave to the bishops the installing of priests; they are not, without consulting the bishop, to remove those who have been installed; and if they come to a church under interdict, they are to be admitted only once a year to perform service therein, and even then are not permitted to bury there the bodies of those laid under interdict.'

Strong language, and precise: not even a St Amand could misinterpret its meaning. Alexander III was one of the Temple's greatest supporters; for him to write such a reprimand, it is clear that even he believed that the Templars had frequently and massively overreached their rights. And even though, in St Amand's time, the Temple had grown immeasurably in secular power in the Holy Land, buying castles and land throughout the country as their owners returned to the West, nevertheless the Templars themselves felt it was time for a change of policy; for the man they elected to be their ninth Master, Arnold de Torroge, was St Amand's opposite in every way. His age is unknown, but he was much older than St Amand, and had the caution and circumspection expected of age; and since he had been Master of the Temple in Spain since 1167, he had no connection with any of the political factions in the Holy Land.

In some ways he was an admirable choice, because his equable nature calmed, for a while, the criticism of the Templars – but the virtue of his age played them false, and his very lack of political affiliation brought about an open conflict with the king.

The rivalries of the period within the Holy Land entered their second stage at this point, heightened by events beyond the borders. One of St Amand's last actions before his imprisonment had been to effect an agreement with the Master of the Hospital which 'terminated, voluntarily and irrevocably, all the debates born between the two Orders, both here and beyond the sea, over our lands, moneys and various possessions' – one of St Amand's few deeds of reconciliation. But the reconciliation, by bringing the Hospitallers to the Templars' side, altered the balance of power politics within the Holy Land; and just after it, in 1180, a drastic alteration began outside the country, when Emperor Manuel Comnenus died, leaving no heir but an eleven-year-old boy. In 1180 as well the patriarch of Jerusalem died, and was replaced, largely because of the king's mother's influence, by Heraclius, archbishop of Caesarea, an almost illiterate but extremely good-looking man with a priapic reputation. In the same year the king's sister Sibylla married an unknown young Frenchman named Guy de Lusignan. He was the third son of a minor nobleman in France, handsome, and reputedly descended from Satan through the water-fairy Melusine, but without any other distinction whatever. And, since the king by now was dying, he stood to inherit the throne of Jerusalem. So now the parties were composed, roughly, of Count Raymond of Tripoli, Baldwin's erstwhile regent, and the native barons on the one hand, still hoping for some sort of peace; and on the other hand, belligerent as ever, the Templars and Reynald de Chatillon, with their new allies the Hospitallers, the dissolute patriarch Heraclius and the foppish new heir-apparent, Guy de Lusignan. The balance was firmly with the latter, the warlike group; but if Byzantium had stood, their subsequent deeds and misdeeds might have had less disastrous consequences. As it was, six years of the interaction of people and events led, grimly and inexorably, to tragedy.

The sole hopeful event of 1180 was a new peace treaty between Baldwin and Saladin, intended to last for two years. One of its clauses permitted the free traffic of Moslem and Frankish merchants across one another's territory; but it so happened that a major Moslem caravan route to Mecca passed through Oultrejourdain, right beneath the walls of Reynald's castle, Kerak. It was too much to expect that Reynald would resist the temptation of those rich camel trains winding past his doorstep; he could not, and did not. In 1181 he captured the goods of an entire caravan. Saladin demanded return of the goods, or compensation; Reynald refused point-blank, and poor Baldwin, nearly blind, confined to his bed, unable even to sign his name, could do nothing. By chance fifteen hundred Christian pilgrims were shipwrecked on the Egyptian coast, and instantly taken as hostages by Saladin; Reynald was adamant. The merchandise and the hostages remained each where they were, and war was on again.

In 1182, extending his empire, Saladin ravaged northern Syria; and Reynald grabbed the chance for the most daring exploit of his life. Whatever else one may think of him, his sheer audacity compels a certain admiration; for by now he was bored with local land-raids. Piracy was the next thing, and piracy in a grand style. As the crow flies, Kerak lies one hundred and twenty miles north-north-east of the Gulf of Aqaba, the eastern horn of the Red Sea. From Aila, the port at the north of the gulf, to Medina, the journey by sea and land is about seven hundred and fifty miles; to Mecca, it is over a thousand. But Mecca and Medina, the holiest cities of Islam, were Reynald's new goals.

East of the Dead Sea, close to Kerak, the forest of Moab flourished. On Reynald's orders, trees were felled, five ships were constructed, tested on the Dead Sea, dismantled and taken by camel those one hundred and twenty miles to Aila. The town was captured easily; the ships were reassembled; two remained to blockade the island fortress of Graye, by Aila, and the rest set off south, sinking and burning other ships, sacking and pillaging towns with a glorious flamboyant nonchalance. No one had ever even thought of doing such a thing before; the Moslem world was totally unprepared; and for almost a year, Reynald's fleet were masters of the Red Sea. Reynald himself, clearly more of a sponsor than a sailor, stayed on shore in the north; but his pirates must have had the time of their lives, on a magnificent spree from coast to coast. On the African coast they sacked Aidib, the main Nubian port, and took merchantmen with goods from India and Aden. On the Arabian coast they burnt all the ships in the ports of Medina, and came as far as ar-Raghib, one of the ports serving Mecca – one Arab report says they even went to Aden. It was a marvellous adventure, but it could not last. A Moslem fleet was assembled under an admiral with the somewhat unlikely name of Lulu, who eventually caught up with the pirates while they were busy at al-Hawra, the port of Medina. What is most astonishing, and what terrified the Moslems most, is how nearly the fleet succeeded; for ar-Raghib is only sixty-five miles or so from Mecca. Indeed, a few of the pirates actually got to Mecca – but as prisoners: for Lulu destroyed their fleet; the survivors were divided into two groups, of which one was taken to Mecca, the other to Cairo; and in the two cities both groups were ceremonially executed.

One of the strangest aspects of the whole episode is that only one Frankish chronicler mentioned it at all. He was a squire named Ernoul and he described the piratical odyssey as a scientific expedition 'to know what people lived on this foreign sea'. To the Moslems it was the greatest outrage against the Faith since the fall of Jerusalem, and Saladin vowed that he personally would kill Reynald.

Moslem accounts of this voyage of destruction concentrate, naturally, on the wrecking and burning, the chaos and carnage that Reynald's men left behind them. Neither the Moslems, nor Ernoul with his brief comment, touch on what now seems the most remarkable part of it all: the feat of organization and endurance involved in shifting those ships from the Dead to the Red Sea.

No one knows Reynald's route from Kerak to the coast, but there is really only one possibility: the old Roman road which linked Aqaba with distant Damascus, and which passed, so to speak, by Reynald's front door. Even today parts of this road survive, and a journey along it from sea to sea reveals a vivid and fascinating view across time, back to that day when Reynald's camels began to lumber south, with the beams and planks of his ships strapped on their swaying backs.

Between the Dead Sea and the castle of Kerak runs the Wadi Kerak, a twisting gorge cut by a stream which, in the rare rain-storms, swells rapidly to become a river. Reynald's ships would probably have been dragged ashore at some point close to the mouth of the wadi and dismantled on the beach there. The mere fact of their being dismantled and reassembled raises the question of their construction, whose answer can only be a matter of guess-work; they could have been to a European design and secured with pegs, but it is possible, and perhaps more likely, that an Eastern design such as the dhow was used. Reynald always exploited his surroundings to the full, and ships of the dhow family had two great advantages for the Red Sea operation: their familiar forms would give no warning of danger, and their traditional construction – laced with fibre, rather than per-manently fixed – would have helped to solve the problem of their overland transport. But for a European, dhows are not easy ships to handle, even compared to a twelfth century rig; and since it takes a fairly determined effort to sink something on the Dead Sea, it is possible that the testing period there was really a training session for the crews.

But training or testing, once it was over and the vessels loaded onto the camels, the long trek had to begin. The Wadi Kerak, the obvious starting point, was also one of the hardest stages: ten miles or more of precipitous track, rising four thousand three hundred feet from the level of the Dead Sea to the castle itself. The track winds up from a rocky beach studded with oleanders, through jagged crags of sandstone and granite; then after a rich but brief stretch of cultivated land, you emerge at last by the rounded limestone mountain peaks. Kerak broods, silent, reflective, and slightly menacing, still high above your head.

Its size is awesome. The building dates from the early twelfth century, but the site has been inhabited since at least 1200 BC. The Old Testament speaks of a curse laid on the town by the prophet Isaiah, and whether from that or from its strategic position on the north–south trade route, Kerak has seen many major battles in its time. In the Crusader province of Oultrejourdain, Kerak's looming form dominated, threatened, protected, oppressed; those without learned a new instinct of survival, while those within savoured conquest, and looked beyond the horizon.

It is impressive, but leaving the castle brings relief. Very likely Reynald's pirates felt the same. Allowing the improbable – that some of them were literate – this makes the complete lack of records detailing their desert journey more understandable. Away from Reynald's eyrie they became their own masters, and the desert became a minor obstacle before the start of their great adventure. They would have expected to return, to tell of it, and perhaps to repeat it; writing – if anyone could – was irrelevant, compared to actual experience.

Their fate was hard. Stumbling over the burning stones, they might have paused at the summit of the Rasn Nagb pass, twenty miles south of Petra, and stared across the arid brown rocks to the blue mountains in the distance; then they would have come down to the wide stretches of *ghor*, the dry mud-flats, utterly waterless, and baked as hard as flint; and at last they would have crossed the yellow sands of the southern desert. Not even they could have ignored the jebels here. These are gigantic outcrops of hard rock, many over two thousand feet high, and worn into dozens of fantastic shapes by the storms of centuries. Perhaps the men rested in their shade, or found with gratitude one of the occasional trickling pools that lie hidden among them.

But literate or illiterate, the general silence of the Franks over this arduous journey springs from a reason simpler and more profound than any other: namely that after more than eighty years of Christian occupation, these lands east of the Mediterranean were home. Their dangers and risks were known and accepted for, to many of the Franks in the twelfth-century Latin East, countryside such as this was all they had ever known, or would ever know. For all that, however, the rigours and perils of the land were no less real; and in a way it is good to know that, thugs and ruffians though they all undoubtedly were, Reynald's marauders had the freedom of the Red Sea for nearly a year, before their gruesome, ceremonial deaths under Saracen swords.

By the time of the destruction of Reynald's fleet, in the summer of 1183, Saladin was master of Aleppo. The boy-king of Syria had died suddenly two years before, probably poisoned, and Saladin had only to fill the vacuum. For more than two hundred years Islam had not had so great a king; his rule extended from Libya to Aden to the Tigris, a huge triangle far larger than all the Crusader states together had ever been. Now they were no more than a fringe intrusion – but they were there, and their existence was shameful to Islam. They had to be eradicated. Saladin knew they could expect no help; the West was bored and preoccupied and – the final movement in the patterns of power – the strong and stable rule of Byzantium was disintegrating. Like the boy-king of Syria, the Byzantine boy-emperor had been poisoned; the new emperor was a tyrant with a nearly bankrupt empire and a negligible army. Saladin concentrated on Reynald.

In Jerusalem, King Baldwin's disease worked slowly through his body, and his arms and legs began to decay. Nagged by his mother, his sister and the profligate patriarch, he gave the regency of the kingdom to the spineless, beautiful youth, Guy de Lusignan. But Guy was so weak, so hesitant, so cowardly and so rude to his dying king that no one, not even his three backers, could tolerate the idea of him in power. In March 1183 he was deposed, and his step-son, Baldwin's nephew, was proclaimed heir to the throne. Another Baldwin, he would be fifth of that name; and his story would be the shortest and saddest of all.

It was now that Arnold de Torroge's ignorance of Palestinian politics led him astray, because for some inexplicable reason both he and the Master of the Hospital, together with Heraclius, tried to intercede for Guy. All three were banished from court; then some months later King Baldwin sent the trio on a mission they must have all known to be hopeless – to drum up interest in Europe and launch another crusade. Thus both the military Orders were deprived of their chosen leaders.

Saladin, meanwhile, was ready for Reynald. The last major event of 1183 was his siege of Kerak. It failed, but during its course one extraordinary incident took place – a gesture of the highest chivalry. The siege began on 20 November, and by chance a marriage was being celebrated in the castle. As rocks from the Saracen mangonels shook the walls, the marriage party continued within. The bridegroom's mother sent dishes from the feast out to Saladin and he, having learnt where the party was taking place, ordered the bombardment of that part to stop.

Count Raymond was regent of Jerusalem once more, and on his advance towards Kerak, Saladin withdrew. It was 4 December 1183. The castle and Reynald were safe; but Saladin could afford to wait.

In the autumn of 1184 he marched against Kerak again; and again he could not break the castle's defence. It did not really matter: Reynald was a godless unbeliever, but he was only one amongst many, and time was on Saladin's side. On 30 September, Arnold de Torroge succumbed to his age, and died in Verona; the mission to the West had no other result. There was no hope from Europe, and the Byzantine tyrant, Andronicus Comnenus, turning Christian politics upside-down, made a treaty with Saladin guaranteeing not to help the Franks. The treaty helped Andronicus not one bit, however, for in 1185 his tyranny provoked a rebellion; he was caught, and torn to pieces.

The downward spiral of fate and intrigue accelerated. A new Master of the Temple was elected; the election was, as usual, secret, but it seems that it was decided only after a violent debate in the Order. In Jerusalem it was rumoured that Gilbert Erail,

Commander of Jerusalem and Treasurer of the Order, and Arnold de Torroge's 'companion of rank', would be the new Master; but when the Templar electors announced their decision, it was for Gerard de Ridefort, whose bride had been sold by Raymond. De Ridefort had risen to be Seneschal of the Temple, and promotion from Seneschal to Master was not unusual – but, with a heart filled with malice and resentment towards the regent of the kingdom, he was the worst possible choice.

On 16 March 1185, Baldwin the leper-king died, released at long last from his slow agony. His nephew was crowned King Baldwin V. In this collection of kingdoms with children at their heads, he was the youngest of all: only seven years old. People called him Baudouinet. The death of the leper-king and the crowning of the infant were attended by famine throughout the kingdom. It seemed that starvation would end the ancient war of cross and crescent without any further help from Saladin, and Count Raymond, in despair, asked for a four-year truce. He did not hope the proposition would be accepted – but it was, for Saladin himself was ill, and thought he was dying. For the Franks, it was as if they had been snatched from the very jaws of the lion.

This last chance was an illusion. At the end of August 1186, shortly before his ninth birthday, Baudouinet died. He at least died of natural causes, for he had always been delicate. It had been half-expected and, in his will, Baldwin the leper-king had left a contingency plan to cover the succession. According to this, the rival claims of the leper-king's sister, Sibylla, and his step-sister, Isabella, would be assessed by the pope, the kings of France and England, and the German emperor; it was a typically sensible plan, and as Baldwin lay dying, all the great barons and leaders of the realm had sworn to carry it out. Heraclius and de Ridefort were amongst those who swore to assist. Reynald de Chatillon was not there, but an old jail-mate of his from the years in Damascus, Joscelin de Courtenay, *was* present, and Joscelin took the oath like everyone else.

When Baudouinet died, the contingency plan was set in motion. Count Raymond called an assembly of the lords of the kingdom to decide on ambassadors for the West. The assembly was to be held at Jerusalem; but Joscelin persuaded the count that Tiberias would be safer, away from the interference of the debauched and dishonest patriarch Heraclius. Raymond walked trustingly straight into the trap, and departed for Tiberias.

Baudouinet had died at Acre. As soon as Raymond left the city, Joscelin's troops occupied it, along with Tyre and Beirut. The Templars took the king's tiny corpse back to Jerusalem, where they buried it with all honour in the Church of the Sepulchre. Joscelin summoned Reynald from Kerak, and Sibylla and her useless husband Guy de Lusignan from Ascalon, directing them to Jerusalem. In Acre he proclaimed Sibylla queen, then hurried south to meet her and the others. When all were gathered together, the Templars closed the gates of the Holy City and set guards to watch for Count Raymond. Heraclius and de Ridefort went to claim the royal insignia; these were kept in a triple-locked chest, one key each being held by the Patriarch and the Masters of the two Orders. At first the Master of the Hospital, faithful to his oath, refused to hand over his key; then in disgust he threw it out of the window, dissociating himself and his Order from the whole sequence of events.

With the insignia secure, Heraclius crowned Sibylla, and then she crowned Guy – the weakest and worst king who ever ruled in Outremer. And Gerard de Ridefort, in a mockery of blessing, raised his voice and shouted: 'This crown repays the marriage of Botrun!'

Raymond would not submit to Guy. The truce with Saladin was still in force, though Saladin was now recovered and fit again, and it was possible that the kingdom might yet revive, in spite of its characterless monarch. But then Reynald de Chatillon played his last card.

Another of those rich, tempting camel trains drew him out of his nest in Kerak. He slaughtered its escort, threw the merchants and their families into his dungeons, telling them to call on Mohammed to help. His booty from that raid was the largest he had ever won.

It was like a repeat of the last caravan raid. Saladin demanded compensation; Reynald refused; King Guy could do nothing; the war was resumed. But this time, it was a war of total extermination.

CHAPTER 7

THE HORNS OF HATTIN

The Holy Land, 1187

'I will give them into the hands of their
enemies ... and I will make the cities
of Judah a desolation.'
Jeremiah XXXIV, 19–22

THE ATMOSPHERE OF MISTRUST and betrayal affected everyone in Outremer – even Count Raymond, whose regency had been reliable and trustworthy. Moslems said that the Franks at that time numbered no one braver or shrewder than he; but after Guy's coronation, Raymond turned to treason and rebellion. First he tried to supplant Sibylla and Guy with Isabella and her husband, Humphrey of Toron; however, the scheme fell flat when Humphrey swore allegiance to Guy. Then, when general war became inevitable, he began corresponding with Saladin, and early in 1187 the pair formed a private treaty in which Saladin guaranteed to make Raymond 'King of all the Franks'. It was certainly shrewd: Raymond knew that the sole chance of Outremer's survival lay in extending peace as far and for as long as possible. But, equally certainly, it was treason. Raymond did not attempt to conceal what he had done and, when it became known in Jerusalem, King Guy assembled his army and prepared to subjugate Raymond by force.

The expedition, typically, was not Guy's idea – he never really had any ideas at all, and Gerard de Ridefort played on his brainlessness unscrupulously. De Ridefort's malice towards Raymond was unbounded, and it was he who pushed Guy into this unaccustomed posture of authority. It would have been madness for Guy to force the issue; Outremer would have committed suicide in civil war, for Raymond already had Saracen reinforcements in his own army, and could call on the unlimited resources of Saladin's empire. It never came to that, though, for a new adviser appeared: Balian of Ibelin, who vigorously pointed out the idiocy of the plan. Guy could be relied on for one thing, and that was to follow the most recent advice. Instead of force, he agreed to use diplomacy, and sent Balian, accompanied by the archbishop of Tyre, the Master of the Hospital and Gerard de Ridefort to mediate with Raymond. De Ridefort took the slight severely, but he had to be present, for any peace without his agreement would be futile.

Balian's squire on this journey was the young man named Ernoul. He was literate, which was uncommon; even more uncommonly, he was interested enough in writing to record what he saw. It was he who had written the sole Frankish record of Reynald de Chatillon's piracy, though he did not take part in it – which may have been why he ascribed higher motives to Reynald than he deserved. His account of the embassy to Raymond, however, is first-hand, detailed and vivid. The delegation left Jerusalem on 29 April 1187. They rode sixty miles that day, and rested at Balian's castle in Nablus. On the morning of the 30th, deciding to stay at home for the day and organize his affairs, Balian sent the archbishop and the two Masters ahead; they arranged to meet fifty miles further north at the castle of La Fève. By the evening Balian was ready to go; he and Ernoul set off late, meaning to ride all night. However, passing through Samaria, Balian remembered an appointment: next morning, 1 May, was the Feast of St Philip and St James. He decided to halt at the house of the nearest bishop and celebrate mass in the morning.

Shortly after dawn on the feast day, he rode on with Ernoul. They arrived at La Fève in the middle of the morning, and were pleased to see the Templars' tents pitched before the castle walls; but as they approached they sensed that something was wrong – everything was silent. They searched the tents – every one was empty. Ernoul went into the castle and searched it – it was almost empty as well. There were only two soldiers in the whole building, stretched out on one of the upper floors and so ill they could not speak.

For two hours, not knowing what else to do, Balian and Ernoul waited at the castle, worried and bewildered; then they took to the road again. And on the road to Nazareth they suddenly met one single knight – a Templar, wounded and bleeding. As they approached each other, Balian shouted out, 'What news?' The Templar replied, 'Bad.' And there in the dusty highway, they learned what had happened.

The evening before, about the time that Balian and Ernoul had been setting out from Nablus, the archbishop and the Masters had arrived at La Fève, where a message had come to them from Raymond. It said that Saladin had asked permission of Raymond for his son to cross the count's land on a reconnaissance of Palestine. Bound by his treaty, Raymond had had to agree; but he had made the condition that the Moslems should not enter his land before dawn of 1 May, and that they should leave by nightfall without harming any of his towns or villages. The people of the country were warned of the visit, and ordered by Raymond to stay within their walls, where they would not be harmed. Raymond's message to the Masters and archbishop contained the same advice; the archbishop and the Master of the Hospital, Roger des Moulins, were happy to go along with it. Gerard de Ridefort was not. From a village nearby he summoned the Marshal of the Temple, Jacques de Mailly, to join him and to bring all his brothers with him. De Mailly obeyed, arriving at La Fève with ninety Templar knights – it was their tents that Balian and Ernoul had vainly searched.

That morning, when Balian had been as mass, the Templars had left La Fève. The archbishop had stopped in Nazareth; the two Masters, the Marshal and the brethren had continued, strengthened by forty secular knights. Everyone else had heeded Raymond's warning; except for the one hundred and thirty-three horsemen, the roads were empty. The company had ridden a short way beyond Nazareth, and then, breasting a hill, had seen the Moslem reconnaissance force below. There were seven thousand.

On his initiation, a Templar swore never to retreat unless the odds against him were greater than three to one. Here, at the Springs of Cresson, the odds were fifty-three to one; Roger des Moulins and Jacques de Mailly saw no purpose in taking them on, and said so. But Gerard would not allow retreat. Angrily turning his back on Roger, he looked at Jacques, tall and blond on a white horse, and sneered at him, saying, 'You love your blond head too well to want to lose it.' Jacques answered, '*I* shall die in battle as a brave man should. It is you who will flee like a traitor.'

Goaded by each other's insults, they led the charge down into a hopeless battle. And Jacques de Mailly's words came true: out of that company of one hundred and thirty-three, only three escaped – and de Ridefort was one of them. De Mailly was one of the last to fall. He fought like a demon – or an angel. By then it was common for the Franks to see St George fighting beside them in their victories, a belief which the Moslems knew of. For the Templars, he was conspicuously absent at Cresson; but seeing de Mailly's appearance and valour, the Moslems, when they finally cut him down, believed they had killed the Christian warrior saint.

For the Franks, the massacre had only one constructive result: Raymond, feeling a terrible guilt for his treaty with Saladin, submitted to Guy without hesitation. He had seen horrid evidence of the slaughter, for in the afternoon of 1 May, when Balian and Ernoul had met the solitary Templar, Raymond in Tiberias had been watching the return of the Saracen patrol. He knew they had kept their word: not a town, not a village, not a building had been harmed. But spiked on their spears he could see the heads of Templar knights.

At least – at last, and at the last moment – there was the semblance of unity within the kingdom. In May another pilgrim caravan passed Kerak; this time Reynald did not dare to touch it, for its passengers included Saladin's sister and nephew, and Saladin himself led the escort. Simultaneously, armies from all over his empire were massing east of the Sea of Galilee. The Christians prepared as best they could, and by the end of June had gathered about thirteen thousand men – ten thousand footsoldiers, about two thousand light cavalry and twelve hundred knights. Both Military Orders supplied all they could, keeping only skeleton garrisons in their fortresses. In addition the Templars gave King Guy their share of funds received from Henry II of England – the soldiers paid with this wore the arms of England. Heraclius, as patriarch and spiritual leader, was supposed to be at the head of the army, carrying the True Cross, but he conveniently fell ill and was obliged to give the Cross to the bishop of Acre. Most people guessed that he was actually dallying with his mistress.

The Christian army had no time to waste; Saladin was ready, and it was he who called the tune. On 26 June he reviewed his army, dividing it into three and taking command of the centre. In battle array he led his men to the south of the Sea of Galilee, and on 1 July they crossed the Jordan. On 2 July the town of Tiberias fell; but the castle, commanded by Raymond's wife, held out, and she sent a message to her husband in the king's camp at Acre.

The royal army was already on the move. In council with the king, Count Raymond had advised caution and a strategy of defence: the summer heat was already almost unbearable, the land was nearly waterless – but to the third-generation Franks it was familiar; Saladin did not know it, and if battle could be avoided, the weather and the terrain would work for the Franks. It was sound advice, but Raymond's treason was too recent. Reynald de Chatillon and Gerard de Ridefort accused him of cowardice and treachery; in King Guy emotion was stronger than reason, and he ordered a general advance. By the afternoon of 2 July the royal army was encamped at Sephoria, a well watered place with good pastures, halfway between Acre and Tiberias, and only three miles from Cresson. There the messenger from Tiberias found them. His news, literally of a damsel in distress, touched the chivalrous knights, and the popular reaction was to strike camp at once and go to her aid. Only one voice dissented, and of all people, it was that of Raymond. Even though Tiberias was *his* city and *his* wife was in danger, he said he would rather lose them both than sacrifice the kingdom – for that, he predicted, would be the result if the royal army left its present strong position. This time his reason and his example prevailed; the decision was taken to remain at Sephoria, and the army settled down for the night. Then, when all was quiet, de Ridefort returned to the king's tent. Yet again he denounced Raymond as a traitor. Tiberias was only six leagues away – its loss would shame the Franks, and he and his brethren would rather sell their white mantles than let a Christian city go so easily. Hearing this, Guy inevitably changed his mind. A new order went out: the army would march for Tiberias next morning.

Dawn came quickly on 3 July a midsummer dawn, the air

hot, dry and still. And somehow, as quickly as the dawn's arrival, Saladin guessed – or knew – the King's order. Perhaps real traitors left Guy's camp in the night. As the royal army was leaving the water and meadows of Sephoria, the Saracens mobilized and moved ten miles north-west, directly between the Franks and Tiberias. They stopped at a little village called Hattin.

The land there falls away sharply from west to east. The great western plain comes to a double-peaked rocky hill, a hundred feet high, called 'the Horns of Hattin'. The village of Hattin is less than a mile from the Horns, but lies six hundred feet below them; the Sea of Galilee, five miles away, is another thousand feet lower. Like Sephoria, Hattin has plentiful pasture and is well watered. Saladin was able to rest and refresh his men and horses; but he was taking a considerable risk. Guy's army was not much smaller than his own, and defeat there would force a retreat downhill towards the Sea. It was a calculated risk, though: for between Sephoria and Hattin, the western plain was dry as a bone, and the Christian army had to march twelve miles across it, in armour, under a blazing midsummer sun. They looked, said one Moslem, 'like mountains on the march, like seas boiling over, wave upon wave . . . the air stark, the light was dimmed, the plain dissolved into dust, destiny hung over them.'

As the Franks approached, detachments of fast, mounted archers rode out from the Moslem camp. Count Raymond had been given command of the Frankish vanguard; Balian and Ernoul rode with him. Guy had the centre, and the Templars the rearguard. The road was limestone, glaring white, shadeless and waterless. The Moslem archers circled the Franks, darting in and out, concentrating on the Templars and pressing them so hard that they were nearly cut off from the rest of the royal army. By the time the army had covered ten miles everyone in it was exhausted, parched with thirst, burned by the sun, chafed by armour and harassed by the archers. Guy called a halt. Raymond, hearing the order, cried out: 'Alas! Lord God, the war is over! We are dead men! The kingdom is undone!' He alone knew of a possible well, at Lubieh, on the southern slopes of the Horns of Hattin; the royal army dragged itself on a little farther. But the well was dry.

They could not continue; they could not retreat. They pitched camp around the empty well, with no pasture for the horses, no water for anyone, man or beast, and the men's throats so dry they could scarcely eat. And all the while, as if to taunt and tantalize, Saladin's army ate and drank below.

The night was a foretaste of hell, full of heat and terror. In the darkness the Saracens surrounded the Franks, and set fire to the dry grass and scrub. With nightfall a wind had arisen, and as the thornbushes crackled with a lurid red light, the stinging smoke blew through the royal camp. Above the noise of the flames and through the billowing smoke, the Franks could see and hear the Moslems singing and praying aloud; Ernoul endured it all. When the morning finally came – Saturday 4 July – he saw the extent of the Moslem encirclement, and thought that not even a cat could slip through it.

But far below, the Sea of Galilee was visible, gleaming in the sunshine. The sight of so much water drove the Frankish infantry to despair: they broke ranks and charged the Moslem ring in a fatal, futile rush. The Moslems were rested, fresh, invigorated and well-armed: every man had a full quiver, and seventy camel-loads of arrows waited to replenish them. None of the Frankish footsoldiers got through.

The Moslem attack began with clouds of arrows 'like thick swarms of locusts'; many of the Franks' horses were killed in the first onslaught, and a knight unhorsed was almost immobilized. Yet despite their thirst, the heat, and the smoke from the still-burning scrub, the Franks fought ferociously. 'They burned and glowed in a frenzied torment,' wrote one of the Moslems, 'but as the arrows struck them down, those who had seemed like lions now seemed like hedgehogs.'

With the infantry dead or powerless to act, the horsemen sought refuge on the Horns of Hattin. As the Saracens closed in, Guy ordered Raymond to take the last possible chance and attempt a direct charge, while he and the remaining knights grouped around the True Cross. The section Raymond charged was commanded by Saladin's nephew who, seeing the move, responded with a classic Moslem tactic: he fell back, let the Frankish squadron through, then closed ranks again. Raymond's charge was made ineffectual and worse: now the Frankish strength was split, and there was nothing Raymond could do but retreat to Tripoli. Balian and Ernoul broke out soon after with Reginald of Sidon; and after that no one else escaped.

On the Horns, Guy and one hundred and fifty knights made their last stand, the king's red tent and the True Cross at their centre. Saladin's sixteen-year-old son was in the Moslem army:

'It was my first set battle,' he said, 'and I was at my father's side. When the King of the Franks retired to the hill, his knights made a gallant charge, and drove the Moslems back upon my father. I saw his dismay – he changed colour, tugged at his beard and rushed forward, shouting: "Give the devil the lie!" So our men fell on the enemy, who retreated up the hill. When I saw the Frank flying and the Moslems pursuing, I cried in glee: "We have routed them!" But the Franks charged again and threw our men back once more to where my father was. Again he urged them forward, and they drove the enemy up the hill. Again I shouted: "We have routed them!" But Father turned to me and said, "Hold thy peace – we have not beaten them so long as that tent stands there." At that instant the royal tent was overturned. Then my father dismounted and bowed himself to the earth, giving thanks to God with tears of joy.'

Among the dead was Heraclius's deputy, the bishop of Acre, who had carried the True Cross. Its bearer was meant to go without arms or armour, but he had worn a chain-mail shirt under his vestments. Christians afterwards saw this as typical of a general lack of faith, the cause of the catastrophe. It is difficult now to comprehend the utter viciousness and horror of a hand-to-hand medieval battle; but after Hattin, Moslem rhetoric took wing, savouring and gloating over the day's work.

'The limbs of the fallen were cast naked on the field of battle, scattered in pieces over the site of the encounter, lacerated and disjointed, with heads cracked open, throats split, spines broken, necks shattered, feet in pieces, noses mutilated, extremities torn off, members dismembered, parts shredded, eyes gouged out, stomachs disembowelled, hair coloured with blood, the praecordium slashed, fingers sliced off, the thorax shattered, the ribs broken, the joints dislocated, chests smashed, throats slit, bodies cut in half, arms pulverized, lips shrivelled, foreheads pierced, forelocks dyed scarlet, breasts covered with blood, ribs pierced, elbows disjointed, bones broken, tunics torn off, faces lifeless, wounds gaping, skin flayed, fragments chopped off, hair lopped, backs skinless, bodies dismembered, teeth knocked out, blood spilt, life's last breath exhaled, necks lolling, joints slackened, pupils liquefied, heads hanging, livers crushed, ribs staved in, heads shattered, breasts flayed, spirits flown, their very ghosts crushed; like stones among stones, a lesson to the wise.'

That last phrase contained an unwitting and macabre irony: the battle was not the first lesson Christians had been taught at Hattin. The twin-peaked hill was, in one tradition, the site of Christ's Sermon on the Mount.

At least the dead could not know the magnitude of the defeat. But to those who survived, and to all the rest of Christendom, something greater than the army was lost on the field of Hattin: the True Cross, captured and dragged in the dust. And even when the battle was finished, the slaughter continued. The Frankish survivors, including over a hundred Templars and Hospitallers, were brought before Saladin. The secular prisoners were sold into slavery; then, in front of Saladin, the holy knights of both Orders were beheaded one by one. Two hundred and thirty Templars died that day, executed or killed in battle; only de Ridefort was spared, with King Guy, a group of barons, and Reynald de Chatillon. De Ridefort and the king were too valuable as hostages to die; the barons could be ransomed; and Saladin had sworn to kill de Chatillon himself.

De Chatillon, de Ridefort and King Guy were taken to Saladin's tent, close to the battlefield. Saladin greeted them all with courtesy, bidding them sit and rest; then he offered Guy a cup of rose-water, iced with snow. Islamic custom held that a gift of food or drink ensured the recipient's safety; Guy drank with gratitude and passed the cup to de Chatillon. At once Saladin said to his interpreter: 'This godless man did not have my permission to drink, and will not save his life that way.' Rising and standing before Reynald, Saladin angrily listed his sins. But nothing could shame Reynald, who made a surly reply. Saladin drew his sword, and in one quick movement sliced off Reynald's head.

Guy was horror-struck; but as the corpse was dragged from the tent, Saladin turned to him and said, 'Twice I have sworn to kill that man: once when he tried to attack Mecca and Medina, and once when he broke the truce to capture the caravan; but a king does not kill a king.'

The Moslem army, with its hostages and slaves, left the site of the battle quickly and began a long march through the rest of

Palestine, a march more like a triumphal procession than a military campaign. On 5 July, the day after Hattin, Tiberias surrendered; Raymond's wife and her household were given safe passage to Tripoli. On the 10th, Acre fell; on the 14th, Nablus; the 20th, Jaffa; the 24th, Toron; the 29th, Sidon; 6 August, Beirut; and 4 September, Ascalon.

By mid-September, the only Frankish properties south of Tripoli were a few castles, the port of Tyre and Jerusalem itself. Tyre was on a peninsula, joined to the coast by a single spit of land; all the defeated barons fled there, and arranged a strong defence. In Jerusalem there were only two knights; but they and the citizens refused to let the city go, though Saladin promised them life and liberty. Among the refugees crowded into the Holy City were the wife and children of Balian of Ibelin; Balian himself had gone to Tyre. He asked Saladin for safe passage to bring his family to Tyre, and received it, on condition that he bore no arms and stayed only a single night in Jerusalem. In good faith, Balian agreed, and went to Jerusalem with Ernoul; but once there it was impossible for him to keep his oath: the citizens simply refused to let him go. To an honourable man it was extremely embarrassing; Balian wrote to Saladin explaining his breach of faith, and Saladin, typically, absolved him of the oath and provided an escort for his family. Not that such a gesture cost Saladin anything, for everyone knew that Jerusalem was bound to fall; but, as an act of unnecessary kindness, it was pure chivalry.

The siege of the Holy City began on 20 September. On 2 October, the anniversary of Mohammed's ascension into heaven, a Templar knight named Terric wrote to Henry II of England.

'Jerusalem, alas! has fallen. Saladin ordered the cross to be cast down from the summit of the Temple of the Lord, and for two days to be carried about the city and beaten with sticks. After this he ordered the Temple of the Lord to be washed with rosewater, inside and out and from top to bottom.'

Only thirty years before, a German pilgrim named John of Wurzburg had visited Jerusalem. The buildings belonging to the Templars were, he said, a town within the town, a fortress within the fortress; their stables were so large that fifteen hundred camels, or over two thousand horses, could be accommodated. Their refectory was a vast, colonnaded, vaulted hall, decorated only with trophies of war – swords, helmets, belts and coats of mail taken from the enemy. Cats and dogs wandered over the rushes strewn on the floor. The dormitories of the brethren were cells furnished with a bed, a chair and an unlocked box for each man. Outside were the tack-rooms, the forge, the armoury, the cobblers' and tailors' workshops and storerooms, the bakery, the kitchens, the wine-cellars, the silos – cut deep into the natural rock – and the slaughterhouse.

Within a week of the Moslem conquest, all that was changed, for Saladin made particular efforts to remove all traces of the Templars. On Friday 9 October, with the al-Aqsa Mosque cleansed and purified, he prayed there; and then he set about the disposal of the survivors of the siege. There could not have been a greater contrast to the behaviour of the Franks in 1099. More than twenty thousand Christians were still alive; seven thousand were ransomed with money from the royal treasury and the Military Orders, and twelve hundred were simply released; the native Christians remained in Jerusalem. Those Franks who could not pay a ransom – there were several thousand – were enslaved; but no one was killed. If Heraclius had behaved better, there might have been no slaves at all; but morals had never played much part in his life. He paid his ransom of ten gold pieces, and left the city, to the disgust of Moslems and Christians alike, bowed down with a sack of gold, and leading a train of carts loaded with carpets and plate. No one knew what became of him afterwards; Fuller's terse comment is sufficient: 'He lived viciously and died obscurely.'

From the battle of Hattin to the fall of Jerusalem, the conquest of Palestine had taken twelve weeks and six days. Only Tyre remained; Saladin had assumed it would be won as easily as the rest, and had not bothered to take it early on. Now, as much to the Franks' surprise as his, it was too late. In mid-July, ten days after Hattin, the port had been ready to surrender; then a ship sailed in, bearing Conrad, Marquis of Montferrat and brother-in-law to Queen Sibylla through her first marriage. He had taken charge of the city's defence at once, and had deflected the Saracen army towards easier spoil.

In November, with the rest of the country subdued, Saladin returned to the walls of Tyre; but by then they had been strengthened so much, and the city so well organized, the Moslems could not win through. On New Year's Day 1188,

Saladin lifted the second siege of Tyre and led his army back inland.

The year 1187 had begun with treachery and intrigue throughout Outremer. By its end, there was nothing left of the Latin Kingdom of Jerusalem; nothing, except piles of dry white bones scattered all over the Horns of Hattin – and one peninsula port. To the Moslems, Tyre seemed no more than a minor irritation; to the Franks, it was the last rock, and the only hope.

CHAPTER 8

LION'S HEART

Cyprus and the Holy Land, 1189–1193

'Dead men and prisoners have no friends, no kin.'
Richard Coeur-de-Lion, in his captivity

As Frankish Palestine disintegrated in the autumn of 1187, those Templars whose lands had been overrun congregated in Tyre. Terric was among them, he who had written to Henry II; he was Preceptor of the Temple in Jerusalem, and during de Ridefort's imprisonment he took charge of the Order. In Tyre he co-operated with Conrad de Montferrat, witnessing legal documents, arranging the city's defence and writing poignant appeals to the West. Conrad and he seemed to have worked reasonably well together – at any rate, no criticism of one to the other has survived. The situation they found themselves in demanded co-operation; but the good relationship did not last. Early in 1188 de Ridefort returned to impose his will on the Templars once more; he had been liberated after ordering his brethren at Gaza to surrender their castle to Saladin. In July, Guy de Lusignan was released as well. Shortly afterwards, Conrad wrote to the archbishop of Canterbury. His letter shows the effect that Guy and de Ridefort were having.

'You know,' he said, 'what it has cost me to defend the Christians in Tyre; and because I strive to maintain them there, I am being attacked by de Lusignan, the erstwhile king, with his barons and with the Master of the Temple: not content with slandering me and attacking my honour, they intercept the help so necessary to me; and what is worse is that de Ridefort has taken the alms of the king of England, and refuses to pass them on to me.'

The last comment was untrue, for the Templars had spent all their share of Henry's alms in preparations for Hattin and ransoms in Jerusalem – although it is quite possible that de Ridefort may have pretended, simply out of malice, that funds still existed and were being withheld. But the rest of the complaint was true; its key is the phrase 'the erstwhile king'. Once a king, always a king; so Guy thought, and on his release he had ridden to Tyre to take control of what was left of his kingdom. However, Conrad knew he was doing better than Guy had ever done, and he refused to relinquish authority, or even to let Guy into the city. For a whole year the legal king had been unable to govern, and without Conrad the entire kingdom would have been conquered. Conrad considered that Guy had lost his right to rule; the throne was a *tabula rasa*, waiting for Conrad's name to be written on it. There was enough reason in this to revive the old rivalry; Reynald de Chatillon's bones lay at Hattin, and Raymond of Tripoli was dead – reputedly of shame – but the Templars, led by de Ridefort, still supported Guy, and the Tyrians by then were content with Conrad. To them it seemed Guy had never been a lucky king, and the split was made worse by rumours that de Ridefort had promised Saladin that he would embrace Islam.

With the city gates closed in his face, Guy did not stay long; but after wintering in Tripoli, he returned to Tyre in the spring of 1189 and renewed his demands. Ignored and rejected just as before, he pitched camp outside the city walls.

About the same time, a fleet of fifty-two ships arrived from Pisa, an important reinforcement for Conrad; his only other western help had been a contingent from Sicily the year before. Guy remained before the city for four useless months, and then suddenly at the end of August he lost patience, and left – taking with him de Ridefort, the Templars, the Pisan fleet and the Sicilians. Blessed as a saviour by some, cursed as a usurper by others, Conrad could do nothing but watch them go, and then write his bitter complaint.

Guy had decided to go to Acre. Like Tyre, it was built on a peninsula; unlike Tyre, it was held by Moslems. But with a large fleet to blockade the seaward entrance, and an army to cover the land approach, Guy believed he could besiege and recapture the city. His decision was a grand and brave gesture of defiance towards Conrad; as a king without a kingdom, he had very little to lose but his life. Success at Acre would give him a proper base, and a credibility he had never had before.

Brave, certainly, but very rash; Guy was depending on Saladin's preoccupation elsewhere. Everything about the decision – its daring as much as its apparent lack of reflection – suggests it was planted in Guy's mind by his evil genius, de Ridefort. Obsessive, determined, irrational, de Ridefort may well have believed by then that as Master of God's militia he bore a charmed life. Luck had always carried him through before – at Cresson, at Hattin and in his imprisonment. This time it failed him.

The siege of Acre began on 27 August. Under its first shock the city almost fell; but the Franks had no siege engines and could not press their advantage. It had been madness to hope Saladin would pay no attention. Within a week he was there, and the Franks, surrounding Acre by land and by sea, had a Moslem army at their backs as well. On 4 October the two forces collided. The struggle was indecisive, but in its course de Ridefort was captured again, and once more thrown into prison. He did not return.

Madness is relative; it may be defined as an overwhelming conviction that differs from popular belief. To our age, lacking the driving faith of medieval Christendom, the entire story of the Crusades can seem like madness – so much energy and effort, and so many lives, were expended on that tiny area called the Holy Land. To them it was not madness, for they believed the land *was* holy. But de Ridefort, the last Templar Master elected in Jerusalem, may actually have been insane.

Once he was gone, Guy's luck seemed to change, for as winter approached, Saladin fell ill, disbanded part of his army and retired inland with the rest. And although the Moslems in Acre had consolidated their defence, and there was no immediate intervention expected from the West, he refused to send men against the Franks when he could not be in command. 'If I am not there with them,' he said, 'they will achieve absolutely nothing, and it might cause much more harm than good.' Guy's men dug trenches, built earthworks and prepared to strangle

Acre slowly. Had they known how long the process would take, they might never have started; for when the new crusade arrived, nearly two years later, they were still there.

Europeans had long been accustomed to dismissing the regular bad news, and worse predictions, that came from the Holy Land. The dreadful reports of Hattin and Jerusalem did finally have an effect – a disorganized confusion of repentance. The historian Thomas Fuller commented:

'The cardinals lamented out of measure, vowing such reformation of manners; never more to take bribes, never more to live so viciously; yea, never to ride on a horse so long as the Holy Land was under the feet of the Turks. But this their passion spent itself with its own violence, and these mariners' vows ended with the tempest.'

In October 1187, even before news of Jerusalem had arrived in Rome, Pope Gregory VIII had appealed for a Third Crusade. The princes of Europe – in particular Henry II of England and Philip Augustus of France – had made pious noises; Henry had even instituted the 'Saladin Tithe', a ten per cent tax on the revenue of every lay person in his realm, in order to pay for a crusade. But little else happened at first. The tithe was collected successfully, although there was a scandal when a Templar knight called Gilbert of Hoxton tried to embezzle the money in his charge; yet no crusade materialized. The reason was the almost perennial state of war between England and France; it had died down after the shock of the capture of Jerusalem, and then flared up again a few months later, keeping the two kings at home. But one person who had taken the cross was determined to fulfil his vow: an obstreperous French count named Richard of Poitou. His journey to the Holy Land, and his actions there, gained him a new name: Coeur-de-Lion – Richard the Lion-Heart, King of England.

It is ironical that Richard should have become one of the great folk-heroes of England, for not only was he hardly ever in England, but also he came close to impoverishing the country – and he did not even speak English. In trying to understand Richard and the popular English reaction to him – in trying to touch the lion's heart – one has to dig through the accretion of legends that have grown around him. Most of these legends were created in the four hundred years after his death; real incidents were elaborated, fictional events were tacked on. The writers of romance borrowed from many tales of true, legendary or mythical characters, and Richard was freely compared to their heroes – Charlemagne, Roland, Arthur, Robin Hood. But piercing through these decorations, one comes face to face with a man whose closest parallel is the robber baron Reynald de Chatillon. Indeed, if Reynald had had a little more poetry in his soul and a better press, he might well have become as popular a hero as Richard, for their deeds were remarkably similar. The differences were firstly that Reynald was motivated purely by greed, whereas Richard's actions had a fairly thick veneer of religion; and secondly that Richard, as a European king, commanded a greater audience than Reynald – an audience, moreover, which was comfortably distant from the actual events; which was more cultured and refined than Reynald's; and which was prepared to celebrate its heroes in song and prose and verse.

Born in England in September 1157, Richard was the second son of Henry II and Eleanor of Aquitaine, who had been divorced by Louis the Young of France in 1152, after his return from the ineffectual Second Crusade. Richard grew up more French than English, living in his mother's court in Poitiers and learning its ideals. As a man he personified those ideals – he was tall, strong and handsome, with red-gold hair; he was extremely energetic, an excellent horseman and swordsman; he was quick-tempered, but easily calmed – especially by gold; he was a first-class leader in battle, a gallant with women and a fair poet in court. He was the incarnation of his age.

The sources of his fame in chivalrous romance are closer to the French and English than Palestinian Franks. There were more urgent problems in Palestine than finding a rhyme for ballads; besides that, half of Richard's adventures took place outside the Holy Land, in his journeys there and back. Four years passed between his taking of the cross and his arrival in Acre. To the romantic court at Poitiers, the perfect crusader, typified once by the pious, austere Templars, now seemed a little old-fashioned; if, in going to fight the infidel, a man made incidental conquests on the way, then so much the better. To the English it was simpler still, for even then they had a well-developed sense of nationalism. Richard might be half-French by birth and almost all French by breeding, but it mattered not; his coronation made him all English, and his character made him the example of all 'doughty knyghtes of Yngelonde'. Hitherto the English had played comparatively little part in the crusades; but once Richard gave them a national stake in the venture, they praised him so highly one could be forgiven for feeling that he seemed to have defeated all Islam single-handed.

He became King of England on 6 July 1189, and was crowned on 3 September. He immediately set about reorganizing the realm and preparing for the holy war, 'by a thousand princely skills gathering so much coin as if he meant not to return'.

At last his crusade could begin. Philip Augustus of France had finally decided his policies would be better served by joining in than by staying out, so the enterprise was not Richard's own or even England's own; but Philip was a quiet man who disliked show, and as Richard's flamboyant character dominated the crusade, it seemed that none but he took part.

Together, the two kings left Vézélay in France on 4 July 1190 – three years exactly after the battle of Hattin. Shortly after Lyons they took separate routes, Philip heading for Genoa and Richard for Marseilles, where their respective fleets waited to convey them and their armies to Outremer. They had decided to break the journey in Sicily; Philip went with his men by sea, and after a peaceful voyage arrived at Messina on 14 September. Richard was already there. Like Reynald de Chatillon, he disliked the sea, and at the last minute had chosen to go overland through Italy while his men sailed. Passing through a little village he had tried to steal a hawk, and had been attacked and nearly killed by its owner. He had escaped, but the unseemly incident set the tone for his whole voyage, and when he had arrived in Mesinna on 3 September, he was quite unrepentant and in a thoroughly bad temper.

It happened that his favourite sister, Joanna, was in Sicily, more or less a prisoner of Tancred, the king. Richard always reacted sharply to insults, although he himself insulted people freely; and despite Tancred's almost immediate release of Joanna, Richard's second action on his crusade was to take over a small Italian town on his sister's behalf. He followed that by installing his troops in a Sicilian monastery, throwing the monks out by force. There was a popular belief in France and Italy that all Englishmen had tails, and Richard's truculent mood was not

Perched on a crag midway between the port of Tyre and the Sea of Galilee, Castle Montfort – the Strong Mountain – gave the Templars control of Upper Galilee.

Teqoa, only a few miles from the Holy City of Jerusalem, was the site of their first recorded military engagement – a defeat which left the ground littered with Templar corpses 'as far as the eye could see'.

The mother house, the Temple in Jerusalem, from which the Poor
Knights' empire grew. No-one ever counted how many lives were lost
for the possession of these stones.

A view of the Temple Mount which no Templar could ever have seen;
but from the ground the knights would probably still recognize the
Dome of the Rock, the exercise yard, the walls within which they
prayed and the hills beyond.

Opposite:

The microcosm of the Order, Castle Pilgrim, on the promontory of
Athlit. On this fortified peninsula four thousand people could live in
safety. The main land defence – the eastern wall – still remains: ninety
feet high and sixteen feet thick.

The excavated moat and walls of ancient Caesarea, one of the major
maritime links in the lifelines of the Holy Land, now dead, dry and
empty.

The sea walls of Acre. Near this place, fighting to the last, the Templars sustained their final defeat at the hands of the Muslims.

The great cathedral at Vézélay. Richard of England and Philip Augustus of France set out from here on the Third Crusade on 4 July 1190; and when, on Easter Sunday 1146, St Bernard had preached the Second Crusade here, he was obliged to preach out-of-doors, for the building could not contain his audience.

The castle of Gréoux in south-east France, the largest extant Templar castle in Europe. Excavations were carried out here recently in the belief that the 'treasure of the Templars' lay hidden within the building. Nothing was found.

Overleaf:
Not easily accessible even today, the village of Couvertoirade lies *en plein désert*, a superb example of an almost completely preserved medieval town. The large building to the right is the Templar chateau, with their church beside it. When they ruled the town it was a peaceful place; the fortifications were all built by the Hospitallers, inheritors of the dissolved Order of the Temple.

Uncompromising as their creator, St Louis, the walls of Aigues-Mortes spring from the salty marshes of the Camargue. To the left lies the river on which the saint-king twice set sail for the Crusades.

A sympathetic nineteenth-century portrait of a weak and corrupt fourteenth-century pope, His Holiness Clement V, destroyer of the Order of the Temple.

Below:
St Louis, King of France.

posite:

1 this year all the Templars in the ngdom of France were aprisoned at the command of the ing of France...' In 1307 five ousand Templars were arrested in ingle night.

ter seven years of trials and cture, confessions and cantations, the last Master of the der, Jacques de Molay, was rnt alive with his brother-knight, eoffrey de Charney. Later the Charney family revealed the oth known as the Shroud of Turin he cloth which may **have** been the al treasure of the Templars.

SAINCT LOVIS ROY DE FRANCE.

Philip the Fair, grandson of the saint-king, believed to have been killed, with his puppet pope, by the curse of the last Master.

The stone-carved head of a Templar knight in the walls of the Temple Church, London.

improved by hearing this opinion repeated by the Sicilians. On 3 October his men sacked Messina, and his banner flew over the town.

Not content with thus incommoding his host King Tancred, Richard proceeded to offend King Philip, his partner in the crusade. For many years there had been an understanding that Richard would marry Philip's sister Alice; now he announced that nothing would induce him to do so. But, incredibly – the ways of politics being as they are – Philip swallowed the affront; Tancred gave Richard and Joanna twenty thousand ounces of gold each; and they all spent the winter together on the little island.

Philip left Sicily on 3 March, and Richard on 10 April 1191. Brethren of the Templars and Hospitallers remained in charge of Messina. As before, Philip's voyage was slow and peaceful; but Richard seemed to attract trouble and action wherever he went. Strong winds and high seas scattered his fleet. One ship was sunk, three were blown on to Cyprus, and Richard himself stopped first in Crete for one day, and then for ten days in Rhodes. He had been so ill in the storm that he could barely contemplate another voyage, and only left Rhodes by sea because there was no other way. Sending word to Acre that he would arrive eventually, he made for Cyprus – for the ships blown there held not only his sister but also his new bride-to-be, Berengaria of Navarre.

Landfall was on 8 May. The self-styled emperor of Cyprus, Isaac, had prevented Joanna and Berengaria from landing, and Richard, after so many days at sea, was in a revengeful mood. On 11 May, ships arrived from the Holy Land, bearing high-ranking Templars and the ever-hopeful Guy de Lusignan, all eager for help. On the twelfth, Richard and Berengaria were married – Queen Berengaria of England; and on the thirteenth, when the rest of Richard's ships arrived, and with the help of Guy and the Templars, he began a general assault on the island.

Cyprus, sea-set Cyprus, is a small island: its area is little more than 3,500 square miles. Yet it is not a place to be encapsulated in a single phrase, either of fact or romance. In ancient times its shape was compared to that of a hide pegged out to dry. On the northern coast there is Kyrenia, with its massive Venetian fortifications rising from the sea-shore. In the south there is Limassol, where Richard landed, and the bay of old Paphos, where Aphrodite was born. To the west, on the Akamas peninsula, there are the caves which St Neophytos dug, and where he wrote about 'the cloud of English' who invaded the island. Over to the east there is the Karpasian peninsula, from which, on a clear day, one can see the mountains of Lebanon; central to the island are the Troodos mountains, with their vast and ugly open-cast copper mines, and Nicosia, the capital; and between the windy mountain-tops, and the suck and hiss of the sea, there is, it seems, almost every variety of vista and vegetation – cornfields, and exotic orchards of apricot and citrus; groves of almonds and olives; beehives and anemones; pinewoods, scrub, golden oak and cherry trees. There are churches and monasteries everywhere, many abandoned or in ruins.

By the time Richard Coeur-de-Lion landed at Limassol, the civilizations of Mycenae, Phoenicia, Rome, Egypt and Byzantium had all left their marks on Cyprus. A few miles east of Limassol, under the waves of Akrotiri Bay, lay the ancient sunken city of Amathus; westward, at Curium, the Roman shrine of Apollo of the Woods, its altar still in place. Aqueducts and baths remained, along with a stadium that could hold six thousand people. More enigmatic than either of these, however, was the palace of Vouni, in the north by Morphou Bay. The walls and terraces, the courts, baths, conduits and staircases were all there, dating from the fifth century BC; yet no one knows exactly who built it, or who lived there, or where these people came from. Templar occupation was the briefest of any in the island's history, and they left the least: a chapel in Famagusta, some carved stones in the Nicosian cathedral of St Sophia, and, out on the Karpasian peninsula, a castle named Gastria, of which nothing but the foundations remain. There is no more; it is almost as if the Templars and Cyprus just did not fit together. For them it was always an ill-fated isle; for Richard the Lion-Heart it was the exact opposite: Cyprus brought him greater fame, and greater fortune, than he had ever had before. And it was quick as well, for his whole rumbustious conquest took less than three weeks.

By the end of May 1191 the island was in Richard's hands, and the emperor Isaac surrendered. Isaac made one rather pathetic condition – that he should not be put in irons; and Richard, with heavy-handed humour, had Isaac bound in chains of silver. On 5 June, with Isaac in tow, Guy and the Templars following, the riches of Cyprus in his holds and two Englishmen in charge of the island, Richard set sail again – this time for Acre, at last.

He must have been glad that the voyage took only three days. Yet even in so short a time, he managed to run into a fight, this time with a dromond, a large Saracen supply ship taking food to Acre. The dromond was sunk – unfortunately before its cargo could be taken off – and its crew killed, or drowned in the sinking. Naturally legends grew out of the episode; they tell of Richard, with his back to the mast, killing all but thirty of the crew of sixteen hundred. Clearly his part could not have been so great; but it was the first time he had fought real Saracens. It seems to have brought home to him the meaning of a holy war: that there really were people who did not share his faith, and who would kill to protect their own. Thus, when he arrived in Acre on 8 June 1191, he was primed, eager and almost ready to start. All he needed was time to get over his seasickness.

Philip of France was no warrior; he preferred the plots and intrigues of politics to the confrontation of battle, and in the seven weeks between his arrival and Richard's, he had entertained himself by devising elaborate siege-engines. He was mean as well, and had paid his armies no more than the agreed amount; reasonable enough, but in a siege that had lasted nearly two years, something extra was needed to tip the balance. Richard provided it.

Richard's reputation had preceded him, and simply by being in Acre he brought new energy to the moribund siege, which by then was in its ninety-third week and had degenerated into an amicable stalemate. Moslem and Christian children would play together between the lines, and warriors of both sides would commence individual duels, then break off to chat. In order to win a war, one should not live too close to the enemy; he becomes human, and often rather likeable. Richard's view of the Saracens was typically of a newcomer, fresh and clear; he had not had time to be jaded out of bigotry – indeed, he had just been jolted firmly into it. His presence reminded the Christians that their neighbours were actually their enemies, and enemies of a particularly despicable kind: infidels who held the True Cross captive.

Philip could be jealous as well as mean. His engines were ready; Richard had insulted him in Sicily, and yet was far more popular than he. Without waiting till the English king was better, Philip launched an attack in which the Templars took part, an attack more memorable for its appearance than its effect.

'You could see there an incomprehensible number of armed men,' wrote one of the participants. 'There were so many shining coats of mail, so many glittering helmets, so many noble horses neighing, so many white mantles, so many knights of great probity and daring, so many banners, that never had such a crowd appeared to be reckoned up.'

But despite the display, the attack was ill-conceived. After fighting all day – it was Monday, 17 June – 'the French laid down their arms and the Turks vilely reproached them, taunting them that they were unable to finish what they had begun. Furthermore the Turks shot Greek fire and, little by little, destroyed the engines as well as the other implements of war which the French king had had made with such tender care. He was so overcome with wrath and rage that he fell into a fit of melancholy, and in his confusion and desolation would not even mount a horse.'

When, several weeks later, Richard was sufficiently recovered to contemplate a new attempt, Philip was still sulking and would not join in. Richard's approach, in any case, was something the parsimonious Philip could not stomach. The same chronicler wrote:

'He [Richard] decided that, since in the business world work makes progress through excellence, he might more readily attract the spirits of the young by posting a reward than by giving orders through commanders. Who, indeed, is not attracted by the scent of money?'

Richard's idea was extremely simple: he raised the soldiers' pay and offered a bonus, first of two, then three, then four pieces of gold for every stone removed from the walls of Acre. He could afford it; he had had plenty of money when he left England, and his almost incidental conquests of Messina and Cyprus had made him very rich.

It worked. One of the defensive towers was mined, and fell, weakened by fire below and a barrage of rocks above; and then 'the young men rushed forward and swarmed to the wall. When the stones were taken out they would go on eagerly, greedy for praise as well as for payment. Even in the midst of the enemy's missiles they worked on bravely. Many of them were wounded; others, in fear of death, stayed away from danger; but some of them, protected neither by shields nor weapons, manfully pushed the Turks away from the wall. This wall was extremely high and immoderately thick, but the men removed a great many stones. . . .'

Richard had shown the Franks the practical benefits of conquest, far more attractive than the demands of duty or the intangible rewards of religion. By sea and by land the assault tightened, throttling the city, while keeping the Moslems on the mainland at bay; and on 12 July the garrison capitulated. The siege had lasted for ninety-eight weeks; Richard had been there for thirty-four days.

The terms of peace were strict. The besieged Moslems were to go free, but they could take nothing from the city except the clothes they wore. Weapons, furniture, food, money – everything else had to stay. The Moslems captured by the Franks were ransomed for 200,000 pieces of gold; the True Cross, along with fifteen hundred named Christian prisoners, was to be returned to the Franks; two thousand seven hundred Moslems were to remain as hostages until all the terms were fulfilled; and the final date for fulfilment was set as the end of the month – less than three weeks away.

At first all went smoothly. The Moslem hostages were handed over, and the city evacuated. Richard, always as ready to respect a good warrior as to insult a poor one, gave orders that no one should injure or insult the departing Moslems. The command was unnecessary; the Christians were fascinated by the sight of their adversaries, some of whom they had got to know, and an eye-witness wrote:

'On this critical day the probity of these Turks was admirable, as was their great bravery . . . Now, as they crossed over their high walls on their way out of the city, they were regarded by the deeply curious eyes of the Christians, who admired them especially as soldiers and who recalled their memories. Their appearance, as they emerged almost empty-handed from the city, was astonishing in its gracefulness and dignity. Although extreme necessity had just vanquished them, reducing them almost to beggary, their constancy had not disappeared; rather, in their spirited appearance they seemed victorious.'

Those evacuees were the lucky ones. The peace treaty had been made without Saladin's consent; the only line of communication between him and the beleaguered city had been to send a man swimming from the coast through the Franks' blockade at the harbour entrance. Such a man had brought news of the proposed treaty to Saladin, who was in the very act of writing to forbid surrender when he saw the Moslem standards taken from the walls and replaced by the banners of England and France. Permitted or not, the treaty had been signed, and in his name; and he agreed to stand by it.

With the city almost empty, the Christians crowded in, jostling through the streets, shouting, singing and dancing, the two kings riding at their head – Richard, the hero of the day, elated and boisterous, Philip dour and sulky beside him.

'The banners and manifold flags of the Kings were run up atop the walls and towers, and the city was equally divided by the two kings. They also made a proportionately equal distribution of the supplies of arms and food, and the captives of the highest degree of nobility were divided between them by lot. . . . The King of France, moreover, for his part had the noble palace of the Templars with all its appurtenances. King Richard got the royal palace, to which he sent his queens [Joanna and Berengaria] with the children and their servants.'

The division immediately sparked off one of the rebellious outcries the Franks indulged in whenever they had no Moslems to fight. Many of the Christian army had owned property in Acre before the Moslem conquest. The order of the Temple had been the biggest single landlord, owning the cattle-market, the market streets and a palace by the sea, and under their new Master, Robert de Sablé, the Templars led the complaints, saying they had not fought to install two foreign kings, but to regain their lost possessions. An amicable solution was worked out before long, but the incident typified the attitudes of the Franks in general and Richard in particular, and underlined the contrast in character between Richard and Saladin. Richard was a king by right, but a knight-errant by nature. He felt little responsibility to his subjects in England, and none to his soldiers except when in the field. There he could be a magnificent general, seeing chances and taking them, seeing dangers and avoiding them, and always setting an example of superb personal courage. But he could also be rude, unreliable, selfish and untrustworthy – and at the next moment, poetic, good-humoured, affectionate and admiring. In all these contradictions he was simply the mirror of his culture.

Knowing this, and knowing Richard's culture all too well, Saladin was cautious in dealing with the treaty. He asked the Templars, 'whose word he trusted though he hated them', whether or not Richard would keep his side of the agreement. The knights refused to say. A more damning assessment of Richard's integrity could not have been found.

Saladin's own reputation for honesty and mercy was well-founded: his behaviour at Jerusalem was the most famous example, renowned even in Europe. His power over his people was founded on his obviously genuine love for them and his unswerving fidelity to Islam. Only in this fidelity could he become fanatical or inhuman, as his execution of the Templars at Hattin had shown. In general he fought only to preserve the purity of his land and religion, not, as the Franks often did, from the love of fighting and loot.

Richard's treaty at Acre was difficult for Saladin to fulfil. Time was short; the number of prisoners to be released was great; the sum of money was immense; and the True Cross, which to Moslems was just a piece of wood, was the most valuable bargaining-counter they had ever had. And while Saladin was not prepared to break his word, there was no guarantee that Richard would keep to his. Saladin, therefore, negotiated an alteration in the terms: the numbers involved remained the same, but the time was extended to three months. Each month there was to be a delivery of one-third of the total of prisoners and cash. Saladin was unwilling to relinquish the True Cross; and therein may lie an explanation for Richard's subsequent action, the most cruel single deed of his life.

On 2 August the first instalment of money and prisoners arrived. A few named prisoners were not present in the group, and Saladin requested that the hostages held in Acre should be exchanged for a new set. Already each side was deeply suspicious of the other. To Richard, Saladin seemed to be prevaricating. In his understanding, that only meant one thing: treachery. His reaction was unbelievably brutal.

On the afternoon of 20 August he and his army rode out from Acre until they were in full view of the Moslem camp. With them they brought all the Moslem hostages – two thousand seven hundred men. Richard gave his order; 'nor was there any delay', a satisfied Frank noted later. 'The king's followers leapt forward eager to fulfil the commands, and thankful to the Divine Grace that permitted them to take such a vengeance.'

The Moslems encamped on the hills watched, uncomprehending at first. Saladin's secretary Baha ad-Din described the atrocious afternoon.

'The Franks brought up the Moslem prisoners in chains . . . then they fell on them as one man and slaughtered them in cold blood, with sword and lance. Our spies had informed Saladin of the enemy's manoeuvres, and he sent some reinforcements; but by then the slaughter had already taken place. As soon as the Moslems realized what had happened they attacked the enemy and battle raged, with dead and wounded on both sides, until night fell and separated them. The next morning the Moslems wanted to see who had fallen, and found their martyred companions lying where they fell; and some they recognized.'

Ever since then people have tried to plumb Richard's reasoning and discover a motive for the massacre. Only two possibilities have been found, and Baha ad-Din put them both succinctly: 'one was that they had killed them as a reprisal for their own prisoners killed before then. Another was that the King of England had decided to march on Ascalon, and did not want to leave behind a large number of enemy soldiers.' Either explanation is feasible; each is contemptible. But there is a third, which has not been suggested before: the question of the True Cross.

Even in the twelfth century there were enough 'fragments of the True Cross' in the world to fill several ships, and the authenticity of the Cross the Franks possessed at Hattin is obviously questionable. What is important, though, is that the Franks did believe it was the True Cross. But what happened to that cross after the Horns of Hattin is a mystery. Moslems said it had been sent to Damascus and then to Baghdad, where the Caliph buried it – on 4 June, 1189: a precise date is given – to be trodden under Moslem feet. But *a* cross, mounted in gold and adorned with pearls and jewels, as the 'True Cross' had been, was held in Saladin's camp and shown to Frankish envoys, who accepted it as genuine. Finally, one of the few Frankish soldiers who escaped from Hattin claimed he had buried the Cross in the sand there, when he saw the day was lost. He undertook to find it again, but could not after three days and nights of digging, and gave up the search.

That last is the least credible of all; no Christian who believed he knew the whereabouts of the True Cross would give up searching after only three days. The question is which of the accounts Richard believed; and it is possible that, after accepting on face value the reports of the cross in Saladin's camp, he may have heard the story of the burial in Baghdad. Believing that, he would also have believed that Saladin was taking him for a fool. True or not, the very thought would have been unbearable; and Richard enraged was merciless.

Whatever the real, unrevealed reason – 'God knows best,' wrote Baha ad-Din unhappily – Richard quit Acre within forty-eight hours and headed south, scornfully leaving the butchered bodies to be gathered up or left to rot. His army was a hundred thousand strong, and riding in the vanguard, a small group of a few hundred, were the white-mantled élite of the force – the Templars, with their new Master, Robert de Sablé.

The exact fate of Gerard de Ridefort was unknown. Nothing had been heard of him since his capture outside Acre, almost two years before. Uncertain whether he was dead or alive, still Christian or an apostate, the Templars had waited a year and a half before electing another Master. Perhaps they were afflicted by the creeping lethargy brought on by the long months of siege; certainly Richard's arrival invigorated them as much as everyone else. He had scarcely landed when they made their choice at last: de Sablé, a comrade of the English king.

De Sablé was one of those few men who were apparently *asked* to join the Order; he was elected Master almost immediately he had entered. He was perfectly qualified for the exalted post: rich, generous, pious, mature, experienced and influential. In France, he had left his Anjou estates at Briollay and La Suze, and, one hundred and fifty miles south-west of Paris, his town, Sablé. He had also left a family – two daughters, both married, and a wife and son, both dead. A convent and a monastery owed their existence and their livelihoods to him; a chapel commemorated his wife. On the long voyage out to Acre he had been one of Richard's admirals. His lands in Anjou made Richard his overlord; but when he called Richard and Philip Augustus 'cousin', he was not merely being polite, he was being accurate. It happened too that he was distantly related to the second Master of the Templars, Robert de Craon, elected fifty-five years before. An incidental qualification; but Robert de Sablé had something of the same skill as the earlier Robert, the master diplomat who had won for his Order the Bull *Omne Datum Optimum*; and more than ever since the days of Robert de Craon, the Templars needed a diplomat. Their recent ill-judged actions remained in people's memories more vividly than the protection they gave every day; one head-strong Master could give the whole Order a notoriety that could barely be effaced by any three more prudent leaders. Bernard de Trémélai, Bertrand de Blanquefort, Odo de St-Amand, Gerard de Ridefort; the Templars had had more than enough of rash and obstinate Masters – at any rate for the time being.

Members of the high nobility were rare among the Templars by then. De Sablé's reputation was already good, and simply by accepting the post of Master, he went a long way to expunging the guilt attributed to the Order by so many – the guilt of the defeat at Hattin and the subsequent loss of Jerusalem. At once, he became a major figure in the Anglo-French camp at Acre. After Richard's arbitrary division of the city and the ensuing near-rebellion, de Sablé was entrusted with the allocation of property and loot. While Philip remained in the Holy Land, de Sablé arbitrated constantly between the two kings; and when Richard disdainfully ordered the Duke of Austria's banner to be thrown 'into the jakes', it was de Sablé and his new brethren who protected Richard from the Austrians' wrath.

It was important for the Templars to alleviate the tensions between the Franks, for although they and the Hospitallers were the only remaining real Frankish military power in the East, they needed to harness the energy of the new crusaders if anything was to be recovered. Perhaps fortunately, King Philip left for Europe soon after the recapture of Acre, announcing that his vow was fulfilled and his part in the Crusade finished. Before he left, he handed over all his remaining war materials and food to de Sablé, to be divided between the two Orders. He had never had much love for crusading, and had often been more of a hindrance than a help; his departure was publicly criticized, but privately welcomed by many, especially the English. For most of the Crusaders, however, Jerusalem was the only goal; only a few of the French left with their king. The rest remained, and moved south with Richard.

De Sablé, despite his experience in other theatres of war, was a newcomer to Palestine. Prudently he took advice from his brethren, who knew the country and the enemy well. Richard in turn generally listened to de Sablé's advice, and generally took it. Through this phase of the war, therefore, the guiding spirit was that of the Templars; and two things at least showed the brethren how much their public image had revived and improved. With de Ridefort presumed dead and de Sablé in charge, all criticism of the Templars' military actions stopped; and although at least once Templar counsel contradicted crusader hopes, that counsel was accepted.

Richard needed advisers; he was a fireball that had to be directed and controlled, lest he burn everything indiscriminately. He was no administrator; much less was he an empire-builder. Cyprus was beginning to hang heavily on him, and money was beginning to run short. De Sablé suggested a solution to both problems: the Templars should buy the island. Delighted with the idea of simultaneously ridding himself of an unwanted possession and filling his coffers, Richard agreed immediately. The price was set at 100,000 gold bezants. On behalf of the Order, de Sablé paid 40,000 in cash, and arranged to pay the rest as and when it was needed. With financial security, military strength and sound advice, Richard's confidence was unbounded.

For the march to Ascalon, the Templars recommended the old Roman road by the coast – longer than the direct route, but safer, with the sea controlled by the Pisan supply fleet. Saladin moved cautiously parallel, trying to tempt Richard to attack, but de Sablé kept the king's eyes set firmly to the south. Not until Arsuf, a hundred miles south of Acre and half-way to Ascalon, was battle joined at last. The site was chosen by Saladin; the first charge was Moslem; but the victory was Richard's. His battle-formation was a masterpiece of classic elegance. In the rear, with their backs to the sea, an infantry reserve guarded the baggage train. Three times that number of footsoldiers and archers formed the front line, stretched along three miles of the Roman road; and between the two lines, on the road itself, the knights were divided into twelve companies, the Templars on the right wing, the Hospitallers on the left, and Richard with his standard in the centre. Wave after wave of Moslems broke against the Franks, who waited like rocks; then, when their charge came, Richard was in the forefront. Saladin's secretary Baha ad-Din, perched in the safety of a nearby hill, had a bird's-eye view as the great armoured horses thundered forward.

'I myself,' he wrote breathlessly, 'saw their knights gather together in the middle of the infantry; they grasped their lances, shouted their shout of battle like one man, the infantry opened out, and through they rushed in one great charge in all directions – some on our right wing, some on our left, and some on our centre, till all was broken.'

It was Richard's finest hour. Thirty-four years old, he was in the prime of life. At Acre he had made Saladin's huge army ineffectual. At Arsuf he had defeated them in pitched battle, and had shown himself to be one of the greatest generals of his time and culture. Just as important, he had shown that Saladin, undefeated since Hattin, was not invincible. The Crusade could go on, and it seemed that nothing could stop it. Twenty years Richard's senior, Saladin, in the scale of the time, was entering old age. He was ill, and weary of war. His main wish was to preserve Jerusalem for Islam. He began to fight in a way unknown for him before: a rear-guard, scorched-earth policy, drawing his forces in to the Holy City, the focal point. Ascalon was razed to the ground; the fortifications of Lydda, Ramleh and Natrun, Jerusalem's eastern defensive arc, were dismantled. All Saladin's energies were concentrated in Jerusalem, which was desperately under-fortified; for Richard, the lion-hearted king of the Franks, might enter at any moment, and all the work, all the fighting, all the Moslem lives lost in four years of holy war would be utterly wasted.

But it never happened like that. The Franks marched vigorously, enthusiastically, drawn by the magnet of Jerusalem, the thought of the Holy City so nearly in their grasp; then, at the fort of Beit-Nuba, a mere twelve miles from their goal, King Richard ordered retreat.

The disappointment was stunning. The English stayed by their king, as did the Templars and Hospitallers; but the French, angry and downcast, began to desert. Yet if Richard the Lion had lost heart, it was not through fear of Saladin; as passionately as any of his men, he wanted to take the Holy City. It was visible from the hills around Beit-Nuba; riding there one day, Richard came into sight of Jerusalem, and covered his face with his shield in order not to see the city, so close, so vulnerable, so tempting and so dangerous. It was future danger that Richard saw; and that, and present troubles in the lands he had left, dissuaded him from a conquest that would have made all Christendom ring with his name.

It was de Sablé and the Templars, backed by the Hospitallers and the native barons, who argued against the conquest. They knew, as well as Richard and every other crusader, that the city was theirs for the taking; lives would be lost, but the city would be won. But when it was taken, who would keep it? The majority of the Crusaders would certainly go home; Richard too would be obliged to return to his distant English throne. The Frankish Palestinians would have nothing but a strip of coast-line and one great city far from the sea, surrounded by enemies and cut off from friends. Infinitely attractive, the conquest would also be incalculably reckless. Even if the Kingdom of Jerusalem was of Jerusalem only by name, it must be united, physically and politically, if ever it was to grow into reality once more.

The new objective was Ascalon, the new winter work its re-fortification. Depressed and dissatisfied, the army turned and plodded mournfully towards the coast. It was the depth of winter; all at once the things which before had seemed mere discomforts now became almost intolerable – the marching through rain and sleet, the camping in mud and puddles, the rotten food. Even in Ascalon it was little better – the city was in ruins, and hard work was essential just to keep the rain out.

In Acre too it was a winter of discontent. Guy de Lusignan, the titular king of Jerusalem, was alone in his household; his queen, Sibylla, and their two daughters, had all died the year before. Conrad de Montferrat, the saviour of Tyre, had engineered the divorce of the other princess, Isabella, and her husband Humphrey, and had then married Isabella himself. Two claimants to one non-existent throne: it would have been farcical if it had not been so close to tragedy.

Hard on the heels of this news from Acre, word came to Richard of his brother John's misdeeds in England. The errant king must return with all speed, unless he wished, like Guy, to lose his kingdom. Pulled every way at once by his inclinations, his ambitions and his duty, Richard balanced all of them in his last crusading months, advised on all occasions by the trusted de Sablé.

Negotiations for peace were opened with Saladin. At the same time, the question of which king should wear Jerusalem's empty crown was put to a general council of all the knights and barons. Richard personally supported Guy, for all his ineffectiveness, since the de Lusignans of Anjou were vassals of the English king. De Sablé had done the same for the same reason, but now, far-sighted as ever, he recognized that the throne should go to the better man. Conrad won the Templar vote – and every other vote as well. Not one of them went to Guy.

Nonetheless, Guy was content; for while voting Conrad king of Jerusalem, de Sablé suggested a new realm for Guy – the isle of Cyprus. Templar rule there had been no more than a military occupation, and a limited one at that, since only fourteen knights could be spared from the mainland. Those fourteen had no taste for colonizing, and could not control the freedom-loving Cypriots; but Guy bought the island happily, and the fourteen knights returned, probably equally happily, to Acre.

Conrad de Montferrat was not so lucky. Hearing the glad news of his election, he prayed to God that he might not be allowed to accept if he were not the right man for the throne. Eight days later he was dead, with an Assassin dagger between his ribs.

Accusations flew in every direction – it was Guy, it was Richard, it was Saladin. In fact it was the Assassins' own initiative, their first and last act in all the Third Crusade, prompted by Conrad's piratical theft of a merchant ship's cargo belonging to the sect. All the same, it threw the problem wide open again; but when needs must, the devil drives, and Richard, as a Plantagenet, claimed descent from the devil. In two days he had found a new husband for Isabella, and five days later, Jerusalem had a new king – Henry of Champagne, who just happened to be Richard's nephew. Conveniently, he was a nephew of Philip of France as well. At last, the remains of Outremer had a leader whom everyone – or almost everyone – would follow.

The remaining few months of the Third Crusade passed in a swift flurry of alternating acts of aggression and overtures for peace. On 23 May 1192, Richard recaptured Daron, the most southerly castle lost to Saladin. On 20 June, in the style of Reynald de Chatillon, he took a Moslem caravan with great quantities of merchandise and food, and several thousand camels and horses. He made another advance to Beit-Nuba, and retreated once more, not knowing that Saladin had been on the point of ordering a retreat to the east himself. On 29 July, following the Franks towards the sea, Saladin took Jaffa; and on the thirty-first, Richard took it back again.

The last battle was on 5 August, outside the walls of Jaffa. Like Arsuf, it was a magnificent display of Richard's leadership; in a final, careless gesture, he seemed to snap his fingers in Saladin's face. The dawn attack was intended to surprise the sleeping Franks, but a last-minute warning gave them just enough time to prepare; and with two thousand infantry, fifty-four knights and fifteen horses, Richard drove off no less than seven thousand Moslem cavalry.

It could not go on. Each army was exhausted. Both Richard and Saladin were ill. No final victory had been won, nor any final defeat suffered, but each king knew that neither he nor the other could continue. On 2 September Richard signed a treaty of peace for five years. As a king he refused to take an oath; de Sablé swore for him. Next day Saladin put his name to the treaty; and thus ended the war of the Third Crusade, the crusade which Richard the Lion-Heart, with his fiery will and personality, had made so much his own.

Outremer was reborn. It was cut to a fraction of its former size, but it lived. Peace had been made with honour, where, but a few years previously, all – all – had seemed lost to Christendom. Christians could visit the holy shrines of Jerusalem; Moslem and Christian caravans could pass freely and fearlessly through each other's lands. The fighting was done; the armies were disbanded.

However, Richard's adventures were not over yet. He still had to travel the long miles back to England, and he had made many enemies on the journey out. De Sablé gave the last help he could, and Richard left the Holy Land disguised as a Templar. But some identities cannot be concealed. Passing through Austria, he was recognized, captured and taken before the duke – the man whose banner he had cast into the jakes at Acre. Fifteen months later, he was released, when all the silver in England had gone to build the battlements of Vienna.

By then, both Saladin and de Sablé were dead, the former in the spring, the latter in the autumn of 1193. Six years later Richard followed them, dying fighting, as he had lived. Saladin died at peace with his people, his enemies and his God, remembered by the Moslems with love and by the Franks with respect. Of de Sablé's end little is known; the records state merely the fact of his death. But, as Richard had rebuilt Outremer, de Sablé, with his wisdom and prudence, had rebuilt the honour of the Order; and even the living, for a short time, could rest in peace.

CHAPTER 9

THE DEVIL'S DOCTRINE

Europe, Byzantium and the Holy Land,
1193–1213

'There must be also heresies among you.'
1 Corinthians XI, 19

ONE OF THE MAIN OBJECTIVES of the Crusades was the unification of eastern and western Christendom, and one of the basic principles of the time was that religious belief – conversion to the one true faith of the Roman Church – could be effectively established by force. Unless one bears this in mind, the events of the twenty years following the deaths of Saladin and de Sablé became the essence of insanity. Nevertheless, even remembering those principles, it is difficult to see the years from 1193 to 1213 as anything but the grossest perversion of Christ's teaching, a macabre parody in which almost everyone in Christendom – even the Templars – took part.

The ugly drama was played in three separate theatres: southern France, northern Syria and Constantinople. The Templars were involved, to a greater or lesser extent, in all three; and behind all three, simultaneously puppet-master and one of the puppets, was one powerful man: Pope Innocent III.

Saladin's great empire had been sustained only by his personality. When he died in 1193 he left seventeen sons and one daughter; the empire began to fall apart at once. The knife was taken from the throat of Outremer, but the Palestinian Franks could not use the opportunity for reconquest; their own minute kingdom was far too weak. Henry of Champagne wielded full royal authority, although he was never actually crowned king of Jerusalem; his policy towards the Moslems was always one of peaceful diplomacy, trading words rather than blows, and in the interests of their own survival, the Templars supported him. Henry even made a new alliance with the Assassins. The Old Man of the Mountains celebrated it in spectacular fashion: he invited Henry to a meeting on a cliff-top, where his followers demonstrated their fidelity by leaping, one by one, to their deaths in the abyss below, until Henry begged for the display to end.

The Templars had little time for such frivolities. They were grateful for the alliance: one more threat was removed. And, following de Sablé's prudent example, they avoided conflict with the Moslems for nearly fourteen years after his death. But they were busy elsewhere – busy with the inception of twenty years of Christian fratricide.

At first, it seemed harmless enough, a little question of the reclamation of lost property. About eighteen miles north of Antioch lay a castle named Baghras. Before Saladin's war it had belonged to the Templars. In 1191, Saladin had captured and razed it; then, immediately he and his men had left, the site was occupied and the castle rebuilt by the prince of Armenia, Leo II. No sooner was the reconstruction finished than Prince Bohemond of Antioch, on behalf of the Templars, asked for the castle to be returned to the Order; Leo refused point-blank; and from this sprang two decades of war between the Christians of Palestine and those of Armenia.

In those days of monarch-politicians, Leo of Armenia was one of the most overtly political of all. Crowned king in 1198, he won his throne through fair words and flattery; he maintained it through glib promises and judicious spiritual blackmail, balancing those greater than he against each other. A king's crown could be granted only by an emperor, or the pope; the Armenian Church was regarded as heretical by the Church of Rome. Leo therefore obtained his crown from the Byzantine Emperor and his sceptre from the German emperor, the greatest temporal ruler of the time. Simultaneously he began correspondence with the dying Pope Celestine III, suggesting that in return for papal recognition he would bring the Armenian Church back to the Orthodox fold. The deal was made, and Leo achieved his ambition; he was acknowledged as a king by everyone who mattered. That achieved, he had further ambitions. Antioch would make an attractive addition to his kingdom. To that end, Baghras was a prime strategic site, and despite papal prompting that he should return the castle to the Templars, Leo was determined to keep it. The Templars were equally determined to get it back.

Very little is known about the man who was Master of the Order then – even his name is uncertain, being reported variously as Gilbert Erail, Horal, Arayl, or Roral. Neither his age nor his country of birth are known; but unlike his predecessor de Sablé, he was a 'career' Templar. For him, the road to the exalted position of Master was long and arduous. Ten years before his election as Master, he had been Grand Preceptor of the Temple in Jerusalem; it was he who had been passed over in favour of the explosive de Ridefort. From that, and their widely differing characters, we may guess that he and de Ridefort disliked each other thoroughly; but Erail was spared the frustrating agony of personal service to de Ridefort, for in 1185 he had been created Master of the Temple in Spain and Provence. For four years he had stayed there, watching from afar the destructive, demented leadership and its culmination at Hattin; then in 1190, in the period between de Ridefort and de Sablé, when the Order as a whole had no Master, he was made deputy Master of the Temple in the West. He appears, therefore, to have been reliable, respected and conscientious; and although the utter secrecy of the Templars' elections prevents certain knowledge of this, it is a reasonable surmise that he was proposed as Master a second time, after de Ridefort's disappearance at Acre. But dependable as Erail must have been, the Templars needed a man whose integrity was recognized outside their own ranks, a man who could restore the Order not only in its own eyes but in the eyes of the world. When de Sablé had done that, Erail's chance came at last; in 1193 he was recalled from the West, and the faithful servant of the Temple became its twelfth Master.

Five years later, when Leo put on his Armenian crown and tightened his grip on Baghras, it may have seemed to the Templars that chance had endorsed their choice of Master. The old Pope Celestine had welcomed the Armenians' return to orthodoxy, but had done little to promote the restoration of

Baghras. More could surely be hoped for from his successor – for Innocent III was a personal friend of Gilbert Erail. However, any such optimism was ill-founded. The two men shared one characteristic: a deep loyalty to the religious bodies of which they were the heads. But where Erail was plodding and prosaic, steady and straightforward, Innocent was dynamic, passionate, visionary and intensely forceful – not at all the man to be bound by friendship when greater things were at stake.

When Innocent became pope in 1198, he was only thirty-seven years old. It was unheard of that such a young man should attain such high office; but Innocent was very exceptional indeed, if not unique. He had studied theology, Roman law and canon law in Paris and Bologna, and had formed definite ideas on the mission of the papacy, ideas which he sketched vividly, almost brutally, on the very day he was consecrated. He based his sermon on a quotation from Jeremiah:

'Here and now I give thee authority over the nations; with a word thou shalt root them up and put them down, overthrow and lay them in ruins; with a word thou shalt build them up and plant them anew.'

And he meant what he said, every syllable. For one hundred and ten years, since Urban II launched the First Crusade, the Church had not had a pope with such breadth of vision and force of character. Innocent's vision was of Christendom as a great republic, in which all people shared one faith, and all nations, though mutually independent, were subject to one supreme temporal and spiritual authority – his own and his successors'. One vast spiritual commonwealth, presided over by the paternal benevolence of the Roman pontiff – that was Innocent's idea, and he succeeded in realizing it more nearly than any other pope before or since. In Germany, Italy, France, England, Norway, Aragon and Armenia, he was recognized as spiritual suzerain; and he opened negotiations with the Byzantine emperor, as head of the Greek Church, working towards its union with the Church of Rome. Innocent himself would, naturally, be head of the unified Church.

But what seemed to Innocent to be a spiritual commonwealth seemed to others like a spiritual dictatorship. Not everyone was willing to follow his plan – the Byzantines were understandably hesitant; the sincerity of the Armenian submission was dubious;

and the people of southern France, ebullient and audacious as ever, had actually begun to question the unquestionable dogma of the Church. And, of course, Jerusalem itself, theoretically the centre and keystone of Christendom, was in infidel hands.

If Leo of Armenia was a good example of a political king, Innocent was the peerless example of a political pope. There was no one to match him in the ecclesiastical world, and among all the secular sovereigns of Europe, his only potential rival – Henry VI of Germany, the Hohenstaufen emperor whose gift Leo's sceptre had been – had suddenly and conveniently died. Germany itself was split then by civil war, for Henry's heir, Frederick, was a minor. But Frederick was under Innocent's protection, who, following the words of his inaugural sermon exactly, uprooted, overthrew and rebuilt nations. He adjudicated over the German civil war, crowned his chosen man emperor, then in the course of time deposed that one and replaced him with the young Frederick. Similarly, in England, Innocent deposed the weak and unprincipled King John, refusing to reinstate him until John became his vassal. The same happened in Norway. In France, Innocent forced Philip Augustus to end his second, bigamous marriage; in Spain, the King of Leon was compelled to repudiate his wife, to whom he was too closely related; and the King of Aragon, witnessing all this, hastened to swear fealty to the whirlwind pope.

In the midst of this succession of events, the question of the ownership of Baghras seemed distant and unimportant. Innocent knew the Templars would never desert the Church of Rome, but he was suspicious of the depth of Leo's conversion, and, not wanting to lose a vassal so easily won, let Leo retain the disputed castle. Time and again Gilbert Erail sent pleas for justice to his one-time friend, yet on that particular issue Innocent was impervious to appeal. The Templars had to continue their own private war against a fellow-Christian – a state of affairs which Innocent did not seem to find objectionable.

Nevertheless, he did help the brethren actively in other ways. He regarded them as his own private army, and was not going to let anyone forget it. In the first seven years of his papacy he reconfirmed *Omne Datum Optimum* eight times, and in his second year (1199) he was called to defend the Order from the only kind of attack they could not resist at all: excommunication.

The very notion that the knights of God should or even could be excommunicated seems absurd. But it happened; and the incident demonstrates why people had, by then, mixed feelings about the Templars.

Money was the root of the problem. The Templars had long since become accustomed to handling large amounts of it, not only on their own account in the financing of their far-flung, expensive military operations, but also on behalf of other people. Their castles in Europe were a byword for strength and security, and it was common for any European king who happened to have some money to give it into the Templars' hands for safe-keeping. Philip Augustus was just one such; at the time of his crusade with Richard of England, the French State Treasury was located in the vaults of the Paris Temple. And not only royalty sought a safe deposit for spare cash inside Templar walls; bishops and archbishops, merchants and private citizens, all placed their funds in the houses of the Temple.

Unless the money was an outright gift, these people naturally expected to get it back again when they asked. Unfortunately the great majority of the Templars were illiterate, and their book-keeping was often extremely haphazard. Sometimes only one man, perhaps the commander of a preceptory, would know that a deposit had been made, and if he died or was transferred before it was reclaimed, the owner of the money might never see it again. Sometimes, too, money deposited by one person would be claimed by his heir. With a little good will on each side, such claims could be settled easily; but good will was not always present. According to the ethics of the time, the root of evil was not the love of money but *superbia* – haughtiness, pride, arrogance – and by Innocent's day it was a commonplace that the Templars had *superbia* in plenty. Even Richard I, himself no humble king, parried an accusation that he was proud by saying he would marry his pride to the Templars, since it was so familiar to them.

The two elements, money and pride, came together in 1199. The bishop of Tiberias sent a claim to the Master, Gilbert Erail, for repayment of thirteen hundred gold bezants lodged with the Templars by his predecessor, and the Templars, for some unknown reason, refused to pay it. The bishop of Sidon was nominated to arbitrate; however, his idea of arbitration was to threaten excommunication not only to Erail and all the Order, but to their friends and colleagues as well, both in Europe and the Holy Land, if the money were not returned within three days. It was – yet the bishop carried out his threat all the same.

Erail and his brethren were stupefied and enraged. If they were excommunicate, they could not fulfil their holy vows. Very well then, they said, we shall forget our vows, throw off our white mantles, leave the Holy Land and return to our homes.

Innocent intervened at once. Accusing the bishop of 'great stupidity or grave malignancy', he suspended the unfortunate man from his duties and absolutely forbade any cleric to be so presumptious again. It was a kind of victory for the Templars, who withdrew their petulant threat; but it served only to deepen the resentment felt towards the Order by the regular ecclesiastics; and the depth that resentment had already attained may be judged by the speed and severity of the bishop's sentence against the knights.

Innocent's equally swift reaction indicates his determination to keep the Templars free of any authority but his own. Through buying cheaply or taking over deserted property as civilians fled westwards, the Templars and Hospitallers had become the major landowners in Frankish Palestine. Territorially rich, militarily disciplined, spiritually and legally inviolable – and all at his sole disposal; the possibilities would have dazzled a lesser man than Pope Innocent III. But Innocent was not dazzled. With his clear, severe legal mind and his overriding vision of the Christian Republic, Innocent saw exactly how he, and only he, could use the Templars; and almost as soon as he had ascended to the papal throne, he initiated the Fourth Crusade.

He had every reason to hope for total success. Never since the days of Urban II had circumstances been more promising. The dismal failure of the Second Crusade, and the limited achievements of the Third, stood in sharp contrast to the overwhelming victories of the First. To Innocent the reason was all but self-evident: no kings had gone on the First Crusade. With no kings, there were no royal rivalries. The jealousies of ordinary men could be controlled by the pope's own legates; and Innocent, from his unchallenged position, could make sure that no kings would sully his crusade. He could also avoid the blunder of sending men of different nations to fight for a supposedly common cause; and for his special warriors, the Templars, he had a special role. Since they were already in the Holy Land, they obviously had no need to travel. Instead, they would await the European armies that were bound to materialize; they would consolidate their own holdings and prepare for a great, united offensive; and, from their already legendary reserves of gold and jewels, they would contribute to the financing of the grand operation.

It all seemed so beautifully simple as to admit no chance of failure. And if everyone involved had been as inspired by God as Innocent believed himself to be, it might have worked. But it all went horribly, tragically wrong, because there were forces in men's minds that Innocent did not take into account, and whose strength he could not understand.

To begin with, the Templars were not at all eager to embark on a new holy war. The lack of Baghras still rankled sorely. Leo had ignored Innocent's one request to give the castle up, and the pope's subsequent apparent indifference bewildered the knights. Confused and uncertain about his old friend's motives, Gilbert Erail died on 12 December 1200; and if Philip de Plessiez, Erail's successor, was cautious and devious in dealing with the pope, he only reflected the perplexity felt by the whole Order.

There were other, yet more pressing, practical reasons for avoiding an unnecessary war. De Plessiez (whose origins, and earlier ranks, are completely unknown) became Master at a particularly difficult time: the first three summers of his Mastership were spent coping with drought, famine, earthquakes, plague and one cataclysmic sandstorm. In the earthquakes the towns of Acre, Tyre and Tripoli were largely destroyed – though, curiously, the Templars' house in Acre was one of the few buildings to survive unscathed. The work of reconstruction, and of finding food for the tens of thousands of starving, impoverished refugees from the devastated countryside was more than enough work; but the natural disasters did at least strike everyone, Moslem and Christian, and de Plessiez was able to renew the truce with the Moslems. Innocent, the war-like pope, did not care for this at all, but was mollified by hearing from de Plessiez that, in return for the truce, the Moslems had started paying tribute to the patriarch of Jerusalem. Perhaps they were. Perhaps they even believed de Plessiez's claim that he could guarantee a lasting peace if the tribute continued – but it was fortunate for de Plessiez that Innocent did not hear of that claim.

Despite their very reasonable prevarication, the Templars could not prevent the Crusade from happening. Their contribution to its cost was duly collected; in Europe the enterprise got under way; and at once it began to go subtly and insidiously wrong. The devil's doctrine was taking hold. The Fourth Crusade was to become one of the greatest crimes of Christians against Christians.

Innocent's Christianity was in men's mouths, but not in their hearts. The leaders of the Fourth Crusade were drawn by the lure of riches and revenge – but not riches in heaven, nor revenge on infidels. The ordinary soldiers started in good faith, and by June 1202 were assembled in Venice. The suggestion made by Richard Coeur-de-Lion ten years before, that a new crusade should first conquer Egypt, had been accepted, and the Venetians had undertaken to supply ships and food for a year. Their price was high: 85,000 silver marks. By the time the crusading army was gathered together, its leaders had discovered that they could not raise such a sum. Fifty thousand was all they could offer, even with the Templars' help. And what they did not know then was that while agreeing to transport the army to Egypt, the Venetians had simultaneously made a trade agreement with the Egyptian Sultan – an agreement which promised that no European army would set foot on Egyptian soil. For many years already, the Italian trading republics of Pisa, Genoa and Venice had found there was good business to be had with the Moslem nations, and the Venetians in particular did not wish to upset their stable, profitable markets. Their enemies were closer.

Unable to fulfil their side of the treaty, the crusaders waiting in Venice could only agree to whatever new terms the Venetians might impose. The offer they were given seemed remarkably generous: payment of the remaining 35,000 marks could be delayed, and the expedition could set out, if the Crusaders would just help the Venetians to take control of the Dalmatian port of Zara. A trifling thing; Zara was only two days' sail from Venice, and was on the way to the Holy Land. The crusading commander, Boniface of Montferrat – brother of Conrad, the saviour of Tyre – accepted quickly, making light of the fact that Zara was a Christian city; for by then he too had seen a better goal than Palestine.

Too late, Innocent realized he had lost control of the Crusade. His desperate prohibitions of anti-Christian aggression were ignored. On 8 November 1202 the fleet sailed, bearing four thousand five hundred knights, nine thousand esquires and twenty thousand infantry, and a week later Zara – or what was left of it after five days of fighting – belonged to Venice.

Using the only weapon he had, Innocent excommunicated the town of Venice and all the crusading army. Since the Crusaders had been blackmailed, however, he soon lifted their sentence; yet though the Venetians remained condemned, they were quite unabashed. To them Zara was only a prelude. In conference with Enrico Dandolo, the old, half-blind but infinitely cunning Doge, Boniface arranged another detour: Constantinople.

Dandolo had personal grudges against the Byzantines. His partial loss of sight stemmed from a head-wound received thirty years before, when, as ambassador to Constantinople, he had been involved in a fight there; and after becoming Doge, the Greeks' dislike of him had proved bad for trade. The Venetians also remembered bitterly the brutal ejection of their townsfolk from Constantinople in 1171; and the Crusaders, when they thought about it, found they had just as much reason to hate the Greeks. The Eastern Church was schismatic and heretic, and heretics, who had rejected Christ's word, were worse than infidels, who had never heard it. Everyone knew the Greeks were traitors as well; more than fifty years before, St Bernard had begun the still-current teaching that Byzantine treachery had killed the Second Crusade, and Odo de Deuil had written that France and Germany would 'always have something to bewail if the sons of these men do not avenge their fathers' deaths.' Boniface easily revived these memories, and capped them with his own personal stake in the project. His brother-in-law, he claimed, was the rightful emperor of Byzantium. The current emperor was a usurper who, in the interests of legality and international harmony, should be overthrown and replaced.

In Rome, Innocent could only wait for reports, helplessly and impatiently. He did not condemn the plan outright; if it worked, the reunion of eastern and western christendom would be worth it. And when the reports began to filter in, he was jubilant – the emperor was overthrown, the new emperor enthroned; the debt to the Venetians would be paid, the Churches would be united, ten thousand Byzantines would join the Crusade. All that could have been hoped for had been achieved, and the united powers of Europe and Byzantium would descend on the Holy Land.

Then slowly the reports changed, and the news was of burning and torture, rape and sacrilege. Constantinople, the heart and pride of Byzantium, had been turned into a huge abattoir. In three days of riots and orgies, the Crusaders slaughtered as many Greeks as possible, little children, men and women, young and old; breaking into cellars they glutted themselves on the sweet Greek wine, then reeled out to set the great library ablaze; they burst into convents to ravish the nuns; they chopped down the doors of Hagia Sophia, drank the altar wine, ripped the silken hangings apart, hacked up the ornaments of gold and silver, emptied the reliquaries, defecated on the ikons, cleaned themselves with pages from the sacred books; and all the while, harlots cavorted in the aisles, as one, seating herself on the patriarch's throne, sang of the joys of love.

When the corpses were finally shovelled together, the body of the reinstated emperor was among them. All his promises had been baseless: there were no men for the army, there was no money for the Venetians. He was deposed and strangled, and in his place a Flemish knight was crowned lord of all the Greeks.

In Europe, the 'Crusading victory' was extremely popular. The Venetians were paid off with silver from melted chalices, and a stream of precious holy relics poured into the cathedrals and abbeys of France, Flanders and Italy. Only Innocent could see that his great dream had been shattered; the eastern and western Churches could never be united now. He turned his back on Byzantium, and grimly began to set his own house in order.

Perhaps sometimes, in the remaining twelve years of his life, Innocent managed to forget, managed to escape the memory of the smoke and stink as Byzantium and its culture writhed and died under his Crusaders. Perhaps; but he was changed, purified – or hardened – in the fires. Although he was not directly responsible for the crimes of the Fourth Crusade, his anger at its result was mingled with a deep sense of guilt. To purge the two emotions he needed an outlet of righteous violence; and he found it almost under his nose, in the geographical centre of western Christendom – southern France, the Languedoc.

France was divided north and south into two cultures, the division corresponding roughly to the course of the river Loire. Richard Coeur-de-Lion, with his Poitevin background, was a typical product of the romantic south; Philip Augustus, ruler of the north and nominal suzerain of the south, was equally typical of his colder, harder people. The differences between the two regions were exemplified by their languages: the word for 'yes' in the north was 'oeil'; in the south, it was 'oc'. The eventual domination of the north gave rise to the modern French 'oui'; but the language of oc, the 'langue d'oc', still designates the south.

Not only their languages but their religions were different. Innocent had forced fidelity on Philip, but no such fidelity prevailed in the south. St Bernard had complained once that churches there were empty and falling into disrepair. The reason was that the southerners had found a religion more satisfying to them than Roman Catholicism – the religion of the Cathars, or, as they became known from their French spiritual centre, the Albigensians.

Catharism was more than just a sect of the Catholic Church. While based on Christianity, it was another religion, with an understanding of Christ which denied the right of the Roman Church even to exist. The Cathars claimed, with truth, that their services were far closer to those of the first Christians than any in the Church of Rome. They also followed St Paul's distinction between body, soul and spirit, believing that a human soul was a fallen angel trapped in a mortal body, and that its spiritual body remained in heaven. Soul and spirit could only be united through knowledge – *gnosis*, meaning not intellectual knowledge, but a special, revealed knowledge and understanding of spiritual mysteries; without this *gnosis*, the soul was condemned to migrate to another mortal body, human or animal, when its first one died. The Cathars drew distinctions as well between the three parts of the Trinity, which they did not believe to be three facets of one being: Christ was an angel, a heavenly messenger who taught the knowledge whereby souls could be freed from their bodies. He did not come to atone for human sins; and though they acknowledged that a man was nailed on the cross, they denied that this was Christ. Thus they rejected both the Resurrection and the Incarnation, the two central tenets of the Christian faith.

If it seems complex, that is only because it is unfamiliar. In southern France in the eleventh and twelfth centuries the doctrine was preached everywhere, and was familiar to everyone. And though the Cathars had no church buildings, they had a comprehensive organization of teachers throughout the Languedoc, men who taught a creed of peace and simplicity, and who manifestly lived as they taught.

Yet however peaceable and tolerant the Cathars were, they flouted Catholic dogma, definitely and openly, and Innocent could not tolerate that. They might live as Christians should, but they were heretics; and in 1209 the pope ordered the destruction of those who professed the Cathar creed. With the precedent of Constantinople, he dignified the operation by calling it a crusade, and called on the Templars to support him. They did, as did many others, tempted by the indulgences offered to all true believers. For the French, the Holy War had come to their doorsteps, and it was much easier to burn heretics at home than to face the rigours of the long journey to Palestine.

One example will suffice to show the thinking behind the Albigensian wars. On 22 July 1209, the town of Beziers – not far from the Spanish border, and close to the Mediterranean coast – was surrounded by the 'army of the faith', and was quickly captured. When asked what should be done with the mixed Cathar-Catholic population, the papal legate said simply, 'Kill all of them; God will know his own.'

The Templars joined in the burnings and hangings with a will, but it took much longer than the forty days Innocent had anticipated to cauterize Catharism. And with the benefit of hindsight, this period at the beginning of the thirteenth century can be seen as a time of great portent for the Knights of the Temple, a devil's dress-rehearsal of their own agonizing end; for out of the flames in Albi and Toulouse sprang a spark that would blaze up and engulf them as well.

In the ashes of the Cathars and Constantinople, the Templars unwittingly wrote their own fate. Far from helping Outremer, the Fourth Crusade and its sequel in the Languedoc actually damaged the kingdom. A deputation of Templar knights assisted in the coronation of the first Latin emperor, who gave boastful promises of imminent military aid, promises which could never be fulfilled; and seeing the spoils to be had in France and Byzantium, many secular knights left the dangers and poverty of the Holy Land for good. After 1204 the only western knights who went there were those who joined the Military Orders. Superficially, it appeared that the Fourth Crusade gave the Templars little return for their money; but it is possible – although this has never been proved, and has only recently been suspected – that, out of the carnage of Constantinople, they won a greater prize than anyone else: a prize whose true nature they barely understood, but which they valued and honoured more highly than life itself. Guarded behind an almost impenetrable wall of silence, shielded from the sight of all but an elect few, the mysterious, secretive, arrogant Templars held one of the world's greatest enigmas – an object which they believed was the source of their power and their glory, but whose rumoured possession led ultimately to their total obliteration.

CHAPTER 10

CASTLE PILGRIM

The Holy Land, 1218–1244

'Let us build us a city and a tower,
whose top may reach unto heaven.'
Genesis XI, 4

FROM HAIFA TO ASCALON, the coast of Israel runs in a
gentle, almost uninterrupted curve, heading slightly west
of south. Haifa itself, old Haifa, lies in the shelter of a
great hook of land. But if you take a boat and sail
westwards around that hook, out over the warm clear Mediterranean; and if, then, as the land falls away to port, you
alter course to south-south-west and follow the coast, nothing
more lies between you and Ascalon. Nothing, except one long
promontory, named Athlit.

Sailing that coast, from Alexandretta in present-day Turkey
to Damietta in Egypt, you pass all the ports of the crusading days
– Lattakieh, Jabala, Tortosa and Tripoli; Beirut, Sidon and Tyre;
Acre and Haifa, Caesarea, Jaffa and Ascalon. But none of those
places, most of which today are large cities, recalls the Crusades –
and especially the Templars – quite so much as Athlit. Lying
nineteen sea-miles south of Haifa – only a few hours' voyage –
the promontory juts out a third of a mile into the sea, and is
entirely covered with the ruins of the strongest castle the
Templars ever built: Castle Pilgrim.

Built in 1218, exactly a hundred years after the Order was
founded by Hugh de Payens and his little group, Castle Pilgrim is
a perfect example of all the Templars stood for. Its express
purpose was 'to bring the Templar chapter from the sinful city of

Acre, until they could move into fortified Jerusalem'. It could accommodate four thousand people, and everything needful for life could be found within its walls: there were pastures and fish-ponds, salt-mines and springs of fresh water, orchards and vegetable gardens, and, by the natural harbour, a ship-yard. You may still moor there, at a jetty two hundred feet long; and even today, the ruins are majestic and imposing. Walking among them, it is easy to imagine the white-mantled knights, the horses, the sergents in black or brown, the pilgrims whose labour created the castle and after whom it is named. There was the church, a polygonal, near-circular building modelled on the Church of the Holy Sepulchre; there were the great towers, each one a hundred feet long and seventy-four feet wide, that defended the landward face; there was the vaulted hall in which the knights held their secret meetings. Proud, aggressive and self-contained, Castle Pilgrim is a microcosm of the whole Templar Order.

Its construction was begun by William de Chartres, the fourteenth Master. Goaded by the bellicose Pope Innocent III, the preceding Master, Philip de Plessiez, had refused to renew the truce with the Moslems and had died in battle, late in 1209. His mastership had lasted eight and a half years, an average length; out of all the twenty-three Masters of the Temple, only seven survived for more than ten years. But death must often have been welcome to them, for though they were honoured as princes, they had to combine the skills of a politician, a general, an abbot and an economist. William de Chartres held this heavy respon-sibility for nine difficult years. For six of those years, the Franks and Moslems were at peace, but without that the Templars in the East probably could not have survived the period. Baghras was not restored to the Order until 1216; before then, Leo of Armenia had destroyed their houses in Antioch and their castles in Armenia, and Henry, the second Latin emperor of Byzantium, had annexed all their castles in Greece. None of the Templars' enemies caused more difficulty than those within the faith.

Castle Pilgrim was certainly the greatest legacy that William de Chartres left his brethren. It was built as a place of defence and refuge, but a strong castle, manned and provisioned, was not just a passive object; the edifice itself was an active threat. Active enough, in the case of Castle Pilgrim, for the Moslems to raze one of their own castles – an almost impregnable one on Mount

Thabor – through fear of the new stronghold towering over Athlit. One may only guess at the feelings of the Moslem spies as they watched the first defensive ditch being dug, and the trains of oxen dragging the yellowish stones that would make the wall – each stone so large that a pair of oxen could pull no more than one at a time.

It took six weeks of digging simply to go deep enough for the foundations; and as they dug, the pilgrims and Templars discovered they were not the first to have seen the possibilities of the promontory. Far underground were two large and long-forgotten walls, the remains of some ancient fortification. Not only that, but a treasure was found: money of a kind no one had ever seen before. The brethren received it with delight, seeing it as the gift of a very practical God, and used it – presumably melted down and recast – to defray some of their expenses. Then came another kind of treasure, even more valuable from the military view: a fresh-water spring came gurgling and bubbling up, bearing with it the promise of life, food and abundance within the walls. And with the God-given water, the tons of excavated sand, and ground sea-shells from the beach, the brothers and the labouring pilgrims mixed the cement that would hold those walls firm. God smiled on their efforts, and 1000 bezants were laid as an offering on the first stone.

When the eastern wall was finished, it was some ninety feet high and sixteen feet thick, with only one small gate. No man who saw the castle built could have thought it would ever surrender – and it never did. It held firm for seventy-three years, until all other Frankish possessions in Outremer had fallen.

Yet one of the castle's most striking aspects, as one wanders through the ruins, is that the eastern, landward wall is the only real defensive line. West and north and south, Castle Pilgrim was more or less open to the sea. That openness, and the purpose of the castle – to house the Templar chapter 'until they could move into fortified Jerusalem' – together are especially significant of the time. The Franks still controlled the sea; and the Templars in particular still had every intention of reclaiming their ancient property, the Temple at the heart of Christendom.

When, as a young man, Lawrence of Arabia visited the castle's ruins, he described the building as 'a stupidity', saying it was 'as much a prison as a refuge for its defenders'. But that could be said of any stronghold; and as long as Templar ships could sail freely along the coast of the Holy Land, Castle Pilgrim – at once a fortress and a port – was the least imprisoning of all, except perhaps for Tortosa. They had owned an island fortress there since 1169, but like Castle Pilgrim it had been a strategic site long before: Phoenician ruins provided the stone for the new protection. A causeway – every inch of it covered from the castle by peering arrow-slits – linked shore and island; and on the island, there are similarities to the castle at Athlit. Not the mines or fields, for this is a fortification, nothing more and nothing less; two large square towers dominate it, along with an irregularly shaped keep, in which the smallest wall is one hundred and ten feet long. Beneath this part there are great vaulted rooms, and a tiny postern gate communicating with the sea – a way in for supplies and reinforcements, and, in absolute emergency, a way out for the brethren. One cannot forget that this was the home of holy warriors: the chapel is lit by narrow windows, as if this too was a place of strength and defence, and in the pillared volume of the great hall, the sole decorations are the Cross and the Lamb of God.

Travelling inland from Tortosa, you come to two Templar castles that truly are as much prisons as refuges. They are known as Chastel Blanc and Chateau Rouge. Chastel Blanc, built on a mountain, is almost theatrically spectacular: it has two enceintes, the inner raised above the outer; attackers would have to break through both, advancing in peril up their slopes, and even then would not have reached the heart of the building. This is a tower which springs in lonely grandeur from the inner wall, a three-storeyed construction which formed the brethren's last retreat. Its ground floor is a chapel, an astonishing room – it is one hundred feet long and fifty-five feet high. The only light comes from very small windows placed high above the ground; it is a gloomy place, but it does inspire a sense of security. And if it was not safe enough, the knights and sergents could retreat still further, up a staircase built into the wall, and emerge in their great hall, the second storey; and failing that, there was the third, top storey, open to the sky. From there, perched at a dizzy height above the slopes of the defences and the mountain-side below, they could pour down fire on the Saracen hordes; they could observe any movement far away; and with smoke and flame they could signal warning or distress to their brethren in Chateau Rouge. Like its sister Chastel Blanc, Chateau Rouge has two enceintes; like Tortosa and Athlit, it was a place fortified and refortified through the ages. When the Knights Templar arrived there, they were able to use it almost at once, for the most recent fortification, a Byzantine building, was still in good order. Only the inner wall needed some repair, and the place was in fighting form again.

And while such fortresses remained in the hands of these Christian warrior-monks, there was still hope as well, real hope that Jerusalem might be regained. Innocent's protégé Frederick had been crowned emperor of Germany, and was being prodded into a crusade; and shiploads of volunteers from Cyprus, Hungary, Italy, France, England, Holland and Austria were on their way to Outremer. There is some confusion about which expedition should be called the Fifth Crusade, Frederick's or the multi-national force. When the former was organized at last, it was well planned and successful, whereas the latter was conspicuous for its shoddy organization and its ultimate failure. But the failed multi-national Crusade was legal; Frederick's was not. Perhaps the simplest titles for the two are 'Frederick's Crusade' and the 'Damietta Crusade', for it was in the marshes of Damietta that the multi-national venture was finally defeated.

Chronologically, the Damietta crusade was the first by a long way. Different parties left home as early as the spring of 1217. The first to arrive in the Holy Land were the Austrians, in September 1217, closely followed by some of the Hungarians, and the Cypriots. Led by three unwise kings – the Cypriot Hugh, the Hungarian Andrew and the Palestinian John – and with the Military Orders following their own Masters, the hotch-potch army accomplished absolutely nothing, apart from capturing a head said to be St Stephen's, and a jug said to have been used at the marriage-feast at Cana. Content with that, the Hungarians left, and Hugh of Cyprus died.

By the time the next contingent arrived, in the spring of 1218, the construction of Castle Pilgrim was well under way. After the Franks' inept display the year before, the Moslems were not much worried by their preparations for war; but the newcomers were Dutchmen, with a large fleet at their disposal. This opened up a completely different possibility, and on 24 May the combined Dutch, Austrian and Palestinian navies set sail from

Acre. Their destination: Damietta, the Nile and Cairo.

They halted at Athlit, and took on the massed armies of Templars and Crusaders, with extra supplies from the new castle. By 27 May the first ships were anchored in the Nile Delta, two miles downstream of Damietta. On the 29th the main fleet arrived, bearing King John of Jerusalem, the Templars and William de Chartres. Egypt, they knew, could not be conquered; but if the Nile valley could be occupied, and a friendly régime installed in Cairo, then Egyptian grain and Egyptian men could be used in Frankish Palestine. Already they were barely a hundred miles from Cairo – as the crow flies; the river's meandering course covered nearly twice that distance, and its mouth was guarded by a tower, with a bridge of boats and a gigantic iron chain across the only navigable channel. These held the crusaders back for weeks; not until 25 August did they break through. And then, dropping anchor before the very walls of Damietta, they waited. That delay was the undoing of the crusade. With an immediate assault, Damietta would have fallen at once, and a determined push up river and across country might well have succeeded. But reinforcements were expected at any moment from Italy. A few days' wait seemed harmless; but it was the middle of September before the Italians arrived, and by then the initiative had been lost.

To the commander of the Italians, this did not seem very important. He was a Spaniard named Pelagius, a man almost unqualified for command. He was energetic, and a good, experienced administrator, but he was grossly tactless and had a fine sense of social position. He considered his own position, as a cardinal and papal legate, placed him in supreme authority among the crusaders, and he based his approach to the campaign on Pope Innocent's interpretation of the Book of Revelations. Innocent had died in 1216, but he had set the Crusade in motion, and his successor Honorious III had continued it enthusiastically. Pope and Master had corresponded frequently on this and other topics; de Chartres may have remembered, or have been reminded of, the correspondence of their mutual predecessors. Innocent III had once written to Gilbert Erail saying:

'At present people are cooling off, hearing that you are making truces with the Saracens. For ourselves, let us not cool at all, but hold steadfastly to our goal . . . for if you want the West to help you, you *must* take up the Holy War again.'

De Chartres' mastership invigorated the brethren marvellously. The return of Baghras in 1216 freed them from a preoccupation that had gone on far too long; and the building of Castle Pilgrim, two years later, refreshed and encouraged them. Once again they were ready to extend beyond their tedious duties of patrol and protection; and Honorius was very willing to help them. He instituted a one-twentieth tax on church goods to pay for the crusade, and appointed a Templar, brother Aymard, Treasurer of the Temple in Paris, to receive it. So far, so good; but a man might be a master of spiritual warfare and still know nothing of any mundane military value. Had they left the actual conduct of the Damietta Crusade to commanders like de Chartres, who understood war from the theory of strategy, tactics and logistics down to the practice of chopping off heads while riding a horse, it would have turned out differently; but Innocent, Honorius and Pelagius all worked from the premise that the Prophet Mohammed must be the Great Beast of Revelations, and that the Beast's number – 666 – was the number of years allotted before Islam could be destroyed. Since, however, Mohammed was born in AD 570, began teaching in 610 and died in 632, it is difficult to see why such high hopes were entertained; on that basis, the earliest possible date for the crusade to end Crusades would have been 1236. For all his other exceptional accomplishments, Innocent III may not have been a very good mathematician.

Such considerations did not put Cardinal Pelagius off at all. Nor did the gales, floods, famine and epidemics of the winter of 1218; nor yet the almost constant skirmishes and battles on land and water. In one of these battles, a Templar ship was sunk, loaded with Templars and Moslems fighting hand to hand; all were drowned. A contemporary left a simple but harrowing description of it.

'They took in the sail and dropped anchor, riding in midstream. The Saracens boarded, until there were a good two thousand men there. The Templars were below decks, and seeing there was no escape, they resolved to destroy their enemies and die in the service of Our Lord.

'Therefore they took up hatchets and chopped through the hull of the ship. She went quickly to the bottom; one hundred and forty Christians drowned – and more than fifteen hundred Saracens.'

A good ratio, perhaps, but this kind of suicide victory lacked the true Templar style, and the knights were becoming very impatient. In January 1219 the Chamberlain of the Temple, brother Martin, and the Marshal, brother John, travelled across Germany, collecting money to send to their colleagues in Damietta – just what was needed for independent action. But Honorius, doubtless with the best of intentions, scotched that firmly; the money should be spent, he said, 'on galleys, or other machines or apparatus – according to the foresight of Legate Pelagius.' Which was to say that it could not be spent to any constructive purpose at all.

By the summer of 1219, the crusaders had advanced no further. Damietta, so vulnerable a year before, had still not been taken. Disease killed many Christians in the camp and on the stinking, cramped, overcrowded ships. On shore, Moslem raiding parties harassed the army continually; and William de Chartres was one of their victims. Warding off an attack on 31 July, he was so badly wounded that he was obliged to resign rather than handicap his brethren. He died shortly after, having contracted a frightful ailment – possibly scurvy – which softened his gums and the bones of his legs. It was a common cause of death there.

In the pestilential heat of northern Egypt in August, a new Master was hastily elected: Pedro de Montaigu, a native of Aragon. Previously he had been Master of the Temple in Provence and Spain; and although like his compatriot Pelagius, he was certainly a devout Christian, he was too seasoned a warrior to expect the easy fulfilment of a poorly-interpreted prophecy.

Suddenly, however, it seemed that the prophecy was actually going to come true. The Franks had an unexpected visitor: Francis of Assissi. The gentle saint paid a visit to the Sultan of Cairo, who received him well; and shortly afterwards an astonishing message was delivered to the Christians. If they would only leave his country, the Sultan said, he would give them back the True Cross, Galilee, the whole of central Palestine and Jerusalem as well. He would retain the castles of Kerak and Montreal in Oultrejourdain – Reynald de Chatillon's old stamping-ground – but he would pay a tribute for them.

The reaction of the Templars, and all the other Christians, was if anything even more astonishing than the Sultan's offer. The Holy City, the Cross, Nazareth and Bethlehem and all the lands between were there on a plate; they had only to accept, and without further strife they would be lords again of almost everything they had lost. But they turned it down.

Pelagius turned it down because he considered that no Christian should treat with an infidel. De Montaigu and the other military leaders, who were quite accustomed to doing so when it was expedient, also refused, but for more practical reasons. The fortifications of Jerusalem had been dismantled, and the city was open. Even if it had not been, the strategic value of Kerak and Montreal made the offer almost worthless. Moslem armies could move in at any time and attack; and in fact that was exactly what the Sultan had intended to do. Guessing correctly again, the knights decided that since such an offer had been made when their own advance was so small, Egypt was possibly weaker than it appeared. The realization seemed to give them new energy, and in a shock attack Damietta was won at last. It was 5 November 1219; that one small town had taken sixty-two weeks to capture.

Within the walls, they found the place littered with corpses. Plague had hit harder than they had. It was a ghastly sight:

'We found bodies in the houses, in the bedrooms, on the beds; the son by the father, the slave by the mistress; the dead had killed the living.'

And they found gold, and silver, and silk, and every kind of precious object – treasures which inspired such greed that the Christian effort was more damaged by them than by anything else. The crusade lasted for two more years, and almost all that time was spent in Damietta. The Franks never penetrated more than another twenty miles up the Nile. They were kept there by little more than rumours, each more fantastic than the last. The Emperor Frederick II was said to be on his way to support them, and indeed a sizeable force of Germans did arrive; but Frederick himself did not, and Pelagius was loath to move without him. Bound by their oath to the pope, the Templars were stuck, and could only listen in impotent fury when Pelagius told them of a Moslem prophecy foretelling the sultan's death, which obviously corroborated Revelations, and of new word of Prester John, who was still supposed to be fighting infidels far away to the east –

although if the original reports about him had been true, he would have been well over a hundred years old by then.

Brother Aymard in Paris did the best he could. On instructions from Honorius to send 6000 marks of Church money, or more if necessary, to his enraged and frustrated brothers, he sent 13,000, and for his pains received a strong papal ticking-off. Pelagius managed to waste the money; John of Brienne, the king of Jerusalem, sailed back to the Holy Land in disgust; and shortly afterwards, Pedro de Montaigu followed him – for Castle Pilgrim was under siege. In de Montaigu's report of the time, one can sense his relief at action; but when he returned to Damietta in November, the siege successfully withstood and the enemy repelled, he found that Pelagius and all the others were still exactly where he had left them. De Montaigu found in Pelagius none of the foresight that Honorius praised; instead there was nothing but blinkered folly. The Egyptian summer that year had been exceptionally hot and dry; drought had brought death by starvation to more Moslems than the Franks there were ever able to. It had been the last possibility for a concerted assault on Cairo; but Pelagius, procrastinating, let the opportunity slip by. the enervated Crusaders lapsed into quarrelling and fighting amongst themselves. New overtures for peace came from the Sultan, this time even more generous: in addition to all the former proposals, monetary compensation was offered for the refortification of Jerusalem, with a thirty-year truce for good measure.

As brusquely as before, 'a certain lord Legate' (as de Montaigu called him, with withering sarcasm) refused. At last he had decided on action, for the German reinforcements had arrived, and action was needed to give the army back its purpose. But the timing could hardly have been worse – it was midsummer, and the Nile floods were due any day.

On 12 July 1221 Pelagius began the advance, blithely leading his men to their deaths. Six hundred and thirty ships sailed slowly up the Nile. On the shore rode five thousand knights, with four thousand archers and forty thousand infantry behind them. For twelve days they proceeded up the Nile's east bank, ignorant of the Moslem horde that outflanked them on the west bank and then began to trail them. On Saturday 24 July the Christians came to the river Bahr as-Saghir, a tributary of the Nile. On the opposite side a Moslem army was drawn up; and as they assessed the situation, the Christians realized with a slow, chill horror that they were surrounded, and outnumbered.

With no other alternative, they attempted a retreat; at once the sluice-gates on the eastern bank were opened, and the river flooded in. Splashing and sliding through mud and water, pursued by Nubian infantry and Turkish cavalry, the Crusaders died in panic and humiliation, as the Templars fought a desperate rearguard action.

'Our provisions were lost,' de Montaigu wrote later to his brethren in England, 'many men were swept into the stream, and we could make no progress. The water continued to rise, and we lost our horses and saddles and our baggage and everything that we had. We did not know where to turn, and, being like fish caught in a net, we could do nothing but sue for peace.'

Pelagius had escaped. Now he had to accept peace with the infidel – peace without honour. Yet the Sultan's terms were merciful: all prisoners were to be exchanged, and the Franks would receive the True Cross. They had only to quit Egypt and accept an eight-year truce. Pending the Crusaders' embarkation, Pelagius and de Montaigu, together with twenty-two other spiritual and military leaders, gave themselves up as hostages; and on 8 September they and the other survivors sailed away from Damietta, as the Sultan rode triumphantly in.

Religious credulity, tactless intransigence, incompetent leadership – all had contributed to the sordid, pathetic end. As the Christian corpses swirled down the Nile, Pelagius knew he had nothing to show for all the effort – not even the True Cross. The Sultan, in the end, had been unable to find it.

After such a gloomy tale, it is quite a relief to turn to Frederick's Crusade. Humour may not have been one of Frederick's personal qualities, but the circumstances and events of his journey to Jerusalem and his relations with the Templars are full of an irony that, seen from today, borders on farce.

Frederick himself was one of the most exotic men of the time – probably the most exotic man that the Templars ever encountered. Somehow, despite (or perhaps because of) having been the ward of one pope and the pupil of another, he grew up with an almost complete disregard for the Roman Catholic church. By birth he was half-German and half-Norman, but, brought up in his mother's realm of Sicily with its half-Arab, half-Greek culture, and inheriting his father's empire in Germany, he united elements of Islam and Christianity, and superceded them both. He spoke six languages fluently – not only German, French and Italian, but Latin, Greek and Arabic. He was a philosopher as well as an intellectual, thinking as fluently as he spoke and wrote. He was a libertine and a gourmet, and, living at a time when a powerful brain could encompass most of the current knowledge, he understood natural science, mathematics, physics, geometry, astronomy and medicine. His nickname expressed it all: *Stupor Mundi*, the Marvel of the World.

Yet the nickname also expresses the limitations of Europe. In Egypt or Byzantium, Frederick would have been unusual, but not totally extraordinary. In Europe, he was scarcely comprehensible, and therefore frightening and untrustworthy. He lacked the simple virtues: his friendship was unsteady, his enmity irreversible; he was cruel and cunning, and – not surprisingly – immensely egocentric. As Holy Roman Emperor, he acknowledged no man his superior, not even the pope; blessed by God, he accepted no religious dogma – unless it suited his political plans. He criticized Christianity openly and freely, and used it when he chose as an instrument of expansion, and nothing other. Crowned king in 1215, he immediately announced his intention to crusade at the earliest opportunity; but taking the cross was merely a method of winning papal protection while he consolidated his hold on parts of Italy. In 1220 he was crowned Holy Roman Emperor, and one way and another, Frederick, the ambitious Caesar, managed to avoid actually setting out on a Crusade for twelve years. Pope Honorius, who had taught Frederick as a child, was a simple, trusting man who accepted every new excuse at its face value; but Honorius died in 1227, and his successor Gregory IX (incidentally, a cousin of Innocent III) was less patient. For years he had watched from the side-lines and was sick of Frederick's time-wasting. On becoming pope, Gregory lost no time at all, and excommunicated the emperor.

Deeply insulted, Frederick set off crusading without further delay, and the great farce began; for the Church did not allow a person under interdict to take part in a Crusade, much less to lead one. Moreover, any person helping an excommunicated person, or any town which gave him shelter, came automatically under the ban as well; and the Templars in the Holy Land watched with foreboding as Frederick approached. There they were, sworn servants of the pope, bound by oath to help every pilgrim and every Crusader – and equally bound to avoid any contact with excommunicates. The dilemma seems comical now; to the Templars, though, solving it meant more than life and death, for the wrong decision could mean damnation.

Frederick's Crusade arrived in Acre early in September 1228. Virtually the first thing Frederick learnt was that he was now doubly excommunicate – the second sentence being for crusading illegally. He must have felt much as a convict with two life-sentences would feel: the second did not make much difference. But he discovered something else as well, something which *did* make a difference: in the Holy Land he was unwelcome, unwanted and almost unsupported. The excommunications were only part of the reason for this; at least as important was the fact that Outremer had become little more than a string of towns, villages and castles whose continued existence depended on peace with the Moslems. That peace was delicately balanced, depending in turn on the continuing divisions between the Islamic states. Even the Templars and Hospitallers were less belligerent towards the Moslems, and for several years had been venting their aggression on each other; but they forgot their differences, temporarily at least, when it became clear that Frederick was going to persevere with his Crusade, come what may. Their verbal opposition had not put him off, and when he and his little army began marching south, the decision had to be made: would they fight with him or not?

The solution was ingenious and ridiculous. As the imperial troops proceeded, the Templars rode parallel with them, claiming that they were nothing to do with Frederick or his men; they just happened to be going the same way.

It did not work for long. The separate forces made each other more, not less, vulnerable to Moslem raiders. A second solution was adopted: the Templars rode with the emperor, and obeyed his orders – provided that he issued them in the name of God and Christendom, and not in his own excommunicated name.

The Templars were old hands at sophistry. A century earlier, when their Rule had been written down, a prohibition on walking in certain places was followed by the clause: 'and where a brother may not walk, he may not direct his horse either.' But the pains they took with Frederick were more than just ways of bending the Rule; for it looked as though Frederick, the most unlikely Crusader of all, might actually regain the Holy City – and the Templars had no wish to be left out.

Without the prejudice of Pelagius to hamper him, Frederick was using diplomacy. Jerusalem belonged to al-Kamil, the Sultan of Cairo, who had twice shown himself willing to hand the city over, if such a move helped his own goal of ruling all Islam. Frederick's goal was to rule all Christendom; he wanted Jerusalem for himself, not for the pope's 'Christian Republic'. Obviously the Sultan and he could do business.

Within a few months it was all worked out. Frederick agreed, on behalf of the Palestinian Franks (though without their consent), to support al-Kamil. The Sultan, for his part, gave back to the Franks Nazareth and western Galilee; the Moslem lands around Sidon; Bethelehem and Jerusalem, and a corridor of land from there to the coast. The treaty was signed on 18 February 1229 – a bloodless victory that accomplished more, with an excommunicate pen, than forty years of legal crusading had ever done.

Frederick entered the Holy City on Saturday 17 March. On the Sunday, attended only by his compatriots, he crowned himself king of Jerusalem; and on the Monday, breathless with rage, the archbishop of Caesarea arrived to carry out the inexorable logic of Roman Catholic dogma, in the final absurdity of the whole paradoxical Crusade. For harbouring the excommunicated emperor, Jerusalem, the focus of Christendom, was excommunicated as well.

The fact was that nobody wanted a victory of that kind. It was improper. Strategically, Jerusalem would be untenable without firm possession of the surrounding land; a miserable alleyway to the coast was no use. Spiritually, it was intolerable that a man forbidden to go there should go nonetheless; and morally, it offended all military training to win a battle by words. The Templars in particular were furious, for according to the treaty the entire Temple area remained with the Moslems.

For a while Frederick ignored all the criticisms, and investigated Jerusalem. He ticked off the local muezzin for failing, out of respect for the new ruler of the city, to give the customary calls to prayer: 'My chief aim in passing the night in

Jerusalem,' he said, 'was to hear the call to prayer, and the cries of praise to God during the night.' He visited the Dome of the Rock, and demonstrated his knowledge of Arabic with a mischievous pun; there were nets at the doors of the sanctuary, which he was told were to keep the sparrows out. The word 'sparrows' in Arabic is *asafir*; the word 'pigs' is *khanazir*. In Arabic, Frederick said: 'God has brought the pigs here instead!' But his overtly anti-Christian attitude did not endear him to the Moslems, any more than his appearance: 'He had a red skin,' commented one Moslem writer, 'and was bald and short-sighted. Had he been a slave he would not have been worth two hundred dirham. It was clear from what he said that he was a materialist and that his Christianity was simply a game to him.'

For all his cynical brilliance, Frederick did not understand that religion, to most people, was a deadly serious affair. Events after his coup in Jerusalem brought that sharply home to him. The pope launched a Crusade against Frederick himself, fighting on German territory in Italy; and the Templars in the Holy Land tried to entice the Sultan al-Kamil to murder him. Returning swiftly from Jerusalem, Frederick threw a cordon of soldiers around the Templars' house in Acre, threatening to kidnap the Master, Pedro de Montaigu, and to raze Castle Pilgrim. The castle, however, was far too heavily garrisoned for any such foolhardiness, and while Frederick remained in the Holy Land, de Montaigu was permanently surrounded by bodyguards.

The emperor could not stay; events in Italy were becoming too serious. At dawn on 1 May 1229 he took ship from Acre, and the citizens showered him with offal and dung. The most successful Crusader of all left the Holy Land, covered with filth and curses.

Late in the year 1240, a letter from Palestine arrived in the London Temple.

'Armand de Peragors, by the grace of God humble Master of the Poor Knights of the Temple, to our dear brother in Christ Robert de Sanford, preceptor of those knights in England, greeting, in the name of the Lord!'

The decade of the 'thirties had been hard for the Templars in the East. Pedro de Montaigu had died in 1232; in 1237, more than a hundred of the brethren in Antioch had been killed in one battle; al-Kamil, the peaceful Egyptian Sultan, had died in 1238; and in 1239 Jerusalem had been lost yet again. But the 'forties had started well, and looked promising; and the letter from de Peragors explained why.

'We want your brotherhood to know that . . . not through fear of the Christian people, but through a miraculous deed of the Lord, the Sultan of Damascus has restored intact to the Christian dominion all the lands to the River Jordan . . . and may God, who has done this, be blessed by all.'

The loss of Jerusalem had been half-expected, for under the terms of Frederick's treaty, no one but he could permit its refortification, and – knowing that the Templars would be the first to benefit – he had consistently refused that permission. As soon as the treaty expired in 1239, the Moslem prince of Kerak attacked the undefended city, and captured it without much difficulty – exactly as the Templars had foretold. But they too could play at diplomats, as they had often shown; and the Damascene cession of western Galilee owed less to divine intervention than to Templar diplomacy. Opportunist as ever, they had approached the Sultan of Damascus with a proposed alliance against al-Kamil's successor in Cairo; and for their part in the negotiations they were given the mighty castle of Safed.

Lying seventy-five miles north-west of Castle Pilgrim and fifteen miles or so from the Sea of Galilee, Safed was partly ruined, but it was swiftly reconstructed and extended by the Knights. Today, although it is in ruins again, it still dominates the landscape there; and when the Templars were lords of Safed and Athlit, they controlled all the Galilean uplands. The garrison at Safed was only half that of Athlit, being slightly under two thousand men; but by contemporary standards of building and population, each castle was a city in itself.

And yet Safed, despite its prime strategic position, might not have been refortified at all if it had not been for the encouragement of one man, Bishop Benedict of Marseilles. At the time of the Templar–Damascene truce, he happened to be in the Holy Land on a pilgrimage. Delighted with his chance, he visited the holy places of Damascus, and was as much impressed by the Moslems' obvious fear of Safed as he was by Damascus itself. But on returning to the coast by way of the castle, he found it all but deserted; only a few Templar knights were camping there. In

Acre he found the reason for this surprising lack of activity: de Peragors was ill in bed, and feeling depressed and discouraged. Their conversation is on record.

'Lord Bishop,' said de Peragors, 'it is not so easy to rebuild Safed. The King of Navarre, the Duke of Burgundy, the counts and barons of the east all promised to come to Safed, so we could work more quickly and more safely; they said they would stay two months, and would give 7000 marks towards our expenses. But they have all gone; and now you tell us to rebuild the castle without any help.'

But Benedict had taken the idea to heart, and was not to be put off. He persisted, and at last – as much to calm him as anything else – de Peragors agreed to talk it over with his brothers. Once more he pointed out the expense of the project, and Benedict, whose support of the Templars was by then something of an exception amongst the clergy, promised to pray and preach on the brethren's behalf. And it worked:

'Great was the joy in the house of the Temple, and the people of Acre, and throughout the Holy Land. Without delay the Templars chose a committee of knights, sergents, crossbowmen and other men of arms; they assembled a caravan of beasts of burden, opened their granges, cellars, treasure and all their offices to pay the expenses themselves; and in advance they sent teams of stonemasons and blacksmiths.'

Benedict blessed the work, laying a silver-gilt cup of money on the first stone as an offering. Shortly thereafter, for the price of a tunic, an old Moslem showed the brethren a hidden well of fresh water; and when Benedict returned, four years later, he found the castle larger than it had ever been, with seven towers and catapult emplacements to protect it.

Finding the well had been the cheapest part of the whole operation; the figures quoted for building and maintaining Safed are staggering. Construction: 1,100,000 bezants. Peace-time complement: seventeen hundred men. War-time complement: two thousand two hundred men. Annual provisions: twelve thousand mule-loads of wheat and barley, in addition to all other forms of fruit, fish, vegetables and meat. Annual deficit against revenues of the estate: 40,000 bezants. And when one considers that this was only one of thirteen major castles in the Holy Land, and not the largest, the legendary greed of the Templars falls into perspective, and de Peragors' unwillingness to take on such colossal extra obligations becomes more understandable. He and his brethren were caught in a terrible vicious circle: Christians everywhere had come to take the Templars' protection of the Holy Land for granted, and without the prompting of an inspired, enthusiastic preacher like Bishop Benedict, they had become unwilling to contribute to the cost of protection – the defence budget, as it were – out of their own pockets. Yet when the Templars raised the money through trade and finance, the same tight-fisted good Christians were the first to complain and condemn. And to add to the Templars' handicaps – although one may guess they did little to diminish this themselves – the Knights Hospitaller were watching their progress with envy and jealousy.

Ever since 1227, the Templars and Hospitallers had had an uncomfortable alliance, based on their common distrust of the Emperor Frederick, who was still trying to interfere in the ruling of Outremer. But the gain of Safed was too much for the Hospitallers to bear. Suddenly the traditional rivalry between the two Orders erupted into open war. The Hospitallers, in direct opposition to the Templars, made a treaty with the Sultan of Cairo, and sided with Frederick in the quarrels of rule. For three years, until these quarrels were settled, the two groups of holy knights fought each other as savagely as, in normal times, they would fight the Moslems: in the streets of the towns, in the country, around each other's castles – anywhere; on one occasion, the Templars even laid siege to the Hospitallers' house in Acre, with all the regular prohibitions involved: no food was allowed into the building, nor were the besieged allowed out to bury their dead. Both sides behaved exactly like independent republics within the kingdom, and it was not until 1243, when the regency was finally decided, that peace between the Orders was restored. Frederick's coronation of himself was nullified, and his son Conrad was declared the legal king of Jerusalem; but Conrad, who lived in Italy, did not want to go east, and the regency therefore devolved onto the next heir – his great-aunt Alice, the queen-dowager of Cyprus. The unlikely decision had been reached by a punctilious adherence to Palestinian law, and, although the Templars considered themselves above the law, it was this decision that they had advocated. Politically it meant that their foreign policy, not the Hospitallers', had won: the ally was Damascus, not Egypt.

Ironically, the loss of Jerusalem had been made good just two years earlier, by the Hospitaller treaty with the Egyptians. Thus, by the combination of both agreements, the kingdom of Jerusalem was suddenly swelled to include almost all its old territory; and with a little more dexterous diplomatic manoeuvring, the Knights Templar regained their old headquarters – the Temple of Solomon. Armand de Peragors wrote exultantly to his colleagues in England: '... moreover, for the fortification and defence of our lands, we propose to build an extremely strong castle near Jerusalem, by which we hope to retain the whole land easily and defend it for ever against enemies. But,' he added, 'in no way will be able to hold our lands for long against the Sultan [of Cairo], who is a most powerful and astute man, without the mighty and excellent protection of Christ and his faithful.'

The warning was simply military and political sense, but now it seems like a prophecy. Rumours were still prevalent of that mysterious Christian potentate, Prester John; and in fact the rumours had a very slight basis in truth. Far to the East, in Mongolia, was a man named Toghrul, chief of the Kerait clan of the Mongols. A hundred years earlier, the Keraits had been converted to Nestorian Christianity. Toghrul was nominally Christian, and his title, Ong-Khan, was altered by Nestorian missionaries to a more comprehensible form: Khan was translated (wrongly) as priest – prêtre, prester – and Ong became the French name Jean. Vague reports of the Mongols' deeds had been filtering through to Europe and the Holy Land and, though they were not exaggerated, the reports were somehow sterilized in the telling. The bloodthirsty slaughters in the distant steppes became victories won in the name of Christ; and when Toghrul was killed in 1203 by the Great Khan – Jenghiz – the supposed Christian virtues of the Ong-Khan, Prester John, were transferred to Jenghiz. People in Europe and Outremer sincerely believed that help for the Holy Land would come not only from the West, but from the East, from Jenghiz and his family, the founders of the Golden Horde; and in 1244, men from the East appeared in Palestine.

'Men? They are inhuman and bestial, better called monsters than men,' wrote a western contemporary. 'Thirsting for and drinking blood, they butcher the bodies of dogs and humans, and eat them. They wear bulls' horns, they are armed with iron; they are short and squat, with compact bodies; they are invincible in war, and blood to them is a delicious drink.'

Not Prester John's Christians, not even Jenghiz Khan's Mongols, these were the men of the Khwarismian Turks, a tribe displaced by the conquests of the Mongols. Now they were wandering warriors in search of a homeland, ready to sell their strength to any who would buy; and they were bought by the Sultan of Cairo.

On 11 July 1244 – less than a year after de Peragors' prophetic warning – the Khwarismians stormed Jerusalem. Only three hundred people escaped. As they fled along the road to Jaffa, the Holy City and the Church of the Holy Sepulchre burned behind them, and the bones of the kings of Jerusalem were scattered from their tombs. Never again would Jerusalem harbour a Templar army. But the knights regrouped at Acre, more than three hundred of them, with three hundred Knights of the Hospital, six hundred secular knights, proportionate numbers of infantry – and a Moslem army as well, drawn from Damascus. The Khwarismians knew neither God nor Allah. They had no religion at all, and for once Moslems and Christians had a common enemy.

The allies began marching south on 4 October. The Khwarismians, leaving Jerusalem to burn, had swept on to rendezvous with their employer, the Sultan of Cairo, and the joint armies waited at Gaza. On 17 October the two forces – the Franks and the northern Moslems, the Khwarismians and the Moslems of the south – met, at the plain of La Forbie, a few miles north-east of Gaza. Within a few hours it was finished. The allies of the north were destroyed. Five thousand Franks and Moslems lay dead side by side. Eight hundred more were taken to slavery in Egypt. Of the three hundred Templars, only thirty-three escaped to make their way back to Castle Pilgrim. Their Master, Armand de Peragors, lay sightless in the Gaza sand.

Slowly, and in agony, the kingdom beyond the sea was dying. But in their castles and houses, on their fields and farms, in Safed and Athlit and every part of Europe, the Knights of the Temple were determined that their Order, at least, should survive.

CHAPTER 11

DEAD WATERS

Egypt and the Holy Land, 1248–1291

'The earth is utterly broken down,
the earth is clean dissolved.'
Isaiah XXIV, 19

THE TOWN OF AIGUES-MORTES rises abruptly from a flat, featureless landscape. A few miles east is the famous plain of the Camargue, where the wild white horses still run free through the salty marches. North and west the land is fertile, and in summer is green with vineyards. Gazing south from the ramparts of the town, it seems the sea begins almost at once, for there is little to be seen but mile after mile of glittering water. The idea is an illusion: at its nearest point, the Mediterranean is four miles away. And yet the lakes stretching southwards are salt. No more than a foot deep, they kill the soil, and give the town its Provençal name. In the language of oc, 'aigues mortes' means 'dead waters'.

It is a place at once proud and melancholy, beautiful and desolate. Until the year 1240 there was nothing here but a fishing village; but in 1248, and again in 1270, this lonely spot was touched by dreams of holy heroism. In the old town – unchanged since his time – stands a statue of the man who gave Aigues-Mortes its brief grandeur: Louis Capet, otherwise known as Saint Louis, King Louis IX of France. From these dead waters, Louis, the saint-king, twice led the fleets of France in the last of the great crusades.

Born in 1214, Louis the child was serious and introspective. Louis the man was tall and slightly built, fair of skin, fair of hair, fair of face; and scrupulously moral, if not always humanly fair, of character. His likeness is preserved in numerous paintings and statues, showing a handsome face, usually beardless, and always calm and open. His character and actions remain in several contemporary biographies, which, if they did not tally so well with other reports, one might suspect of being mere eulogies; for Louis brought the practice of Christian virtue to an almost unprecedented height. He was a totally conscious man: everything he said or did was done in the sight of God, and for the glory of God; everything he experienced he received as a lesson from God. Insofar as it is possible, he was the Ideal Christian, in this he was comparable to Saladin, the Ideal Saracen.

In a way, however, he was an anachronism. Such a man was bound to understand crusading in its pure sense, as a duty to his God; such a king was bound to launch, and lead, crusades. A hundred and fifty years earlier, no one could have been better suited to the time; but by the middle of the thirteenth century, the popular mood of Europe was prejudiced against Crusades. None had succeeded so well as the First, and since then too many lives, and too much of the Holy Land, had been lost; and with the Crusades against Byzantium, the Albigensians and Frederick, the papal call to fight for the Cross had lost much of its credibility.

Nevertheless, Louis took the Cross in 1244, after recovering from a near-fatal illness, and within a few years had managed to revive enough of the old crusading spirit in his subjects to make a new expedition feasible. At the beginning of the thirteenth century, the French kings had no territory of their own on France's south coast; but Louis had received Aigues-Mortes as a gift from the monastery of Psalmody, a little north of the village. He quickly decided to transform the salty waste into a port. A tower was built to defend the new town; a stream was widened into a navigable channel; quays were installed along the water's edge. All of those are still there; otherwise, not an echo remains of the bustle and hubbub as the thirty-eight chartered Genoese ships were loaded with arms, food, horses and men. The vessels, each of which could take about seven hundred men or one hundred horses, had been hired by Renaud de Vichiers, the Preceptor of the Temple in France; and when the fleet set sail, on 25 August 1248, de Vichiers was an honoured guest with the king.

The royal fleet was soon joined by a second, which had set out from Marseilles. A distinguished passenger in that detachment was Jean de Joinville, who subsequently wrote one of the most important of the contemporary biographies of Saint Louis. The king and he were friends, but de Joinville had been unwilling to take part in the king's enterprise, and was frequently scared half out of his wits by the people and events he encountered in its course. In that, he was no more than typical of the majority of these latter-day Crusaders; his unhappiness at leaving home, his curiosity in port and his conviction, once at sea, that he was completely mad to be there would be as true for most people now as they were for most people then.

'On the day I left Joinville,' he wrote, 'I sent for the abbot of Chéminon, who gave me my pilgrim's staff and scrip. I left Joinville immediately after – never to enter my castle again until my return from overseas – on foot, with my legs bare and dressed in my shirt. Thus attired I went to Blécourt and Saint-Urbain, and to other places where there are holy relics. And all the way to Blécourt and Saint-Urbain I never once let my eyes turn back towards Joinville, for fear my heart might be filled with longing at the thought of my lovely castle and the two children I had left behind.'

When he reached Marseilles, however, the journey began to seem more like an adventure, and his heavy heart was lightened by watching the process leading to departure.

'On the day we embarked, the entry port of the ship was opened and all the horses we had to take overseas were taken on board. Then the door was closed and well tamped, in the same way as you bung a cask, for when the ship is at sea the whole door is under water.

'When the horses had been embarked, our master mariner called to his sailors, who were in the prow of the ship, "Is all fast?" "Aye aye, sir," they answered; "the clerks and priests may come forward." As soon as they had done so, he called out to them, "In the name of God, strike up a song!" They all sang in unison *Veni, Creator Spiritus*; the master called to the sailors, "In the name of God, make sail"; and so they set the sails.'

That, more than leaving his castle, was the real point of farewell for de Joinville.

'Soon the wind filled the sails and had taken us out of sight of land, so that we could see nothing but sky and water; and every day the wind took us farther from the homes in which we were born. How foolhardy, then, is the man who runs so grave a risk! – for when you go sleep at night you do not know whether you may find yourself in the morning at the bottom of the sea.'

But they made Cyprus without more discomfort than sea-sickness, and after wintering comfortably there, set off cheerfully in late May 1249, with a very much larger fleet.

'It was a beautiful sight; as far as your eye could see, the whole sea seemed to be covered with towels, by the canvas of ships' sails, whose number, large and small, was given as eighteen hundred vessels.'

The army had grown proportionately; now there were two thousand eight hundred knights, and innumerable infantry and archers. The course they chose was the same as their fathers had taken in 1218: Damietta, Cairo and then the Holy Land. This time there was an additional reason for the choice; Ascalon had fallen in 1247, and, after the conquest of Cairo, its recovery was to be their first objective. But between Cyprus and Damietta came their first calamity – a gale blew up and scattered the vast fleet, taking some ships as far as Acre. Only seven hundred knights landed with the king at Damietta, and '... there we found all the Sultan's forces on the seashore: fine people to look upon, for all the Sultan's arms are gold, and the sun shone on the golden blazonry. The noise they made with their trumpets and Saracen horns was terrifying to hear.'

Jumping into the water with his shield and lance, Louis waded to the beach, and had to be forcibly restrained from attacking the Egyptian army single-handed. At home he was an able and wise ruler; in war, as yet, he was a holy innocent. The crusaders had a stroke of luck, though: the belligerence of the shining army on shore was only a show. In Cairo the Sultan was dangerously ill. The Damiettans, believing he was dead, hurriedly evacuated their city, and the Christian army simply walked in and took possession. It was an auspicious start.

Yet Damietta seemed to be able to induce lethargy and inertia in every European who went there. The Nile was in flood; the scattered parts of the fleet had not yet rejoined the king; and Louis determined to remain in the captured town. It was the only thing to be done, if Cairo was still to be the goal. There were other possibilities, Alexandria for one, which the Palestinian barons and the Templars, under their new Master William de Sonnac, strongly recommended. But Louis was deeply shocked to discover that de Sonnac had negotiated a secret treaty with the Sultan of Cairo. The high-principled king would not debase himself so low as to treat with the infidel; he rebuked de Sonnac publicly, and took instead the advice of his favourite brother, the warlike and impetuous Count Robert of Artois. Cairo it was to be, and after long months of waiting in the foetid summer heat, king and army began a slow crawl up the Nile's east bank. The snail-like advance – only three miles a day – irked the Templars unbearably. Moslem raiders harassed them constantly, but Louis forbade any retaliation; and then in one skirmish a Templar was unhorsed, and de Sonnac, contrary to Louis' orders, shouted 'Forward, in the name of God, for I cannot stand this any longer!'

The Templars charged and fought with ferocity. Six hundred Moslems were killed or drowned, and, heartened by the unexpected success, the army proceeded more quickly. By 21 December they were on the banks of the Bahr as-Saghir. On the other side of the wide canal they could see Mansourah. The name means 'victorious'; the town had been built on the site of the Frankish defeat a generation earlier.

Psychologically, this was undoubtedly the most important point of the Crusade, for both sides. To go past the place where their fathers' generation had died would have given the Franks the courage they needed, and conquered the Egyptian spirit more surely than anything else.

Facing the French, at the head of the Moslem army, were two of the greatest Saracen generals of the time: Fakhr ad-Din, a personal friend of Frederick II since their negotiations twenty years before, and the Mameluke Turk Baibars, whose joint Egyptian–Khwarismian army had slaughtered the Templars and their then Master, Armand de Peragors, at Gaza.

For six weeks the Christians were held at bay. But they located a ford across the canal, and at dawn on 8 February 1250, under strict instructions to await Louis on the other side, William de Sonnac and Robert of Artois led the Christian vanguard over. Robert, impatient and fearful of losing the advantage of surprise, ignored his brother's orders and urged his men to press on.

De Sonnac argued briefly with him, then gave in before Robert's taunts of cowardice. Together, Templars and French swept into the just-awakened Moslem camp, and in the swift carnage that followed, the Templars found Fakhr ad-Din, and cut him down as he leapt naked from his bath.

The Crusaders spurred their horses on to Mansourah. If that obstacle was overcome, nothing would hold them back from Cairo. But though Fakhr ad-Din was dead, Baibars lived. He hid his soldiers in the town and left the gates open. Templar knights and French knights thundered in, straight through the town, up to the walls of the citadel itself; then with no room to turn in the narrow streets, they found themselves shut in, with Moslem troops on every side. The battle coursed through the town as archers sniped from windows and roof-tops, and horses reared in panic, throwing their riders and trampling them in the chaos and confusion. One wounded knight escaped to warn Louis; a few jumped over the battlements, only to drown in the Nile; and of the Templar force – two hundred and ninety knights – only five survived. De Sonnac, the Master, was one of the five, but an arrow had hit him in the eye, and he was now half-blind.

It had all been a great gamble, a gamble whose prize was not merely a town, but that intangible essential, morale. Both sides had gambled, and the Franks had lost. Louis drew his men up outside the walls of Mansourah, and fought off a series of counter-attacks. In one of them, de Sonnac lost his other eye; this time, he did not survive the wound.

For two months the Crusaders held their ground. The final hope was that a revolution might take place in Cairo, for the Sultan had finally died of his illness; but his son took power without opposition and organized a fleet to thwart the Crusader supply ships from Damietta. In the eight weeks that Louis remained outside Mansourah, one hundred and twelve of his ships were captured or sunk. The army began to starve, and succumbed to dysentery and typhoid. Louis contracted both, but would not leave his men. Finally he attempted to negotiate – a lowering of principles inconceivable in any other circumstances. The overture was flatly refused, and, in a grim repetition of 1221, the Christian retreat began. The sick were conveyed in galleys down the Nile; all those able to walk or ride did so. But it was utterly hopeless. Long before Damietta, every man in the

Christian army was dead or imprisoned, and Louis, the saint-king, lay in chains in a Moslem dungeon.

Somehow, in those conditions, his spirit revived. His captors demanded that he should hand over the ownership of the Frankish castles in the Holy Land. He refused, saying they were not his to give away; and the Moslems threatened to put him in the bernicles.

'The bernicles,' said de Joinville, 'are the most cruel torture you can suffer. They consist of two pliable lengths of wood, armed at the end with teeth. They fit together and are lashed at the end with strong oxhide thongs. When they wish to put people in them, they lay the victims on their sides and insert their legs between the teeth. They then have a man sit on the planks. The result is that there is not six inches of unbroken bone left in the leg. To make the torture as severe as possible, at the end of three days, when the legs are swollen, they place them in the bernicles again and break them afresh.' Even the idea would make most ordinary people give in; but Louis was extraordinary. 'To these threats the king answered that he was their prisoner, and that they could do with him as they wished.'

Astonished and admiring, and perhaps a little perplexed, the Moslems decided to set Louis, and his army, free – on payment of a ransom of 1,000,000 gold bezants, the equivalent then of 500,000 French pounds. Louis agreed, and the young Sultan, bemused at the lack of haggling, promptly cut the sum by a fifth. It was still colossal, though, and when all the Franks' money had been gathered together, they were still 30,000 pounds short.

'Then I [de Joinville] told the King he would do well to send for the Commander and the Marshal of the Temple, since the Master was dead, and ask them to lend him the 30,000 pounds.'

It is extremely difficult to give a modern equivalent for such a sum. National economies as we know them barely existed, yet those days were as bedevilled as ours by fluctuations in rates of exchange, inflation, and changes in market prices. As a very rough guide, however, a French pound was worth about one-third of an English pound; and an English pound could probably buy three cows and a calf.

The Templars had more than enough money on their flagship; the Commander refused to make the loan – on the grounds that moneys deposited with the Order could only be returned to the depositor. Fortunately the Marshal of the Temple was a more imaginative man. It was Renaud de Vichiers, who had hired the Genoese fleet for Louis, and had recently been promoted by his brethren from the post of Preceptor in France.

'My Lord,' said he to de Joinville, 'enough of this dispute . . . As our Commander says, we could not hand over any money without being false to our oath. But, if we are unwilling to lend you the money, you should simply take it. There is nothing unusual in this; if you take any of our moneys we have sufficient of yours at Acre for you to reimburse us.'

And that was exactly what de Joinville did. He was rowed to the Order's flagship, and, climbing aboard, he picked up a hatchet and said he would use that as a key for the king, whereupon de Vichiers presented him with the keys to a single chest, this one alone containing – literally – enough money for a King's ransom, and the Moslems were duly bought off. The curious incident illustrates several aspects typical of the Order, firstly and most obviously their immense wealth. It also shows their continued absolute adherence to the letter of their Rule, and their willingness to find loop-holes in the Rule when pragmatic politics demanded. But perhaps most importantly, it shows how easily they could be accused of pride. Surely no depositor would have objected, even if his money was lost in Louis' rescue; and if it was traced back to the defeat at Mansourah, the king's imprisonment was partly yhe Templars' responsibility.

Louis, fortunately, was not a man to harbour grudges against other men, Christian or Moslem. He was the total defeat of his crusade, and the merciless Moslem slaughter of the sick Christians he left behind in Damietta, as a divine lesson in humility, and, in an excess of piety, thanked God for it.

The time soon came for this most humble king to pass his lesson on to the proud Knights of the Temple. Arriving at Acre on 12 May 1250, Louis stayed in the Holy Land for four years. The esteem in which he held the Templars was clear: he made his residence in their impregnable Castle Pilgrim, and, when, in 1251, his queen bore their seventh child there, he invited Renaud de Vichiers to be godfather. In obedience to the Rule, de Vichiers regretfully had to decline the honour; but he had already been honoured again by his brethren, for he was now the nineteenth

Master of the Temple. The knights had obviously approved of his compromise in the matter of the ransom.

Louis was having to compromise as well. He had learnt that God's will on Earth had to be helped along occasionally, and in 1252 he began negotiations to ally himself with his old enemies in Cairo. The ancient rivalry of Cairo and Damascus was still flourishing, and each side approached the Franks for help against the other. Louis favoured Cairo, remembering the Crusaders still in prison there; the Templars favoured their traditional ally, Damascus, and once again negotiated a secret treaty. When de Vichiers presented Louis with the accomplished treaty, the king, normally calm and self-controlled in the most difficult circumstances, was enraged. He demanded that de Vichiers summon all his brethren to a public hearing, and that they should bring the Damascene ambassador with them. The knights assembled barefoot and sat before the king. De Joinville was an eye-witness of the open humiliation.

'In a loud voice, the King said to the Master: "Master, you will tell the ambassador that you are disturbed by having made a treaty with him without speaking to me; and because you have not spoken to me, you acquit him of all the agreements, and return the signed papers to him."'

De Vichiers did so and then, on Louis' command, he and all the knights knelt before the king and begged his forgiveness. Louis pardoned them all except the brother who had actually written the treaty, who was to be banished from the Holy Land. The sentence was enacted; de Vichier's fate, though, after the shame to which he had exposed the Order, is a little obscure. He lived until 1256; but the records of the last years of his life are contradictory. Some imply that he remained Master to his death; others suggest that he resigned, or was removed from office, very soon after the ceremony with King Louis. The latter is quite possible; but the Knights' chapter still retains its secrecy. Yet oddest of all is the simple fact of de Vichier's submission to the king, and the question of why he allowed Louis to dictate to the Order, an Order whose nonchalant attitude to royalty was already well known. Two reasons suggest themselves, and again they reflect the Order's character, spiritual and military. Louis was the greatest living exemplar of Christian values; and while he was in the Holy Land, all the Frankish factions accepted his leadership. Out of respect for both these qualities, the Templars bowed to him.

Louis left Acre in April 1254. The Moslems in Damietta had once told him that if he would only accept their faith, they would have him as their next Sultan. Naturally he refused; but they were only half-joking. The young Sultan whose fleet had starved Louis' crusade out was dead, assassinated by Baibars. He had been the last of Saladin's dynasty. Now the Mameluke Turks ruled in Egypt, powerful, energetic, self-made men who had risen from slavery to commanding majesty. 'They are Islam's Templars,' wrote a Moslem of the time – it was the highest praise he could give; and before long the Mamelukes showed the kind of opposition they could offer.

The Mongols were on the move. Jenghiz's grandchildren, dissatisfied with their inheritance, wanted more. The four men – Ariqboga, Mongka, Hulagu and Kublai – already ruled all the land from Persia to Korea, and from Siberia to the Indian Ocean. Now, while Ariqboga and Mongka stayed in Mongolia, controlling the centre, viceroys and cousins moved north and south; Kublai moved east to China; and Hulagu moved west. The brothers' announced intention was to conquer the world; and had it not been for the Mamelukes, they might well have done so. Kublai's career in China is well known. Hulagu, in his westward progress, liquidated the Assassins in Persia and Syria, burned Baghdad, captured Aleppo and Damascus, occupied Nablus and Gaza. Influenced by his Nestorian Christian wife, he left the Franks alone; but the fall of Islam in Asia seemed imminent. Hulagu then demanded homage from the Mamelukes; their response was to meet his army in pitched battle at the Pools of Goliath, ten miles south-east of Nazareth.

That battle was one of the turning-points of global history – for the Mongols, the aspiring world-conquerors, were conquered, and Baibars, who entered the battle as one of the generals, returned to Egypt as Sultan.

The incidents of the Mongol–Mameluke war gave the Templars two unexpected new possessions, the town of Sidon and its castle of Beaufort. It was the last small mercy they were to enjoy in Outremer. When Louis' truce with Cairo expired, Baibars struck, and he struck at the heart.

In February and March 1265, Caesarea, Haifa and Castle Pilgrim were attacked. The two cities fell; the castles survived. Arsuf was taken and its inhabitants enslaved; despairingly, a Templar poet wrote that the Christians' agony seemed pleasing to Christ. Louis' defeat had discredited the idea of divine wrath chastizing a sinful people; now it was written, and said aloud, that God had deserted His children, that the Holy Wars displeased Him, and that Outremer was doomed to die.

'Rage and sorrow are seated in my heart,' wrote the unknown Templar, 'so firmly that I scarce dare stay alive. It seems that God wishes to support the Turks to our loss . . . ah, lord God . . . alas, the realm of the East has lost so much that it will never be able to rise up again. They will make a mosque of holy Mary's convent, and since the theft pleases her Son, Who should weep at this, we are forced to comply as well. . . . Anyone who wishes to fight the Turks is mad, for Jesus Christ does not fight them any more. They have conquered, they will conquer. For every day they drive us down, knowing that God, who was awake, sleeps now, and Mohammed waxes powerful.'

It was indeed the last round of strife. Baibars returned in July 1266 and attacked Safed three times. When the walls broke and the Mamelukes burst in, every Templar was beheaded, and a ring of Christian heads was placed around the castle. With the captured Templar banner, Baucent, held in front of his army, Baibars advanced to the very walls of Acre before he was recognized. The town lived through the onslaught; but the fields around it were strewn with Christian dead.

A letter of 1267, sent from the Holy Land to the Master of the Temple in France, reveals the anguish and despair felt by the eastern Templars, as well as their astonishing will to keep fighting. As death reduced their ranks, they had to draw in more mercenaries; but their local financial resources were drained nearly dry.

'We *must* have enough money deposited in Acre to feed our crossbowmen; we also need fifty pounds to pay the sixty knights who came over with the Count of Nevers and my lord Erard de Valérie; the knights of Geoffrey de Serghes cost us 10,000 pounds a year; you must also send us 1,800 pounds that we borrowed from merchants to pay fifty knights in Acre for five months; and, for the love of God, make peace between the

Genoese and the Venetians, and hasten the departure of a new Crusade.'

Between March and May 1268 the Mameluke Sultan captured Jaffa, Banyas and Beaufort, that unexpected Templar prize, and took the knights of Beaufort into slavery. South of Acre, nothing remained of Outremer at all except Castle Pilgrim; and on 18 May, after one hundred and seventy-one uninterrupted years of Christian possession, Antioch was vanquished. To the north of the city, the castle of Baghras – so bitterly fought over in the early years of the century – became untenable; the Templars were forced to abandon it.

'Nearly the whole of the illustrious chivalry of the Temple is annihilated,' Pope Clement IV wrote in despair; but only France and England heeded him. By then St Louis was fifty-four years old. He had had eleven children; in 1268 his first grand-child was born, a boy named Philippe who, inheriting his grandfather's good looks, soon became nicknamed 'le Bel' – the Fair. But Louis' conscience did not allow him to spend much time with his family. On 1 July 1270, at the age of fifty-six, he 'left Aigues-Mortes on his second crusade and sailed to Tunisia, whose ruler was supposed to be friendly to Christians. Louis arrived at Carthage on 17 July. Almost at once he contracted the dysentery that had plagued him at Damietta. The sickness was aggravated by a fever, accompanied by regular convulsions; and on 27 August, Louis the saint-king died, whispering, with his last breath, 'Jerusalem! Jerusalem!'

The English contingent, led by Prince Edward, arrived in Acre on 9 May 1271. The Hospitallers' mightiest redoubt, Krak des Chevaliers, and the Templar castle of Safita had just fallen. Louis' presence in Africa had temporarily diverted Baibars from the Holy Land; Edward's presence in Palestine was just enough to induce the Sultan to offer a ten-year truce. It was gratefully accepted – yet the Franks did almost nothing with the time. Contemporary reports describe them as being a race still physically strong and handsome; but, like many decaying imperial powers, their physical strength and beauty no longer had moral power to back it up. The civilian rulers indulged in civil wars over meaningless, empty titles, and amused themselves with parties where knights and ladies appeared dressed in each other's clothes. Only the Military Orders maintained a sense of unity and discipline; and even they, on occasion, took part in the civil disputes. Chance, however, favoured the Franks for once. Baibars died in 1277, and in 1281 the Mongols launched a fresh offensive against the Mamelukes. Recognizing the dangerous possibility of a combined Franco-Mongol campaign, the new Sultan, Qalawun, signed another truce with the Franks before the first had even expired. The breathing-space was extended; peace on the borders of Outremer could be expected to last until 1291.

But within the shell of the kingdom civil war continued, inflamed by trading quarrels between the Pisans and Genoese. Outremer was quite unprepared for any serious assault, and in 1289 Qalawun returned. Incredibly, his return was by invitation. In a pathetic demonstration of their inability to cope, the Franks asked him to intervene in their civil troubles; and by his intervention, they lost Tripoli.

The loss was not immediately inevitable, nor even necessary. The Master of the Temple, William de Beaujeu, was warned by a spy of Qalawun's intention. He in turn warned the inhabitants of Tripoli, but they, trusting in the truce, did not believe him. Only when Qalawun's army was before their walls did they accept the truth; and by then it was too late. Before long every building in Tripoli was flattened, and the Tripolitans lay rotting on the ground.

Qalawun maintained that Tripoli was an exception, and that elsewhere the treaty still held good. It is scarcely credible, but the Franks took him at his word, hoping that if they gave no offence they would be left alone. Commerce resumed between Christians and Moslems. In the market-place at Acre, people of both faiths mingled to buy and sell. In the summer of 1290 a Christian man discovered that his wife was having an affair with a Moslem. A fight started in the market; it developed into a riot; several Moslems were killed; and, with a year of the peace treaty still to run, war was resumed. The final days were beginning.

As the Egyptian army mobilized, its objective was given as being somewhere in Africa. Once again the Templars' spy – an emir in Qalawun's court – informed William de Beaujeu of its true destination, Acre; and once again de Beaujeu played the part of Cassandra. His warning to the citizens was greeted with jeers and insults. Privately, he arranged with Qalawun that the city should be spared, on payment of a gold piece for every

inhabitant. When he announced the agreement publicly, he wa
denounced as a traitor 'and,' said a witness, 'hardly escaped aliv
from the hands of the people'; and the citizens' conviction o
their own safety was increased when, a few weeks later, Qalawur
died. But his son swore to do as Qalawun would have done; and
in March 1291 the Moslem advance began.

In his 'Description of the Holy Land', a contemporary
pilgrim named Burchard of Mount Sion, wrote:

'The city of Acre is fortified with walls, outworks, towers
ditches, and barbicans of very great strength, and is triangular in
shape like a shield, whereof two sides look upon the
Mediterranean Sea, and the third upon the plain round about it
This plain is more than two leagues wide, in some parts; it is very
fertile, both in ploughed land and in meadows, vineyards and
gardens, wherein grow diverse sorts of fruits. There are in the
city many strong places, castles, and citadels belonging to the
Knights of the Hospital and the Temple, and a good and
roomy harbour on the south side.'

The city's main defences on the landward side were two huge
walls, spaced fifty yards apart, and each over a mile long
Nineteen towers supported these walls, and the city within wa
divided by a third wall with a castle and four more towers. The
Templars' own castle occupied the best position, the south-wes
corner, farthest from the walls and edging the sea.

On 6 April 1291 the entire plain outside the city was suddenly
covered with the horses, men and siege-engines of the Moslem
army. The citizens' wilful blindness had to end. As they stared in
horror from their battlements, they estimated that sixty thousand
horsemen and a hundred and sixty thousand infantry stood armed
and ready before them; and they knew their city could no
survive.

While there was yet time, all those who could not fight – the
old, sick and disabled, the women and children – were evacuated
to Cyprus. The Genoese went too; they had negotiated a treaty o
their own with the Sultan. The Pisans and Venetians remained
with the king, the patriarch, all the able-bodied men of the city
and the knights of the Military Orders; but all told, their
numbers were completely inadequate to the coming fight. They
must have known, but still they stayed, and at last forgot their
quarrels, standing together to face the inevitable end. They could

not be starved out, for the sea-lanes were still open to Cyprus; but no one could send them enough arms and men. They knew they were alone, and they knew that, almost certainly, they would die.

The Templars took the northernmost section of the wall. Battle was joined at once, and continued unceasingly, night and day. From the plain below, the great catapults, the Victorious and the Furious, pounded the towers incessantly, and mangonels called Black Oxen hurled rocks and bolts at and over the walls. Arrows fell in a constant, deadly rain; trumpets, drums, cymbals and war-cries kept up a never-ending cacophony; and beneath, silent and invisible, a thousand engineers dug mines under every tower.

During the night of 14–15 April, a body of Templars made a sortie by moonlight into the heart of the Moslem camp; but in a ghastly tragicomedy – to us – almost all of them tripped over the guy-ropes of the tents, and were killed where they fell. Under cover of full darkness a few nights later, the Hospitallers tried a similar attack; they too were defeated, for the Moslems lit torches and fires until their camp was as bright as day. There were no more attempts of that sort; every man lost weakened the Christians whereas the Moslems, like the Hydra, seemed able to replace each man killed with two. Time was with the Moslems; the initiative was theirs alone; and despair crept into the Christians' hearts as they slowly understood that they could not even attack, but merely defend themselves to the death.

In the second week of May four of the outer towers, and part of the outer wall, collapsed. The defence retreated to the inner wall, and on 18 May a general assault was launched along its entire length. Templars and Hospitallers fought side by side, two centuries of rivalry suddenly effaced. The Master of the Hospital was wounded and carried to a ship; the king, whose duty was not to die but to live for his kingdom, escaped as well. The old patriarch was bundled into a rowing-boat, but he allowed so many others aboard that they sank the boat, and all drowned. Many died in the panic-stricken flight; and William de Beaujeu, the Master of the Temple, was shot by an arrow while defending a breach in the walls. Even as he was dying he was accused of cowardice, until, falling to the ground, he gasped: 'My Lords, I can do no more, for I am dead – see the wound.' Two of his brethren laid him on a shield and carried him to their castle; and outside, the Moslems burst through the inner wall and invaded the streets of the city, killing every person they found. By nightfall on the 18th the entire city was in Moslem hands – except for the Templars' castle. Civilians – including the women and children who had remained – were crowded in there with all the surviving Templars. They held out for several days – the squalor, the stench and the sheer terror were scarcely endurable.

Then came the offer that everyone, even the Templars, must have hoped for: a safe passage to Cyprus for all in the castle, with their possessions, if the castle were handed over intact. The Marshal of the Templars, Peter de Sevrey, accepted the terms. A hundred Mameluke soldiers and one emir were allowed into the Temple to act as overseers of the evacuation, and the Sultan's flag was raised above the building. But the Moslems, wild with victory, began to abuse the women and boys. Seeing this, the Templars attacked, and every Moslem within the narrow confines of the staircases, passages and halls of the building was killed. The flag was pulled down, and once more Baucent, the black cross on the white ground, flew defiantly from the Temple walls.

That night de Sevrey ordered the Commander of the Temple, Tibald Gaudin, to sail north to Sidon. With him, Gaudin took as many non-combatants as possible, and the treasure of the Temple. No record states exactly what this treasure was; but with a small ship and only a few hours' cover, it was easily portable, and probably fairly light. No doubt there were chests of gold and jewels, the residue of the wealth of the Order in Outremer; and there may have been, also, one single treasure more valuable than money or lives – the mysterious prize of Constantinople.

Whatever the nature of that treasure, by dawn, along with Gaudin, and a few fortunate civilians, it was safely at sea. As the sun rose over Acre, the Sultan sent to de Sevrey, renewing his offer of the day before. Taking a few brother knights with him, de Sevrey went to the Moslem camp to surrender. The moment they stood before the Sultan's tent, the little group of Templars were set upon, overwhelmed and beheaded in sight of their brethren.

The castle gates were closed instantly, and from the battlements the remaining brothers continued the fight. Underground Moslem sappers probed closer and closer, and on 28 May, ten days after the fall of the city, the Temple's eastward walls began to crack and crumble as their foundations were dug away. Suddenly a section of the wall caved in. Two thousand Mamelukes charged the breach. The timbers supporting the mine could not take their weight – and with a thunderous roar, the entire Temple of Acre collapsed, and crushed all within it.

Every vestige of Acre, once the capital of Outremer, was destroyed. After Acre, all that was left of the Kingdom beyond the Sea were five city-fortresses: Sidon, Beirut, Haifa, Tortosa and Castle Pilgrim. Tyre had surrendered during the siege of Acre. Sidon, Tortosa and Castle Pilgrim were all Templar strongholds. In Sidon, Tibald Gaudin was elected twenty-second Master of the Order. Part of his garrison retreated to a fortified rock a hundred yards offshore, the Castle of the Sea; he himself continued to guard the secret treasure of the Order, and with it and the other knights of Sidon escaped by night to Cyprus. Sidon was quickly occupied by the Mamelukes; and when they started to build a causeway to the rocky islet, the last members of the garrison took ship to Tortosa. On 14 July the Castle of the Sea was obliterated.

Haifa and Beirut, the last civilian outposts, surrendered and were occupied on the 30th and 31st respectively. Only Tortosa and Castle Pilgrim remained, and neither could withstand a siege. On 3 August Tortosa was evacuated, and on the 14th, Castle Pilgrim – the last Frankish property on the mainland. Outremer was dead; but the Templars had held out to the end. And they continued to hold out. On the waterless island of Ruad, two miles off Tortosa, the last Templars in the Holy Land defended themselves for twelve years more; and when they finally left, in 1303, it was not the Moslems who drove them off. They left through fear of Christians of the West – for in Europe, their whole Order had come under attack.

PART FOUR

The Temple in Europe, 1153–1303

CHAPTER 12

THE QUARTERMASTERS
OF THE CRUSADES

France, England and Spain, 1153–1303

'How is it then, brethren?'
Corinthians XIV, 26

OR MOST OF THE SURVIVORS of the fallen kingdom, life
became a grim and wretched parody of former days.
Many of those who had escaped to Cyprus had lost all
their possessions in the flight; some had sold everything
they had; some had even sold themselves. All were refugees, and
none was wanted anywhere. In order to survive, they debased
and humiliated themselves; the once rich citizens of Outremer
became servants and concubines.

The men of the Military Orders were more fortunate. Every
country in Europe had its Templars, and when a new brother
made his vows, he effectively took on a new nationality; he
became a member of a state without boundaries. Thus, even the
brethren born in the Holy Land could find a haven somewhere in
the West, and wherever they were sent they would be welcomed
by other Templars. They would find familiar customs and
familiar clothes; they would have a familiar, and honourable,
status.

But even for them, life was not the same as before. They had
to join the way of life of the western Templars – a world where
warriors were a minority, and where the Order's function was
not to fight, but to farm and make money. Although Outremer

could not have existed as long as it did without the Templars, the Templars in the East could hardly have existed at all without their brethren in the West. If the brothers in the Holy Land were the spearhead, those in Europe were the shaft, supplying arms and armour, men, money, horses and food. The majority of these men never left the land of their birth; but their work had been essential to the success of the Crusades. To them, the easterners – sun-burnt veterans of the front lines, men who had fought Saracens hand to hand, and who were more at home in deserts than in meadows – must have seemed awe-inspiring, and a little unreal. It must have been equally strange for the returning warriors; they had to grow accustomed to peace. For both groups, integration was made easier by the fact that there were similar elements in every house the Temple owned, be it in Ireland, Spain, Germany or Palestine; but although the Templars everywhere all obeyed one Rule, and ultimately, one Master – although they wore the same clothes and said the same prayers – although their rights and privileges were theoretically identical, east and west – nevertheless, the various branches of the Order had developed variously, and a Templar returning to Spain, for example, would have to make different adjustments from those made by a brother sent to France or England, Ireland, Germany, Hungary or Italy.

England, France and Spain were the three western countries of the most importance to the Order as a whole; they were its granaries and armouries. In each the Order had found favour from its earliest days, gaining land, buildings, members and supporters; yet in each, by 1291, the Order had distinctive characteristics. The three provinces performed different functions within the Order, and – more importantly – had different relationships with the monarchs of their parent states.

As in the East, the Templars of the West owned very extensive properties. A map of their territories in England looks as though a handful of sand had been scattered over it; and every grain represents at least a farm, and often a manor or a castle. The best illustration of their dominion in France is that today, almost seven centuries after the Order's dissolution, one may still visit nearly one hundred and fifty Templar sites; and in Spain, in the Corona de Aragón alone – the crescent of land opposite the Balearic Islands – the brethren possessed thirty-eight complete lordships and seven partial ones. And even a partial lordship could include one hundred and twenty small towns.

But unlike the East, the Order in the West was not predominantly, or even primarily, a knightly brotherhood. The Spanish brethren had certainly fought against the Moors in the reconquest of Aragon, and further south continued to do so until the dissolution of the Order. For their pains, moreover, they had been given a third of the kingdom of Aragon. In the East such a gift would have been accepted gladly; the western Templars in general, though, were farmers and businessmen, not warriors. They did not want the responsibility of ruling and maintaining such an area; but they knew how to bargain for what they did want. Renouncing their rights to rule, they received instead six castles, a thousand shillings a year, a tenth of all royal revenues, a fifth of any further reconquered land, and exemption from certain taxes. Benefits without duties – a clever move, and typical of the Templars in Europe.

Just as typical, and also coming from Spain, was one brother's description of himself – he was 'simple and ignorant'; he and his colleagues led a life 'given up to the land and the custody of animals'. These Templars were smiths and tanners, tailors and shoemakers, gardeners and vintners, cowherds, oxherds, shepherds – or 'preceptors of sheep', as one pair wryly called themselves. Most of them were illiterate; even some of their priests needed to have Latin translated into the vernacular. A brother who could write was so exceptional as to be worthy of comment, like James of Garrigans, who was able to 'write shaped letters well, and illuminate with gold'; and as for reading, the commandery of Corbins – an average place – had a library of sixteen books. Twelve of these were books of holy service; two were copies of the lives of the saints; and two were volumes of sermons. The men were openly and honestly pious; their daily round, as in any monastery, was divided between work and prayer. Their amusements were touchingly innocent: chess and cards were forbidden, but they could play at knuckles, or hop-scotch – as long as they did not bet. They regularly gave alms to the poor; they sold their wine, wool, meat and grain; they performed services to the community, such as building public ovens, or, on a grander scale, providing loans to merchants, royalty and the nobility. Not that these services were free – from the ovens the Templars received one loaf in every twenty baked, and arrangements for the repayment of a loan was always to their benefit. They may have been simple, but they were hard-headed and clear-eyed as well, and they knew their duty: to keep the supplies flowing to their brothers beyond the sea.

In all these things, the Spanish Templars were representative of the Order throughout the West; but their provincial organization had two unique aspects – aspects apparently unimportant, but anomalous, and in the end, vital. Firstly, almost all the members in Spain were Spaniards by birth, and they were rarely sent to other countries. Secondly, despite the liberties decreed in *Omne Datum Optimum*, every one of the Spanish brethren swore fealty to his king. The reason for this latter is unclear; it may have been a condition of royal confirmation of gifts. The former was a consequence of the Moslem presence in the peninsula: since the Spanish Templars had an enemy ready-made on their doorsteps, so to speak, it was economic and military sense for them to help defend the faith in their homeland, rather than be shipped abroad.

In England, no Templar swore fealty to the king. There, all the privileges of *Omne Datum Optimum* were realized, and more, for king after king gave the Order special rights. Since there were no Moslems in England, English Templar knights would automatically go overseas. No one can say how many were sent to the Holy Land (although one of the Masters, Thomas Berard – Master from 1256 to 1273 – was English); but England exemplifies perfectly the non-knightly quality of the Temple in the West. When the Order was dissolved – in other words, when more knights than usual were at home – there were only one hundred and thirty-five Templars in all England. Of those, eleven were priests, and only six were knights.

Those figures also demonstrate how disproportionately great the power of the Temple could be, compared to the number of brethren in it. Between them, the hundred and thirty-five English Templars organized and controlled the thousands of properties throughout the country. Many of these are still remembered; the names and the places still exist.

In Oxfordshire there is Temple Cowley, more famous now for the manufacture of cars; in Warwickshire, there is Temple Balsall, a charming and peaceful little village. Next to the church there the Templar house still stands, and is lived in; the original walls have been clad in brick, but the great chimney where the inhabitants would warm themselves on a cold winter evening still signals comfort to the chilly passer-by. In Kent there is Temple Waltham and Temple Ewell; in Wiltshire, Temple Rockley; in Lincolnshire, Temple Bruer, and – simplest of all – in Cornwall, Temple. Not all the Order's settlements had the prefix 'Temple'; but a look at a modern map still reveals scores more of these easily recognizable names, while local histories disclose the continued existence of literally hundreds of less obviously named Templar sites. And the reason why so few men controlled such huge tracts of land can be said in one word: money.

England's greatest value to the Order of the Temple was as a source of revenue. English Templars contributed to the development of London as an international money market, and to the development of the English economy overall. Hugh de Payens' initial success in the country had mushroomed when King Stephen came to the throne – naturally, for Stephen was the son of Stephen of Blois, that unwilling participant in the First Crusade, and Queen Matilda was the niece of Godfrey de Bouillon, the uncrowned king of Jerusalem. Stephen and Matilda's interest was strengthened by another indirect connection: Stephen's family controlled the area that Hugh de Payens came from, and Matilda's controlled St Omer in Flanders, where Godfrey, another of the founding Templars, had been born. In the civil strife following Stephen's accession, the Templars benefited from both sides, apparently playing one off against the other, and by 1154 were solidly established throughout the country.

They would have benefited much less from their lands, though, if they had had to pay all the usual taxes. Crippling taxation in England is not solely a modern phenomenon; feudal economy was just as stringent, imposing tolls, dues and fines on every conceivable thing. From the total list of medieval taxes, a few taken at random are hidage and carucage; danegeld and horngeld; scutage and lastage; murage and stallage; averpenny, wardpenny, hundredspenny, and thingpenny. Euphonious they may be, but they touched every aspect of daily life. Most were taxes on land, or in lieu of various services, such as bearing arms, or providing beasts of burden. Everything bought or sold, imported or exported, was taxed, and in case anything was left out of the list, there was tallage, an arbitrary tax imposed as, where and whenever the king considered it necessary. The Templars, however, were free of them all. They also had freedom of warren, waste and regard – that is, they could enclose land for breeding animals without paying the usual dues, and their lands would not be inspected by royal officials. They had the right of assarts, of converting forest to arable land, and they paid no amercements, the general, lesser taxes. And just as importantly, they could ignore frankpledge and the wapentake – which were, respectively, the mutual responsibility for peace and the rights of the county courts.

The Templars in England were judges, not only of themselves but of every person living within their territories; they could, if they wished, inflict any punishment, from pillories and fines to the death penalty by hanging or drowning. However, this right was not as extraordinary as it appears, for private jurisdiction was still usual in those days; every lord could administer justice, in whatever form he understood it, to his vassals and tenants. The Templars' privilege went one step further, though; freedom from the wapentake meant that if anyone had a complaint against the Order, it could only be heard in front of the chief justice of the land or the king himself. And there *were* complaints against them, from merchants whose prices they could undercut, from clerics who resented their ecclesiastical privileges, and from local authorities which lost tax-paying land and tax-paying tenants to the expanding Templar manors. However, it would be inaccurate to· see these criticisms as evidence of wide-spread antagonism towards the Order; the same quarrels, from the same causes, took place just as frequently between all the different groups of lay lords, ecclesiastical lords and ordinary burghers. Equally illusory is the idea that the Templars, having won their rights, held them with ease. Richard the Lion-Heart granted the Order a comprehensive charter of exemptions and privileges in 1189, a charter renewed by King John ten years later, and again by Henry III in 1227 and 1253, and by Edward I in 1280. Despite this royal approval, the brethren often had to appeal to the king to support their rights; and his support did not come cheaply. The kings of England rapidly realized that the Templars, weak in numbers but rich in land and property, could be exploited; the confirmation or extension of privileges had to be bought, and under King John the system became a regular 'protection racket'. Enormous sums – 400 marks one year, 4000 another time, a thousand pounds on a third occasion – found their way from the Temple Treasury to John's Exchequer, while the Templars' best horses were claimed for the royal stables.

The brethren paid up; they could afford to, and it was worth it. Inventories of their houses reveal the simplicity of their lives, and underline the truth of their individual poverty. Apart from their agricultural implements, they had hardly anything of value at all – perhaps a priest's vestments, worth ten or twenty shillings, but no luxurious goods whatsoever. Their furniture was functional, usually home-made and not especially good; their food was the basic fare of any contemporary farm – salt mutton and pork, salt or dried fish, cheese, a little beef, and very occasionally, a small quantity of wine. But in thirteenth-century England, when a man's food for a day cost a penny or twopence, and with 240 pennies to the pound, the Order's annual income was £5200.

The money came from rents, trading and banking. Trading and banking were the major sources; apart from the regular buying and selling of foodstuffs and livestock at fairs and markets, the Templars ran a flourishing export business in wool, grain, fish and dairy products. Wool was especially profitable; the greatest concentration of English Templar properties was in Yorkshire and Lincolnshire, both areas producing high-quality wool. It was here that exemption from export duties and restrictions really paid off; duty on a single sack of wool could be seven shillings and sixpence, but for the Templars gross profit and net profit were identical. Yorkshire and Lincolnshire together gave the brethren nearly half their income, almost as much as the combined total of the other twenty-nine English and Welsh counties in which they owned land.

And yet in all Yorkshire there is only one remnant of the Order – a few stones of the village of Temple Hirst. These are all that remain of the preceptory there, a famous place in its day; it was founded in 1152, the Order's second property in the country, and in the nineteenth century its memory was still sufficiently strong for Walter Scott to describe it in *Ivanhoe* – although his description is far from the truth. Today, the major English relic of the Poor Knights is in London: the Temple Church.

London was the centre of operations. The foundation date of the first house there is unknown, but it is probable that Hugh de Payens received it during his inaugural tour in 1128. The first house had a garden and an orchard, a cemetery, a round church of Caen stone, and outbuildings protected by a ditch. It was near the north end of the present Chancery Lane; it soon became too small, however, and in 1161 the Templars moved to a larger site on the north bank of the Thames. There they built their church, consecrated in 1185 by Heraclius, the dissolute patriarch of Jerusalem, during his otherwise futile mission to Europe.

Technically the London Temple was not, and is not, actually in London. The boundaries of the City of London stretched from the Tower in the east to a line a few hundred yards west of St Paul's Cathedral; the City's area was little more than half a square mile. Inside that tiny area, lining its narrow, tortuous, muddy streets, were crammed one hundred and four churches. The Temple Church, just west of the City boundary, was actually in the city of Westminster. When it was built it dominated the surrounding streets; now it is hidden amongst the edifices of two of the Inns of Court, and serves as the lawyers' chapel. In the life of the Church two archaic privileges, inherited directly from the old days of the Order, still survive: the church owes no more allegiance to the bishop of London than it ever did to the pope – its jurisdiction is in the direct charge of the monarch; and the official title of its chaplain is the Master of the Temple. The building as the thirteenth-century Templars knew it consisted of a choir sixty-five feet wide and nearly one hundred feet long, with, at its western end, an impressive circular structure sixty-five feet in diameter. This was in fact the original twelfth-century church; it contains effigies of knights but they are not Templars.

A round church was very rare; only ten are known to have been built in England during the twelfth century, and six of those were Templar. They were modelled on the Church of the Holy Sepulchre, at the Templars' mother house in Jerusalem. Since the Order's dissolution, there has been a popular but fallacious belief that all Templar churches were round; this is merely part of the wide-spread but factually baseless folk-mythology inspired by the Templars' secrecy.

The Templars' banking activities, however, were entirely factual, and played a large part in the function of the London

Temple. From the buildings around their circular church, they operated a system of national and international credit and finance. Kings, merchants and noblemen deposited gold, silver and jewels with them for safe-keeping, and came to them for loans, or to make payments to people overseas. Cash did not always have to be involved; the Templars used, and possibly invented, a primitive form of cheque for credit transfers, in the form of a paper on which was written the place, date, name and signature of the person sending the credit, its destination and its designated recipient. The Temple acted, in two senses, as the Royal Treasury: it was both the store-house for royal moneys and precious objects, and the agency through which those moneys were collected and audited. Thus, the Templars collected from other people the taxes from which they themselves were exempt, and kept them in London on the king's behalf. These could be very large sums indeed – in 1238, for example, the 'thirtieth' tax for Nottingham and Bristol together (a thirtieth of the value of the citizens' movable goods) amounted to £4288. Similarly, the Templars, with their ready-made armed convoys for land and sea transport, were usually given charge of royal funds sent abroad. Not only royal funds, but royal messages too; time and again the English records speak of Templars acting as envoys and ambassadors for the king. And they were active politicians as well: the Master of the Temple in England took part in the parliaments, and acted as an adviser to the king – on one of the most famous, but least successful, occasions Richard de Hastings, Master in England, attempted (in 1164) to reconcile Henry II and that 'turbulent priest', Thomas à Becket. The parliaments, indeed, were often held in the New Temple, as the Round Church and its ancillary buildings were named. Church councils took place there too, as well as less official political meetings; in 1260 Simon de Montfort and the leading barons of the realm met there to discuss action against Henry III's misrule. As in Stephen's reign, the English Templars assisted both sides.

The Order's European properties stretched from Templenoe, on the shores of the Kenmare Estuary in south-west Ireland, to an estate called St Martin, somewhere in either Croatia or Slovenia. In Hungary, Bela III, impressed by Templar activities during his pilgrimage to the Holy Land, had laid the basis of their eastern European branches; he and Bela IV gave the standard donations of land and buildings at Gegna, Dubicza and Banna – but, apart from the names few records of them survive.

In the states that now comprise Germany, it was natural that the Teutonic Knights, a Military Order founded in 1198 in imitation of the Templars, should be more popular; but nevertheless the Templars had extensive possessions there as well, notably at Mainz, Worms, Trier and Berlin, where there was a church on their site at Tempelhof until 1944. Some German properties were acquired very early: Supplingebourg, east of Hanover, in 1130, and Metz (which, although only a hundred and twenty miles north-east of Troyes, was not then in France) is said to have been donated in 1123 – five years before the Order was recognized.

Moving south, it is surprising to find that the Templar presence was much weaker than in distant England. To be sure, there were estates and vineyards at Rome, Anagni, Naples, Lucca, Benevento, Bari, Taranto, Petri, Perugia, Verona, Milan and Bologna; but there were also a great number of bishops reluctant to have their sees reduced, and the Templars' proportionate control, in the peninsula the popes called home, was far less than might be expected. Indeed, the Templar house and garden at Anagni were not donated until 20 July 1296, when Pope Boniface VIII made a gift of them; his reason was that, before then, the Order had no land in the seaward part of Campagna at all.

About forty miles north-west of Rome, near the little town of Tuscania, lie the ruins of two tiny preceptories, San Savino and Castell'Araldo. In both cases, none of the buildings was more than a hundred feet or so long – hardly the stuff of great dominion in an over-crowded country – and their scale was typical of many Italian Templar bases. It was left to Sicily to provide the real concentration of property for the Order in this part of the world: despite the island's small size, they owned parts of Messina, Trapani, Syracuse, Butera, Lentini and Palermo, as well as large complexes of estates around the foot of Etna.

With a common Rule everywhere, the Order's legal and economic status was similar in almost every country. It was only in the great capitals, London, Rome and Paris, that life ran on more sophisticated and cosmopolitan lines; there, financial dealings took precedence, with the brethren accepting current accounts, deposit accounts, deposits of jewels, valuables and title deeds, making loans and advances, and acting as agents for the secure transmission of such things. Pope Alexander III borrowed 150 pounds from the Order, and was required to repay 158. The difference, in Templar terminology, was not interest; to charge interest on a loan would have made them guilty of the sin of usury. Instead such sums were accounted as a fee for the time, trouble and risks involved – a characteristic sophistry too subtle for most people to accept, and one which made the Order much money and many enemies.

Outside the capitals, with their experimental and highly successful wheeler-dealing on the nascent money markets, each preceptor or commander exploited his allotted lands in the appropriate way, farming, praying, brewing, baking, spinning, potting; life in the rural preceptories would have been similar everywhere, an even tenor governed by the dictates of the season and the church calendar, with little essential difference in Scotland, Ireland, Dalmatia or rural England.

Scotland is intriguing, however, for although in the last, terrible days only two Templars were arrested there, the country contained a substantial quantity of Templar property. Around Aberdeen alone, their cross stood on houses and churches in Turriff, Tullich, Maryculter, Aboyne and Kingcausie. In Aberdeen itself they had a chapel, recorded in 1907 as 'lying between Dancing Master Peacock's Close and Gardener's Lane'; and south of the town, at Culter, they had an estate of no less than eight thousand acres. Clearly there must have been more than two men to run all these; but what became of these men – no one knows. There are traditions of escaped Templars and secret preceptories in the outer isles; but these are fantasies born centuries after the Order's suppression; there are no facts on which to base them.

Templar history in Ireland is similar, being very much a hotch-potch of traditions in which places and actions ascribed to the Order have grown in the telling, mixed with confused memories of the Hospitallers, and mingled with a multitude of myths and folk-tales. The Order does not appear to have had any footing there until after the conquest of eastern Ireland by Henry II, who granted the brethren lands in part-recompense for his non-appearance in the Holy Land. He gave them mills in Wexford and near Waterford, as well as a church and ten carucates of land at Clontarf; and from these beginnings, the customary gifts and purchases followed, so that by the time of their suppression, the order possessed lands in the counties of Carlow, Dublin, Kildare, Kilkenny, Limerick, Louth, Meath, Sligo, Tipperary and Wicklow as well, mostly of the relatively poor agricultural type found throughout Britain. (A carucate was as much land as one plough and eight oxen could till in a year, that is, the amount sufficient for the subsistence of one peasant, his wife and their family. This would clearly be a variable amount, depending on the quality of the land, the oxen and the ploughman, but it would always be a substantial tract.)

Although the brother knights in Ireland were all originally of Anglo-Norman families, the brother sergents were native Irishmen – people like Tathug o'Dufgyr, James Pannebecer, Kenedy o'Kynagh and William Boy o'Molyran. These men all figure in the lists of the Irish brotherhood, and men such as these could well have been among those who died for Christ in the Holy Land.

In Ireland, those who were not in the Order often did the same as their counterparts in England, and illegally placed the Templar cross on their houses in order to evade taxes and duties. The practice became so widespread on both sides of the Irish Sea that Henry III was obliged expressly to forbid it. But perhaps the most interesting parts of the Irish connection are these: the Irish money that went to build the New Temple in London, and the Irish Master who died there.

In 1243, Henry III ordered his Irish Exchequer to pay 500 marks to Roger le Waleis, Master of the Temple in Ireland, to assist in the construction of the New Temple. The money was duly received and delivered, and the building was erected. One of the rooms there is a grim little cell, two-and-a-half feet by four-and-a-half feet – too small to lie down in – overlooking the body of the church. From its narrow slit windows you may see and hear the congregation – and they, of course, may see and hear you – but once locked in that room, there is no way out. It was a penitential cell, for the punishment of disobedient brethren. It must have been singularly effective, for the convicted brother was separated, but not distanced, from the centre of his religion – the communion from which he was barred took place tantalizingly close – and the privileged communicants could not fail to be aware of his tortured presence. And in this cell in 1301, the then Master of Ireland, Walter le Bachelor, was starved to death, able to the last to hear the psalms of his brethren below. His crime, for which he died excommunicate, was alienating Templar land without permission. No one could flout the Rule and hope to escape unpunished.

Templar houses everywhere were used as lodgings by travellers, attracted by their unmatched security; the brethren of the New Temple in London were hosts to the highest. Kings and archbishops, papal legates and foreign diplomats all stayed there, sometimes for years at a time. But despite their political status in the country, the brethren looked on England as a great milch-cow, an abundant source of profit, but too inconveniently located to lead the Order in the West. That honour was reserved for France.

On France's east coast, in the centre of the Bay of Biscay, lies the old port of La Rochelle. There are two main approaches to the port from the sea; the northern one, skirting the Ile de Ré – the route to or from Brittany – is called the Breton Strait. The southern approach, between the Ile de Ré and the Ile d'Oleron, has a less obvious name: the Strait of Antioch. Like Aigues-Mortes on the French Mediterranean coast, the Strait of Antioch is a whispered echo of the proudest and most hopeful days of the Crusades; for under the Templars, La Rochelle became a major point of embarkation to the Holy Wars. English ships, en route to the East, would call in there to take on food and fresh water; French ships would depart for Portugal and Spain, Africa, Cyprus and Palestine. The Templars' first properties there were a house in the port and a mill outside it, both acquired in 1139 as gifts from Louis the Young and his wife Queen Eleanor. Within a few decades the Order was strongly established in the region, its lands forming two crescents focussed on the port, which grew correspondingly in influence. The commandery of La Rochelle dominated it all; yet today, apart from a few streets bearing Templar names, there are only three things to show that the Templars were ever there. Under the hotel that has sprung from the ruins of the commandery lies a simple cellar, where the brethren stored grain, or perhaps arms. To enter the hotel one passes through an archway; under that same arch, six, seven and eight hundred years ago, the white-mantled knights and the brown-clad sergents entered their courtyard. And in the courtyard, unobtrusively in a corner, there is a shield carved in the stone, a shield with an eight-pointed cross: Baucent, the Templars' battle-standard.

It is a poignant little epitaph. Even in Paris, where the Order's chief house in Europe was located, and where today one may study, by the hundred, original documents concerning the Templars – even in Paris, barely a trace remains. To see the most evocative relics, the places which re-create most clearly the daily life of the brethren in Europe, one must leave the main centres, and search elsewhere. Even then, though, some care is needed. Some of the best-preserved of the Order's reputed nine thousand European manors are in the south of France. Heading that way from Paris, one might pass through Dôle, and there stumble upon a very medieval-looking restaurant named after the Order. It is situated in an impressive stone cellar, its arched roof supported with massive pillars. It dates from the Templar period, and the food is good; unfortunately, the name is completely bogus. Nonetheless, the area is significant in Templar history: a few kilometres south-east of the town is the hamlet of Temple-les-Dôle, where, still standing and still inhabited, is one of the Order's earliest commanderies, dating from 1134; and south-west of the town, on the banks of the river Doubs, lies another tiny hamlet named Molay. There, around the year 1244, a boy was born – Jacques de Molay, who became the last Master of the Templars.

Deep in the south are today's treasure of the Temple. There is La Bargemone, on the road from Avignon to Aix, once a commandery whose main function was viticulture, and which still produces a very pleasant red wine, marketed, with sound Gallic commercial sense, under the sign of the Templar cross. There is Gréoux, Richerenches, Sainte Eulalie, La Couvertoirade; every one different, and every one illuminating a different part of Templar life.

Sainte Eulalie and La Couvertoirade are sisters, founded in 1151 and 1181 respectively. They lie in the heart of the Languedoc, a little way east of the more celebrated town of Roquefort. Only twenty kilometres separate the two fortresses, but their situations could hardly vary more: Sainte Eulalie is in the bottom of a long, wide, fertile valley, while La Couvertoirade stands isolated in a desert of rocks and scrubby grass. The former is surrounded by fields, stream and green meadows; the latter only has dew-ponds. But the Templars were able to use both places to advantage, growing food for man and horse around Sainte Eulalie, and raising sheep at La Couvertoirade; and both places today are almost exactly as they were in Templar times. La Couvertoirade especially is a jewel, a medieval town almost perfectly preserved. Fifty or sixty houses huddled together, with outside staircases to their upper storeys; narrow alleys that can hardly be called streets; a wall, with five towers, surrounding and protecting them; and, on a slight eminence to one side, the church and the chateau.

After the initial astonishment at finding a place apparently lifted entire from the Middle Ages, the most striking thing about La Couvertoirade is how small it is. It would scarcely be called a village today. Then, it was a town. And the chateau – the word conjures an image of a huge, luxurious building; but, al-though its walls are certainly thicker, the Templar chateau of La Couvertoirade is not very much larger than an ordinary modern house. Grandeur, of course, is relative; compared to the minute dwellings that make up the tiny town, the chateau is grand. But one understands, suddenly and clearly, how many modern ideas of medieval strength need to be revised downwards. One moderately-sized stone building was all that was needed to dominate a few hundred shepherds; but in those days, that was power.

Sainte Eulalie is similar, a collection of little houses within four strong walls, fortified with towers and backed by the Templars' church and commandery. Again, it all seems to be a miniature settlement. The same is true of Richerenches, situated about sixty-five kilometres north of Avignon; but whereas La Couvertoirade and Sainte Eulalie convey a certain impression of lightness and delicacy – a distinctly pastoral air, despite the fortifications – Richerenches is squat and stolid, a four-square construction in a dull plain, dusty, dirty and poor.

Perhaps the strangest thing about these three preserved places is that the impressions they give are historically accurate. Richerenches was the first of the three. Acquired and fortified in 1136, it was built as a statement of deliberate intent, designed to impress the Templars' military nature on the local population, while remaining essentially the focus of an agricultural community. Coming one and two generations later, in a time of burgeoning fame for the Order, Sainte Eulalie and La Couvertoirade had no need of battlements at first. They were farming centres pure and simple, built as monasteries might be, with a church, a refectory, a dormitory, stables and so on. They were peaceful, unthreatened and unthreatening. The walls and towers around the little towns were never there in Templar days; they were unnecessary. But after the Order was destroyed, its houses were taken over by the Hospitallers, and they built the walls – 'in order,' as the people of Sainte Eulalie will succinctly explain, 'to protect themselves from the Templars'.

In contrast to these commanderies, the chateau of Gréoux stands by itself, in every way. The other three were local administrative nuclei, lowland towns intimately tied in with the life of ordinary folk. Gréoux straddles a mountain-top fifty kilometres north-east of Aix-en-Provence. It is the biggest existing Templar castle in Europe. Directly and without compromise, it shows those aspects of the Order that are so much rarer in the West than in the East: sheer military strength – and profound loneliness. Many of the thousands of other, lesser houses would have only the brown-clad sergents to run them. The castle of Gréoux, remote, proud, strong and solitary, was one place where the white mantles of the knights would always be seen – 'until the end of our lives,' in the words of a Templar prayer, 'and until the end of our Order, whenever it pleases God that that should be'.

PART FIVE

Conspiracy and Arrest:
1303–1307

CHAPTER 13

PHILIP THE FAIR

France and Spain, 1303–1306

'Let me alone, that I may destroy them.'
Deuteronomy IX, 14

THE AGE OF THE GREAT CRUSADES was over. Never again would there be a 'general passage' of Europeans to the Holy Land, fighting in the name of Christ. The Christian defeats of 1291 were decisive – not in themselves, but as part of a pattern of change. Europe at the beginning of the fourteenth century was vastly different from the Europe of Pope Urban and Saint Bernard, two hundred years before. Slowly and very painfully, feudalism was giving way to nationalism, and medievalism to humanism. Crusades were often mooted, but never created; militant Christianity was still on people's lips, but – with some notable exceptions – it was no longer in their hearts. In this changing world, the existence of the Military Orders was becoming an anomaly. Since they were no longer fulfilling their prime function, 'the defence of the Holy Land,' it seemed to many people that the Templars had no further reason or right to exist.

The kingdom of France was at the forefront of the changes, and at the kingdom's head was one man who may stand as the emblem of alteration. In 1303 Philip IV, nicknamed 'the Fair', was thirty-five years old – a young man still, in the prime of life, yet old in kingship, for he had been crowned the eleventh Capetian king of France when he was only seventeen.

By 1303 he had been king for more than half his life, and he could look at his realm with a certain grim satisfaction, for if he was not loved, he was feared – not only in his kingdom, but beyond its borders, in Guienne and Flanders, England, Spain and Italy. He ruled a wider and more homogeneous area than any of his Capetian ancestors; for most of them, direct rule had been confined to the Ile de France – Paris and its immediate surroundings. Hardly a kingdom at all; but after three centuries and more of Capetian rule, it had grown to include Normandy, Anjou, Maine, Touraine, Brie, Poitou, Auvergne, Toulouse, Champagne and Navarre. And Philip could count himself a worthy inheritor: he held it all in a grip of iron.

Throughout their three hundred years, the Capetian kings of France had carefully fostered the belief that their monarchy was divinely ordained. Their coronations were elaborately ceremonial, quasi-religious occasions, in which the new ruler was blessed by the Church and anointed with holy oil – oil which legend said had been brought from Heaven by a dove, and which never diminished. As the Lord's anointed, the monarch became semi-divine, a being apart from ordinary mortals; his touch, reputedly, could cure disease. Louis IX, Philip's grandfather, had taken this the furthest, uniting power and piety and laying the foundation of a political theocracy, a nation in which God's law was paramount, interpreted and executed by the king alone. The king's word would also be the word of God, and both spiritually and temporally would be absolute law.

Philip accepted his role completely – whether through genuine belief, political utility, or both, it is impossible to say. Presumably he himself knew; but this man is the greatest real enigma in the history of the Templars. He never revealed his thoughts, his feelings or his motives for action to anyone. To have done so would have been inconsistent, politically and spiritually, and Philip was ruthlessly consistent. Around himself he built a circle of coldness and silence, which no one who knew him ever penetrated; one contemporary wrote of him, 'He is neither a man nor a beast; he is a statue.' The description can hardly be improved; even today his character remains aloof and inaccessible. Only his actions are clear and unambiguous. From those, and from the few contemporary comments which are neither eulogies nor tirades, one can form some picture of Philip the man, the beautiful statue.

Certainly he was beautiful, exceptionally so; everyone agreed on that. He was clearly an intelligent and determined man, and he must have been sincere in his beliefs, for, as half-god and all king, his actions have a terrible logic behind them. He possessed, moreover, an instinctive understanding of psychology, and from the beginning of his reign surrounded himself with a small group of the most cunning men in France. Through these, his ministers, he ruled his kingdom like a spider at the centre of its web. Absolute autocracy was not possible for him: ordinary people, nobles and commoners, still thought in feudal terms, and the machinery for autocratic rule was not yet established; but Philip was establishing it and, as far as possible, he was a pure autocrat, evolving a method of rule that was the antithesis of feudal consent.

His concealment of self, his apparent lack of humanity, may well have been a deliberate device. By giving no revelation of personal satisfaction or discontent, Philip emphasized the priestly aspects of kingship. And the harder his façade, the easier it was for him to deceive his supporters and enemies alike. The less certain they felt of his thoughts, the greater their fear; and the greater their fear, the easier they were to rule.

But Philip's inheritance was not only the makings of a political theocracy. If God ruled through the king of France, it was in this world, not the next; and in this world Mammon had always to be remembered. Philip's mundane inheritance was one of wars and debts – wars against England on sea and in Guienne, which was held by the English, and against Flanders, which was coveted by the Capetians; debts to all who would lend. The Templars were high on the list of royal creditors, but they were not the only ones; the Jews and the Lombards, equal adepts in finance, also underwrote the king's bills.

The need for money was part of the provocation for war. Loans, usually with interest in one form or another, sometimes had to be repaid; and the feudal system, with no provision for a regular income tax and an approximately predictable revenue, was largely dependent on sporadic taxation for specific purposes, of which war was the most obvious and the most easily understood. Yet fighting often cost more than anticipated, not only in money but in lives. Rather than diminishing, indebtedness increased all too easily, even with a successful campaign. To have to fight other people in order to drag money from your own was crude, uncertain and inefficient; and Philip loathed inefficiency. France had all the same kind of taxes as England at the time, which most people considered quite sufficiently iniquitous already. Philip, casting around for money, resurrected some old ideas and introduced some new ones: forced loans, the sale of patents of nobility and licences for export, taxes on particular business, and a general purchase tax on everything bought or sold. This last, being completely unrelated to income, was the worst for common people; but neither it nor any of the already existing means of raising money could be more than stop-gaps.

In the early years of his reign, the 1290s, Philip had found two more novel and more drastic solutions: devaluation, and the pressurizing of rich but powerless groups. The coinage of the realm was debased again and again, losing two-thirds of its value in ten years, and special taxes were levied on the Jews, the Lombards – and the Church. Traditionally exempt from secular taxation, the clergy had often been taxed by the papacy to help pay for crusades, the money being collected by secular authorities. Philip simply continued collecting, but without papal permission. Church land accounted for nearly a third of the kingdom, and every two years or so, Philip diverted a tenth of clerical rents and incomes into his own coffers. This was what he wanted: a source of large, fairly regular revenue. His schemes worked for a while, and might have gone on working. Nobody, apart from the people involved, objected to the despoliation of usurers. But to despoil the Church was a different matter, and Philip, believing himself a priest-king and dreaming of Caesaro-Papism, had one implacable opponent: Pope Boniface VIII, whose will was as strong as Philip's, and whose dream was identical, the union of all authority, temporal and spiritual, in his person.

Europe could not contain two such men. For nine years they fought, the 'Most Christian King' and the Vicar of Christ. Nominally their struggle was over the misappropriation of the Church's income; actually, it was a war – to the death if need be – for sole supremacy in Europe. In 1296 a papal Bull forbade the taxing of the clergy; Philip responded by prohibiting the export of bullion from France, thus preventing French tithes from going to Rome. In 1300, the papal jubilee year, Boniface paraded

hrough Rome like an emperor, with two swords carried before
im, signifying his claim to power over all people, living and
lead. Philip showed no reaction, either by look or word; but in
301 his men arrested the bishop of Pamiers, the papal legate to
'rance, on charges of treason, blasphemy, simony, sorcery and
ornication. The bishop's real crimes were his personal friendship
vith Boniface, and his comparison of Philip to an owl. 'Our King
of France,' he was reported to have said, 'who is more handsome
han any man in the world, knows nothing at all except to stare at
nen.' An ill-advised remark, for that stony stare concealed a
merciless brain.

Boniface retaliated with the issue of two Bulls, one condemn-
ng the arrest and the other revoking all Philip's privileges and
concessions of the previous five years. Philip's next move was
unprecedented: in April 1302 he called an assembly of the three
Estates, nobles, clergy and commoners. Never before had the
commoners been called on to participate; but none of the three
Estates was there to advise. Philip's purpose was to ensure that all
France spoke with one voice – his voice. There was no real
alternative for the assembly. The Bull of condemnation was
publicly burnt and, as one, the French nation rejected all papal
pretensions – and challenged Boniface's right to be pope.

'Unam sanctam!', Boniface proclaimed – one sacred and
inviolable Church was all that did or could exist. The Church had
one head; it was not a monster with two; its head was Christ, its
ruler His vicar the pope; and all kings were inferior to the bishop
of Rome.

Words, words; Philip could match them with ease, serenely,
icily confident in his God-given right to the throne. The
technique used against the bishop of Pamiers was used once
more, and in March 1303 the Estates General of France levelled
twenty-nine charges against Boniface, accusing him, amongst
other things, of sodomy, sorcery, heresy, simony and blasphemy.

Without more ado Boniface used his last weapon, and
excommunicated Philip – a pointless move, for he could be sure
Philip would ignore it, and the pope had, in any case, once
declared that a Frenchman had no soul. The French naturally
thought otherwise, and when they heard, in the summer of 1303,
that the pope was preparing to excommunicate the entire French
nation in addition to the king, there was panic and consternation.

The Bull was due to be published on 8 September. The news forced Philip's hand; to prevent revolution he had to act quickly and decisively.

From Paris to Rome is some eight hundred miles. Thirty-seven miles east-south-east of Rome is the town of Anagni. At the beginning of September 1303 Pope Boniface was staying there; from there, on the 8th, he intended to publish his historic Bull against France. As was his custom, he arose early on the morning of the seventh and went to pray in his private chapel before dawn – and while he was praying, a troop of French soldiers burst in upon him and took him captive.

To kidnap a pope – and to do it, moreover, in the name of defending the papacy; it was unimagined, unthinkable, unbelievable. But Philip, believing the French throne to be more sacred than the papal one, could think of such a thing, and could cause it to be done. Neither distance nor sanctity could protect Boniface; through his profound belief in papal authority he never recognized – until it was too late – the full force of Philip's personal conviction. Set apart from ordinary men, ruling by divine grace, the embodiment of earthly law and the sole interpreter of heavenly law, Philip had no need of scruples or conscience. His intention was to bring Boniface to France by force and there to try him for his crimes. This part of the plan failed, for the people of Anagni rescued the pope; but Philip, apart from unfettered imagination, had age on his side. Boniface was eighty-six years old. The shock of his outrageous imprisonment was too great; he was dead a month later.

The operation was typical of Philip – secret, audacious, carefully planned and carried out. It was efficient, unexpected and terrifying. Such a man could do anything, it seemed; but even Philip, the royal demi-god, could do nothing without support from men of a similar calibre – men of unquestioning loyalty and the utmost daring; men to whom the breath of life was conspiracy, legalized violence and self-aggrandizement. These were the king's ministers, his agents and familiars; and chief among them was the leader of the assault in Anagni, a brilliant, evil man named William de Nogaret.

Philip and de Nogaret formed an almost perfect partnership of power and intellect. De Nogaret was only a few years older than the king, and they worked together for twenty years; but their origins could scarcely have been more different. De Nogaret came from ordinary middle-class stock; his father was a tradesman in Toulouse, and the family took their name from (or gave their name to) a small piece of land they owned twenty-five miles south-east of the town. The village of Nogaret still exists, although the family died out at the end of the fourteenth century.

William de Nogaret's rise to power and infamy was another part of the changes sweeping Europe at the time. Alterations in ancient custom had to be made law; lawyers, being the only men who could pretend to understand the intricate new developments, became a powerful class; and de Nogaret was a lawyer of outstanding ability. In the 1280s he had been legal counsellor to the king of Majorca, and professor of law at Montpellier University; in the early 1290s he joined Philip's legal service; in 1299 he was ennobled, and in 1302 he was made 'first lawyer of the realm'. It was he who made the first public charges against Boniface; he who led the national campaign of vilification and masterminded the kidnapping. He did not compromise in loyalty or hatred. His loyalty to the king was well rewarded – by the end of his life he, a simple merchant's son, owned four hundred square miles of France and had the direct power of life and death over more than ten thousand people; and his hatred of the papacy and all it represented was well founded, for his parents – like most Toulousains – were Cathars and, under Templar supervision, had been burnt alive as heretics.

In this awful fate, Nogaret *père* and *mère* may simply have been unlucky. There is plenty of evidence to show that the Templars worked with the Dominicans, who were in charge of the rooting out of heresy. The Templars, therefore, must have been familiar with, and possibly practised in, the administration of the rack, the thumb-screw, the strappado and the pit, as well as the stake; and the Dominicans rewarded their co-operation by encouraging good Christians to leave money or property to the Order in their wills. But there is also fairly firm evidence for suggesting that the Templars only co-operated if the price was right, for they would frequently obstruct and impede the inquisition of heretics who happened to be their tenants. (This obstruction was enough of a nuisance, from the official point of view, for a totally new Order to be created: the Knighthood of the Faith of Jesus Christ. The sole objective of this brotherhood was the extirpation of heresy – a kind of religious thought-police – and, trespassing on Templar rights and harassing all others, it was such an unpopular group that it was disbanded less than forty years after its creation.) However, nothing indicates that the Nogaret family were ever Templar tenants. Had they been so, the brethren might just have protected them; and then the fate of the Order itself might have been utterly different.

Meanwhile the conspiracy against the papacy did not end with the death of Boniface – rather, it gathered force. The new pope, Benedict XI, seemed cast in the same mould as Boniface, a stern man, determined to maintain the rights of his See. Meeting fire with fire, Philip pressed for a posthumous trial of Boniface. If such a thing happened it would set a horrifying precedent, and Benedict, forced into a dilemma, attempted to compromise by annulling Philip's excommunication. De Nogaret meanwhile made a remarkable demonstration of his loyalty to the king by accepting full responsibility for the attack at Anagni. Benedict's attention was drawn from the king, and he issued a severe condemnation of de Nogaret and his accomplices. De Nogaret was excommunicated; and unwisely Benedict let it be known that de Nogaret would have no chance of appeal before the formal announcement a few weeks later. It never came; for suddenly Pope Benedict died of an unknown disease, with agonizing internal pains. De Nogaret issued propaganda pamphlets rejoicing in the justice that God gave to malicious and worthless pontiffs; and suspected poisoning was never proved.

Pope Benedict died on 7 July 1304, exactly a month after his open condemnation of de Nogaret. His papacy had lasted only eight and a half months; another sixteen months would pass before a new pope was installed. The delay was not of Philip's making, but it suited him admirably: ultimately it worked only to his profit, and in the meantime he had other things to think of.

His wife of twenty-one years, Queen Jeanne of France and Navarre, died in 1305. Philip was thirty-seven by then, and his reaction to the loss was the same as that of many widowers of his time and the previous century and three-quarters: he applied for membership of the brethren of the Temple. Not only that, but he proposed to abdicate in favour of his son. It would have seemed natural for the Templars to have welcomed such a powerful man into their ranks; but they refused him. The secrecy of the chapter still prevailed, and no one, not even Philip, ever knew the reason. The Templars may have thought his request a mere aberration following his wife's death; or they may have sensed that this powerful man wanted, through them, to acquire not humility but still greater power. For although Philip may well have loved Jeanne, he was not a man to act on impulse; he always had a reason, and often several, for every action; and reaching far beyond local battles with popes, he had a plan in which the Templars' co-operation was essential.

Eighteen years earlier, in 1287, a Spaniard named Ramon Lull had come to Paris and had been granted an audience with the young king. Lull was in his mid-fifties, and well-known as a mystic in his native island of Majorca, and on the Aragonese mainland. In his early life he had been a soldier, a courtier and troubadour – a completely worldly man, poetic, passionate and impetuous, married, but with innumerable mistresses, loving and taking everything that life offered. Brought up in Majorca – the most Moslem of Christian islands – he was nominally Christian until the age of thirty, when a profound religious experience converted him into one of the most active Christians of his time. His first action thereafter seems odd for a convert – he spent nine years learning Arabic. It was with a grand purpose, though; for if another Crusade was to take place, Lull believed that it should be a Crusade of conversion. The idea was not new, but it had never been enthusiastically received. In Paris, with Philip, Lull hoped to find the support he wanted.

Although this period, the turn of the thirteen and fourteenth centuries, can be seen clearly now as the end of the great Crusades, it was not nearly so apparent to people alive at the time. Attitudes did not change overnight; after two centuries of a western presence in the Holy Land, such a presence seemed right and natural. A basic assumption of life was that some day the Holy Land would be recovered; the question was not when, but how, it should be done. Since a purely military approach had failed, it seemed likely that the principle of Holy War was mistaken, and only earned divine disapproval; therefore the final crusade should be a seduction of the spirit, a crusade of conversion, backed – just in case conversion did not work – by the knights of the Military Orders. But the rivalry of the Templars and Hospitallers was notorious, and the similarities of the two organizations suggested that considerable economies of time and money could be effected if the two Orders were united.

It was at this point that Philip began to be really interested. His piety need not be doubted; to establish God's kingdom on earth was his firm hope. It was his understanding of the way in which this should be accomplished that caused most of his conflicts – everything in his inheritance and upbringing forced him to believe that he, and only he, could create and rule 'Heaven on Earth'. Lull's developed plan, published in 1305 in his *Liber de fine*, expounded the framework within which this could be achieved.

The main points, the ones which attracted Philip, were these: firstly, the two Military Orders should be made one; secondly, the Master of the new joint Order should be a king, or the son of a king; thirdly, the Mastership should be hereditary; fourthly, the Master should, as soon as possible, take up residence in Jerusalem and be crowned king of Jerusalem. Finally – a small point, but a wonderfully cogent attraction – the King-Master should have the title of 'Bellator Rex', the Warrior King.

The plan as a whole seemed tailor-made for Philip, although it is probable that Lull originally devised it with his own king, James II of Aragon, in mind, and with the more limited objective of a new Spanish Crusade. But Philip took the idea over and made it his own; if it was successful, it would give him everything he wanted – access to regular and virtually unlimited supplies of money; the direct rule of lands in every part of Europe, and beyond; the undying glory of the house of Capet, and the spiritual and temporal well-being of all Christendom. To the already dazzling grandeur of the notion, Philip added two points that would guarantee his total personal control: all ecclesiastical incomes should be fixed, and any surplus should go directly to the 'Warrior King' to help maintain the reconquered Holy Land; and in papal elections the 'Warrior King' should have four votes.

The first step in achieving this extraordinary design was the unification of the Orders, and this was why Philip tried to join the Templars; he intended to become Master in due course, and from there to arrange the union and all that followed. He probably assumed that his acceptance into the Order would be a mere formality, and he must have been deeply shocked and angered at the brethren's summary rejection of his overture. As always, he

gave no sign of his feelings. There was another route open to him
– long, devious and complex, but one which not even the
recalcitrant Templars could deny. Their sole lord on earth was
the pope; if he commanded them to change, they would have to.
But as yet, there was no successor to Benedict. Philip suddenly
became interested in the electoral struggles in Rome.

The cardinalate was divided in two, one side supporting the
memory of Boniface, and the other – French-influenced – continually proposing candidates who would put Boniface on
posthumous trial. The deadlock was not resolved until the
Bonifacians put forward the colourless archbishop of Bordeaux,
Bertrand de Got. Without the support of the French-controlled
cardinals, he could not have been elected, and to suggest him
seemed futile, for he had sided with Boniface in the days before
the kidnap. Yet when the French faction asked Philip's opinion,
he surprisingly declared himself in favour. The election went
ahead; and on 14 November 1305, at Lyons, Bertrand de Got
became Pope Clement V.

King Philip knew exactly what he was doing in supporting de
Got's nomination; he knew the man well. The archbishop was a
weak and greedy man, fond of honour and disliking responsibility; he had attained his archbishopric through family
influence, for his uncle was a bishop and his brother an
archbishop. Given that he was acceptable to the Bonifacians, his
election was in Philip's control, and some years after it was
accomplished, a legend sprang up about a secret agreement
between king and archbishop.

The story was that, in the appropriately arcane setting of a
ruined monastery in the middle of a forest, Philip and the future
Clement V met alone one dark night. The king offered to make
de Got pope on six conditions, five of which he told him then,
reserving the sixth until after the election. If he accepted, the
archbishop had to swear fidelity on the Host, and give three of
his relatives as hostages. The first five conditions were that the
French crown and the papacy should be reconciled; the kidnap-
pers at Anagni should be absolved; Philip should be allowed
to tax the French clergy; the cardinals dismissed by Boniface should be reinstated; Boniface's Bulls should be erased,
and he should be condemned. De Got, according to the
story, accepted all five conditions there and then. The mysterious

sixth, which he did not know until later, was that the Order of the Temple should be dissolved.

Sadly, the story is only a story. Philip and Clement never met before the pope's election, and some of the 'conditions' – the reconciliation for one – had already been achieved. Nevertheless, it is probable that an agreement of that kind was made, not between the two men personally, but through their diplomatic channels; and in any case, Philip could be sure that with a man like Bertrand de Got as pope, the power of the papacy would diminish to almost nothing. After Clement's coronation was over, on the afternoon of 14 November 1305, the new pope rode in procession through the streets of Lyons, his horse led by Duke John of Brittany, and the king's brother, Prince Charles of Valois. King Philip himself rode immediately behind, and – just in time to rein his horse in – he saw the wall beside him begin to crack and tumble. Under the falling masonry, Duke John was fatally wounded; Prince Charles was badly injured, and Clement was thrown from his horse. The king was unharmed, and, as many other people certainly did, he may have seen the incident as a portent of the papal reign. His grand design was beginning well.

In the meantime, however, the daily problem of money continued to plague him. The repeated devaluations had benefited the crown as debtor, but had worked against the crown as tax-collector. In June 1306, Philip coolly announced that he had decided on a return to 'good money', to be effective from 8 September. In practical terms, for ordinary people, this meant that prices would triple overnight. For Philip, it meant that he suddenly had to fly for his life from mobs rioting all over Paris; for once, he had miscalculated the power of priestly royalty, and had pushed the people too quickly and too far. For three days, while citizens were lynched and the riots were quelled by force, Philip took refuge in the Paris Temple, and there had time to study the men who had refused to let him join their Order. He and his court had often stayed there before, but never in such humiliating circumstances. The complex covered fifteen acres and was entirely surrounded by a wall eighteen feet high; the wall had only one gate, and that was protected by a drawbridge over the encircling dry moat. The 'Great Tower', one hundred and sixty feet high, cast a long shadow over Paris; the buildings were sufficient to accommodate three hundred knights with their retainers and their horses. As the riots raged outside, life within the walls could continue relatively undisturbed. When peace was restored and Philip could return from his borrowed safety, he must have thought often of that fortress, and all its hundreds of sisters throughout his realm, which even he could not enter unpermitted.

Devaluation, revaluation, forced loans and taxes – nothing seemed to work for long. A new expedient was necessary. On 21 June 1306 the king gave a secret royal commission to his lawyer, William de Nogaret, the veteran of Anagni. Copies of the command were sent to all the bishops, barons and royal officers of the realm, invoking their absolute obedience and their absolute silence. Exactly a month later, on 21 July, every Jew in France was arrested, and all their goods and money appropriated for the Crown. The operation was swift, efficient, unexpected, nation-wide and entirely successful – king and lawyer were perfecting their technique.

About the same time as Philip gave de Nogaret his commission, Pope Clement wrote a letter to the Master of the Hospital and to Jacques de Molay, Master of the Temple. As their supreme lord, the lack-lustre pontiff commanded the Masters to come to Europe, because 'We desire to consult you regarding a Crusade in co-operation with the Kings of Armenia and Cyprus, since you are in the best position to give us useful advice on the subject and, next to the Court of Rome, you above all others must be interested in the project.'

Shortly after these events, twelve new brothers were accepted into the Order of the Temple, one in each of twelve preceptories scattered across France. Each one was an agent of King Philip.

In due course the Masters of the two Orders replied to their lord, the pope. The Master of the Hospital expressed his regrets that he was unable to obey the command to come to Europe; his brotherhood was in the process of transferring to Rhodes, and he could not leave. Jacques de Molay, however, had no pressing business to detain him; he intended to arrive in Europe early in the new year.

Clement, Philip and de Nogaret began their preparations for his reception – the weak and feeble pope, the ruthless king, and the unscrupulous lawyer with his memories of heretic fires. The unholy trinity awaited their guest.

CHAPTER 14

THE CELEBRATION
OF PERFIDY

France, 1307

'Ye are forgers of lies....'
Job XIII, 4

J ACQUES DE MOLAY, twenty-third and last Master of the
Order of the Knights of the Temple of Solomon, was born
around the year 1244 in Franche-Comté, the eastern part of
France. He was received into the Order of the Temple in
1265, and, being a trained knight, was soon sent out to the
Holy Land. Once there, he found much to criticize in the way the
Order was run; he was a straightforward, active young man, and
he understood the Templars' role on the simplest level: he felt
that their business was fighting Saracens, and as with many other
newcomers to the East, would accept nothing less. The Master at
that time, William de Beaujeu, with his policies of peace, seemed
to de Molay to be at best a coward, and at worst a traitor to the
principle of the brethren. Dogmatic and rigid, de Molay
expressed his disapproval openly, freely and frequently.
De Beaujeu's apparent passivity disgusted him, and he let it be
known that – if he were ever in a position to do so – he would reform
the Order, if only for its own safety. He spent twenty years in
Outremer, the last twenty years of the kingdom. In 1285 he was
in Acre, and he probably took part in the final futile yet heroic
defence of the city in 1291; he may even have been one of those
who accused de Beaujeu of cowardice in the last moments of his

life. Despite the ultimate defeat of the Christians, that terminal period must have been intensely satisfactory for de Molay; with more than enough action, and with the death of a Master he disdained, two decades of frustration were sent hurtling into oblivion.

Part of his frustration had been that, under de Beaujeu, he had never held a leading office in the Order – perhaps because of his outspoken comments. But he had ambition, as his talk of reform showed; and shortly after the death of de Beaujeu's successor, Tibald Gaudin, on 16 April 1293, his assertive character won through at last. After Acre, promotion came swiftly to men of experience. De Molay had been a Templar for twenty-eight years by then; he could speak with conviction, and – to the brethren – convincingly. That year they chose him as their Master. The reforms could become reality.

Elected in Cyprus, de Molay began his mastership with an immediate journey to the West, seeking, yet again, practical support from the pope and the king of Europe. He visited Spain, France, Italy and England; his journey lasted three years. During that time he convoked three general chapters – in Montpellier, in the autumn of 1293; in Paris, over the winter of 1295–96; and in Arles, in the autumn of 1296. He met James II of Aragon, Charles II of Naples, and Edward I of England; in December 1294 he assisted at the election of Pope Boniface VIII. But nothing at all came of the contacts or the effort. James was only interested in a Spanish Crusade; Charles was bent on conquering Sicily; Edward was at war with Philip of France; and Boniface, instead of giving money to the Order, asked for a tribute to help his own intrigues in Italy.

Returning disappointed to Cyprus, de Molay found his brethren in trouble there; the land they held in the island which they had once owned outright was insufficient for their needs, but King Henry – a descendant of Guy de Lusignan – forbade them to acquire more, either by gift or purchase. The island could never be an adequate base for both a Military Order and a king, side by side. The Hospitallers had recognized this quickly, and set about the conquest of Rhodes; but de Molay still believed his Order's future lay in the Holy Land. The Templars, he decided, would remain in Cyprus until they had regained some part of the mainland.

A working relationship was patched up with King Henry, and he and the Templars of Cyprus celebrated the year 1300 with raids on the Syrian and Egyptian coastlines. In de Molay's estimation, these were no more than the Templars' duty; but the raids were grotesquely unsuccessful. The Templars were not superhuman. Without western help, the doctrine of undeviating war had become absurd; yet still the new Master continued his policy of aggression. But it was *only* directed against Moslems in the Holy Land. Late in 1302 the little garrison of Ruad fought a sea-battle with a Moslem fleet. The brethren were severely defeated. Those who survived fled to Cyprus soon afterwards; and that battle was the Templars' last act of war.

Meanwhile the brothers looked in vain for the radical reforms they had expected. The Hospitallers, with an organization as unwieldy as the Templars', recognized the route to survival: what was needed was a change in structure, joined with a continuity of function. After the loss of the Holy Land, the Military Orders – simply to claim the right to exist – had to rationalize their clumsy internal frameworks, and simultaneously to carry on their sworn traditional role of fighting the infidel. They would not have thought of it in those terms, but the Hospitallers understood this necessary course and acted on it; their brotherhood was divided into eight nations or languages, each with specific responsibilities, and after the conquest of Rhodes, their new island centre, they became a kind of maritime police force, keeping the Mediterranean sea-lanes free of Moslem pirates. The structural subdivisions made their Order as a whole more flexible, less ponderous; the new focus of action was in keeping both with their past and with the present.

The Hospitallers, in short, modernized their brotherhood; they changed to meet the needs of a changing world. The Templars did not. The only 'reforms' that de Molay ever instituted were to remind his brethren, at every general chapter, of their vows of total obedience to him, and to enjoin them to economize wherever possible. Under him, the Templars followed the exact opposite of the formula adopted by the Hospitallers: the structure of their Order grew more rigid, more cumbersome than ever before, and, as their banking operations prospered, they seemed to forget their original vocation.

The startling difference between de Molay's words as an

ordinary knight and his deeds as Master had a very simple, very human cause: he was not an especially intelligent man. The forceful criticisms of his youth and middle age sprang from a lack of imagination, a narrowness of character which prevented him from really understanding the problems his Master faced. When he himself became Master, he discovered too late how much easier it is to criticize than to act constructively. Now he began to say publicly that de Beaujeu, whose conduct he had despised, could not have done anything better in the circumstances. But an understanding of the situation of fifteen, twenty or thirty years previously did not help him to tackle new problems effectively – indeed, it did the opposite. His capacity for imaginative comprehension was diminished further rather than enlarged, for he had grown older, and his youthful directness and intolerance had hardened into conservatism and bigotry.

This, then, was the man whom Pope Clement V summoned to Europe in 1306: an elderly, old-fashioned man, who had spent all his adult life in military service; a man of simple ideas, narrow-minded and more or less incapable of sophisticated thought; a man who saw little need to alter the organization he commanded, and whose notions of reform were limited to cheese-paring economies and a strict disciplinarian demand for obedience. When he arrived in Europe, late in 1306 or early in 1307, Jacques de Molay certainly did not consider that there was anything fundamentally wrong with the Order he controlled or the way he controlled it. His mind was absorbed with the problems his brethren faced in the central and eastern Mediterranean – their unsatisfactory position in Cyprus, their difficulties with the warring Venetians and Genoese, and the apparent impossibility of reclaiming any part of the Holy Land. He could see no easy way around any of these troubles, but he had several firm beliefs – namely, that everything done by the Order as a whole was right; that somehow, sooner or later, they would get back to the Holy Land, and that until then they should carry on as they were. It did not occur to him that outsiders might think the Templars had lost their direction. He would have stoutly denied any suggestion that his Order had forgotten the art of war, and was only composed of parasitical financiers; and if anyone had reminded him of Christ's Sermon on the Mount – 'lay not up for yourselves treasures upon earth, where moth and rust doth corrupt, and where thieves break through and steal' – he would not have seen any personal significance in the text at all.

De Molay had been instructed to come to Europe incognito and with as small a retinue as possible. No reason was given; perhaps Clement thought that a Moslem army, knowing the Master was absent from Cyprus, might be emboldened to attack the island. De Molay thought otherwise. Arriving in France, he brought with him sixty knights and a baggage-train of gold and jewels. The procession of bearded warriors, their armour covered with the famous white mantle and red cross, was instantly recognizable to everyone, and seemed to be intentionally conspicuous, a conscious demonstration of the Order's known power and unknown wealth.

Clement was in Poitiers. De Molay, however, completely confident of a good reception from the pope, went to Paris first, in the knowledge that the French king's backing would be essential if the proposed crusade was ever going to happen. With the knights and the treasure safely installed in the Paris Temple, de Molay proceeded to the royal court.

It is likely that this was the first time Master and king had met, but each man already had a fairly clear idea of the other. Years before, de Molay had probably met the king's grandfather, St Louis, whom Philip himself had never really known. Now in the spring of 1307, seated before the young, handsome king, de Molay must have been struck by the apparent family resemblances, the good looks and piety of the Capetian monarchs; and he may have indulged in a little reminiscence, talking with the spurious authority of his age, his status and his experience about the old days – perhaps with an injudicious comparison to the present.

He knew of the king's constant lack of money, and, notwithstanding that, the size of the court he maintained; he must have remembered how, five years earlier, Philip and his entourage had stayed in the Paris Temple, and in nine days had consumed eight hundred and six pounds of bread and two thousand and seventy-seven litres of wine – to the parsimonious Master, such consumption, when the books could not be balanced, would have seemed extravagantly profligate. He would also have known how ruthless and how efficient Philip could be – the Jews had been expelled only a few months previously – but that essential aspect of Philip's character does not seem to have concerned him at all.

Philip, for his part, received the grizzled old knight with the honour due to a sovereign prince. He knew that, by birth and by membership of the Temple, de Molay was no vassal of his. He also knew that de Molay stood in the way of all his plans, and that there was no legal way to coerce the proud old man. He was aware, too, of the part de Molay had played in the election of Pope Boniface VIII, and that Templar funds had helped the English and Flemish as much as they had helped the French. And, very speedily, he must have realized that de Molay, for all his age and experience, was a naive man, who accepted everything at its face value. Enquiring about the Order's present condition, he asked whether everything was as it should be; and de Molay blandly admitted that it was not. In confession, he said, various brethren had revealed errors of behaviour, moments when they had fallen short of the Rule. The admission was nothing more than the regretful comment of an old disciplinarian on a less than perfect discipline; but Philip found it of considerable interest.

De Molay and Philip had an acquaintance in common – Ramon Lull, the Spanish mystic. He had visited Cyprus in 1302, and since then had published his *Liber de fine*, with its plans for a crusade of conversion under the 'Warrior King'. It is possible that in this first interview, the king and the Master talked of the proposals; and de Molay may have been shown a new book, entitled *De Recuperatione Terrae Sanctae* – 'Concerning the Recovery of the Holy Land'. It was written by Pierre du Bois, an unofficial member of Philip's formidable band of lawyers, a colleague of William de Nogaret. It took Lull's suggestion as a starting point, and elaborated that into a detailed, partly realistic, partly utopian blueprint for a crusade. But under that cover lay its real intention, which was nothing less than Capetian world hegemony. This would have been clear even to de Molay; yet if he saw the book at that time, he did not take it seriously at all.

The interview ended to each man's satisfaction. Philip had learnt most of the things he wanted to know, and de Molay moved south to Poitiers, happy in the belief that the good relations of Temple and monarch were undisturbed. And those relations had been good; for more than a century – from 1190 to 1296 – the French royal treasury had been housed in the Paris

Temple, and when Philip moved the state treasury to his own palace of the Louvre, he left his household finance in the hands of the Templars. The brethren enjoyed exemption from almost every legal restriction, and as recently as 1304 Philip had confirmed all their rights, adding to his confirmation the promise that 'the moveable goods of the Order will never be seized by secular jurisdiction, nor will their immovables ever be wasted or destroyed'.

One man had been central to maintaining those good relations: brother Hugh de Pairaud, who in 1307 was Treasurer of the Temple, and whom Philip had appointed receiver and warden of the royal revenues. De Pairaud, an intimate of the French court, had at one time aspired to the post of Master. Being passed over in favour of de Molay, he believed de Molay had only won the election through intrigue. The two men were about the same age, and in their own ways equally intransigent. Since his disappointment, de Pairaud had overtly obeyed de Molay; but in secret, he was a law to himself. On 10 August 1303 he had signed a private agreement with Philip, an agreement of mutual defence and support at all times, and specifically in the battle with Pope Boniface VIII – the pope whom de Molay had helped to elect, and who Philip was now pursuing beyond the tomb.

Unaware of this, de Molay arrived in Poitiers at the end of May. After the fire-breathing examples of Boniface and Benedict, the new pope seemed an uninspiring and unsatisfactory successor. Clement had trained in both Roman and canon law, and before his election to the papacy had been a papal diplomat. He was a man accustomed to compromise, which, to de Molay, was merely a sign of weakness and vacillation; and when the Master met his new lord for the first time, Clement was a worried and frightened man. In the nineteen months of his papacy, he had already submitted time and time again to pressure from King Philip. He had absolved the king of the sin of extorting money from the Church; he had reinstated the cardinals dismissed by Boniface; he had created ten new cardinals, of whom nine were French; he had forbidden the Flemish to rebel against Philip; and he had agreed that, if the security of the realm demanded it, neither Philip nor any of his descendants should be held to a crusading vow. There were only two major things in which he had resisted Philip: the absolution of de Nogaret, and the posthumous trial of Boniface.

And if Philip was no longer insisting on these, it was only in order to concentrate his energies elsewhere.

Only a few weeks earlier, Philip and Clement had had a stormy interview, in which the king had told the astonished and incredulous pope of a long series of horrific accusations against the Order of the Temple – accusations which Philip claimed had been made by reliable witnesses, and which, if true, threatened all Europe and the very existence of the Church. Even if they were not true, they were so serious that Philip believed a full investigation was merited. Such an investigation could only be conducted under papal auspices, since the Templars were only responsible to the pope, and Philip had demanded that Clement should authorize a full inquiry. Clement was unwilling to comply, partly because he could not bring himself to believe Philip's allegations. They were so fantastic that only two interpretations seemed possible to him: either the Templars were part of the greatest betrayal of Christ since Judas's kiss, or else King Philip, obsessed with his 'God-given' throne, was tottering on the brink of insanity. And either way, if Clement gave in to the oppressive monarch, the consequences were terrifying. If the charges were proved, the seal would be set on Philip's power as the 'Most Christian King', the defender of the Church. But if the Holy Knights were vindicated, what then? It would be their triumph, not the Church's; and with their trained armies and their ubiquitous strongholds, they might easily launch a war of revenge and ridicule against the French king. And Clement knew that Philip, cornered, would fight as viciously as a rat and as cunningly as a fox.

Clement could see no way to avoid a catastrophe; and for him personally, the dilemma had a further cutting edge. Much as he had come to dislike Philip, he owed his papal throne to the king; and if Philip was thwarted, if Clement dismissed the allegations as nonsense, that throne could be emptied as dexterously as it had been filled. Kidnap, poison; Clement was haunted by the memories of his predecessors.

With considerable courage, he had refused to give the king a definite answer at once, and had decided to wait until he could consult the Master of the Temple personally. Possibly Philip had not expected more at that stage; he knew Clement's measure. He and his lawyers had some work to do, and so he had returned to

Paris, and with pomp and ceremony and not a hint of suspicion, he had entertained Jacques de Molay.

Seeing de Molay in Poitiers, Clement must have been more shaken than ever, for beyond his usual grumbles the Master seemed content, and happy to be in France. He had come prepared with answers to the questions of uniting the two Orders and launching a Crusade of limited objectives; but Clement was not in the mood to hear them just then. He told the Master of all that had happened. De Molay was outraged and offended. Even the slightest of the things Philip claimed – that the transfer of treasure from Cyprus indicated the Order was about to abandon the East altogether, and operate only in Europe – was untrue. De Molay's indignation, welcome as it was to Clement, was of no use to the pope though. Unless Philip retracted his allegations, something would still have to be done; so Clement determined to wait again, in the feeble hope that delay and his own open support of the Order might persuade Philip to change his mind.

Without having given his prepared answers, de Molay, apparently more puzzled than frightened, returned to Paris, and there held a general chapter. It took place on 24 July; it was secret, as always, and no report exists of what was said in its course. But shortly afterwards, a circular was sent to all preceptories in France, reiterating the passage of the Templars' Rule which forbade any brother to speak of the Order's rites and practices to anyone outside the brotherhood; and around the same time, brother Hugh de Pairaud, that associate of the royal court, was heard to say that any Templar who had reason to leave the Order should do so swiftly, for a frightful calamity was imminent.

De Molay came back from Paris to Poitiers again, seemingly sure that his artless, outright denial had been enough to dispel any doubts. This time he presented the pope with two memoranda. The first was a terse dismissal of the idea of crusading with the Cypriots and Armenians – the Cypriots could only provide a small army, the Armenians were unreliable. Moreover, after his own attempts at localized war, he considered a limited crusade would have no chance of enduring success; a big push was the only way to recover the Holy Land, and in the current climate of political opinion in Europe, that was unlikely to materialize in the near future.

His second memorandum dealt with the question of uniting the two Orders. This, he felt, was as undesirable as a limited offensive, and he gave his reasons at length. He recalled the first time the suggestion had been made, back in 1274, and he noted how its rejection then had been due to the opposition of the king of Spain. Now, he said, he could see only two points in its favour: economies of scale would certainly be effected, and the combined Order would be so strong it could resist any secular interference whatever. Points against the union, however, were myriad. There was a spiritual side; it could not be right to force a man who had chosen one way of life to renounce it for another. There was the human side; the Templars, he said, were known to be more valiant than the Hospitallers, and if the two were forced together, they could easily begin to fight each other, jealous of their own reputations. There was the administrative side; for a union would mean that all official posts would be twice filled, and how, he asked, would it be decided which man would remain, and which would be demoted? His implication was that he, for one, would definitely not give up his post willingly. And then there was the problem of the duplication of property; for if both Orders had houses in one town, someone would have to decide if one or other was to be closed, or if both were to be kept on.

Such far-reaching alterations were beyond the old man's grasp. He was clearly, and naturally, prejudiced against them from the start, and he did not seem to have given much thought to the wording of his memorandum; for, given that all his comments were accurate within their limitations, it was hardly wise to admit that the Soldiers of Christ could be so petty as to kill each other through jealousy of worldly honours, or that he himself was too proud to relinquish his status to another. But the answer was given, and Clement accepted it; and a little later, copies of the memorandum were sent to King Philip.

For some weeks everything was quiet. Clement fended off Philip's continuing demands for an inquiry; and on 2 August, in reply to a request from the English Templars, he sent a Bull to Edward I exempting them from a tithe imposed by the English king. Not only that, but Clement referred to the Templars as his 'dearest sons', and described them as brave Knights of Christ, men who were accustomed to enduring every danger in the defence of the holy places of Christendom.

His opinion was clear, and he could have continued his strategy of passive resistance until, one way or another, Philip was forced to change – he could have, if de Molay himself had not made the next move.

The sense of being under covert suspicion, when nothing open was being said or done, became too much for the Master. He paid another visit to the pope, and on 24 August Clement wrote an unhappy letter to King Philip. Jacques de Molay had had enough of whispered lies and slanders; if there were accusations against his Order, they should be made aloud. This underhand, hole-and-corner behaviour was unbearable. De Molay was quite sure that any changes were baseless and could be disproved, and the Order acquitted; and now he requested a formal inquiry. 'There is so much that seems impossible', said Clement to the king, 'that we cannot believe it'; but he promised to begin an investigation.

Exactly three weeks later, on 14 September, Philip was at the abbey of Maubuisson near Pontoise, a few kilometres north of Paris. From there he issued a mandate to all his seneschals, baillies, deputies and other officers throughout the kingdom. The mandate was sealed, and carried instructions that it was not to be opened until the night of 12 October. On 23 September, nine days after the mandate was issued, Philip gave William de Nogaret a new appointment. He was still 'first lawyer of the realm'; he was still excommunicate. Now he was Chancellor of France as well, Guardian of the King's Seal – an excommunicate filling the top civil post of the kingdom, second in authority only to the king.

Early in October King Philip's sister-in-law, Catherine of Valois, died. Her funeral, a state occasion, took place on 12 October, and the Master of the Temple was accorded the signal honour of being one of her pall-bearers; and at dawn the next day – Friday 13 October – he, and every other one of the five thousand Templars in the length and breadth of France, was arrested by the king's men.

PART SIX

The Trials:
1307–1314

CHAPTER 15

THE HERESY OF INNOCENCE
France, 14 October 1307–7 April 1310

'Thy tongue deviseth mischiefs; like
a sharp razor, working deceitfully.'
Psalm LII, 2

AT THE BEGINNING OF the fourteenth century the
University of Paris was renowned throughout Europe as
a centre of learning and subtle argument, a place where
questions of theology, politics, and law were analysed and
answered – not in a theoretical way, but with practical application
in people's daily lives. Kings, statesmen and ecclesiastics would
go there for guidance in matters of the utmost importance. The
learned academics would give their interpretations of the Bible's
words, their opinions on problems of state or diplomacy, and
their intellectual support for new laws – if they judged them to be
correct. Without such support new legislation of either State or
Church had little chance of acceptance or survival. For this
reason, on Saturday 14 October 1307, William de Nogaret
summoned the leading members of the University to a meeting in
the chapter room of the cathedral of Notre-Dame. The site was
well chosen, lending emphasis to the holy nature of the speech he
had prepared; for de Nogaret's purpose, before that assembly of
bachelors, scholars and religious and secular masters, was to
denounce the entire Order of the Temple as heretical, nauseous
and corrupt.

The arrest of the Templars the day before had shocked and
astonished everyone in France. The operation had gone almost

entirely without a hitch; out of five thousand Templars, only about twenty had managed to evade capture. All those taken had been put into solitary confinement, unable to communicate with any of their brethren, or with any friends or relations in the world from which they had been snatched. Secrecy had been complete; action had been simultaneous throughout the kingdom. The efficiency of his organization must have been a source of pride and satisfaction for de Nogaret. For others, it was frighteningly impressive. Such a skilful, awesome masterpiece would scarcely be challenged, especially as an accomplished fact; but if nothing else was done, de Nogaret and King Philip knew that criticism could easily arise when the shock had worn off, particularly since the Templars were men of the Church. As such, their arrest was a direct contravention of every right of ecclesiastical immunity; and de Nogaret's task now was to show that they did not deserve that right, or any other right at all.

As he stood before the gathering of academics, he had no misgivings; having terrified their hearts, he was confident he could seduce their minds, for his use of language was expert. He had written the mandate of Maubuisson, although Philip had signed it; and every word in the mandate was designed to place the Templars, spiritually and morally, beyond any human sympathy.

'A bitter thing, a lamentable thing, a thing horrible to think of and terrible to hear, a detestable crime, an execrable evil, an abominable act, a repulsive disgrace, a thing almost inhuman, indeed alien to all humanity, has, thanks to the reports of several trustworthy persons, reached our ears, smiting us grievously and causing us to tremble with the utmost horror....'

That was only the beginning of the mandate; to the simple men who were the baillies and seneschals of the kingdom, reading such a text in the dark hours of the morning of Friday 13th, it must have been like a foretaste of divine judgement, an appalling revelation of secret sins. And it did not deal with ghosts or phantasms, nightmares to frighten children, it dealt with men they knew, men in their village or their town; and so, encouraged by the light, they had set out at dawn as bravely and as righteously as they could to arrest their neighbours, the knights and servants of the Temple, armed with the knowledge that these men had performed the most abominable acts imaginable against

Christ and God. On entering the Temple, each and every one of the brethren had denied Christ, and had spat on His image. They had then kissed each other, on the mouth, the navel and the anus, and had subsequently joined in a homosexual orgy; and finally they had all bowed before an idol in the shape of a human head, and had adored it as their god.

There was no resistance when the Templars were arrested; nor was there any in the cathedral of Notre-Dame when de Nogaret repeated the substance of the mandate to his scholarly audience. Stunned by the enormity of the accusations, the University men could only acquiesce and accept the news in silence; and, de Nogaret announced, it would all be corroborated very soon by the frank and spontaneous confessions which his men were receiving, even then, from the Temple's highest officials.

Eleven days passed. On 25 October the academics assembled again, this time in the great hall of the Paris Temple. Five men were brought up from the dungeons below – four Templar knights, and the Master, Jacques de Molay. Speaking in the name of God, on behalf of all his brethren, and using the vernacular so that everyone might understand clearly what he was saying, de Molay confessed that, although his Order had once been noble and holy, '. . . the cunning of the enemy of the human race, who was always seeking whatever he could devour, had led him to a fall of such perdition, that for a long time now those who were received in the Order denied the Lord Jesus Christ, our Redeemer, at their reception, not without the sad loss of their souls, and they spat upon a cross with the effigy of Jesus Christ . . . in contempt of him, and in the aforesaid reception they committed other enormities in the same way.'

By the grace of God, he added, these things had been brought into the open by the Most Christian King Philip, 'the agent of light, to whom nothing is hidden'; and he begged his listeners to intervene with the king and the pope, so that he and his men, who were all wretched and repentant, could be absolved of their sins and undergo ecclesiastical justice.

Disgusted, frightened and oppressed in spirit by the thought of the dreadful subversion that had been going on all around them, the scholars in the Temple, and later, people all through France, heard the confessions with haunted fascination.

De Molay wrote an open letter to his brethren, instructing them to confess all their evil practices as he had done; and the confessions poured forth. Within a few days, thirty-eight had been made in Paris alone, and another hundred over the next few weeks. The pattern was repeated everywhere, as knights, sergents, priests and serving brothers all admitted their corruption and guilt. Hugh de Pairaud, Treasurer of the Temple, made the most sweeping confession of all, for not only had he undergone the sacrilegious reception, but also he had personally received many brothers into the Order in the same way; and he had 'seen, held, stroked and adored' an idol shaped like a head, an idol which brought the Templars all their worldly power and wealth, which caused the trees to flower and the land to be fertile, and which brought death to their enemies.

King Philip wrote a series of letters to the monarchs of neighbouring lands 'in order that you may equally arise in the faith', and keeping them informed of the progress of events. Everything said about the Templars was true; it had to be, for people would not confess to things they had not done. Doubtless in the next month or so the whole unsavoury but necessary process would be complete, and the Order condemned and dissolved, to the satisfaction of all concerned – including the Templars themselves, for they had damned themselves, and now humbly sought penance, absolution and reconciliation to the Church.

Unfortunately for Philip his royal neighbours did not believe he was telling the truth. The grandson of a saint he may have been, but everyone was aware of the way he himself had ruled so far – through war, gross taxation and multiple devaluation; the kidnap at Anagni was common knowledge, and so was Philip's influence in the election of Pope Clement. Apart from those factors, the cause of the Templars' astounding confessions was obvious; for everyone in Christendom knew the Inquisition, and Philip's confessor happened to be the Inquisitor General of France.

The Inquisition – or to give it its more clinical official title the Holy Office – was a tribunal in the Roman Catholic Church for the discovery, repression and punishment of heresy, unbelief and other offences against religion. It was established as a permanent court in 1248 by Pope Innocent IV, and its direction was mainly given to the Dominicans. Their merciless application of its formally approved methods soon gave them a new name punning on the old; they became the 'Domini Canes', the 'Dogs of the Lord'.

Few other human inventions have rivalled the subtlety and ingenuity of the Inquisition's central double-bind. Its basic premise was that no one was ever accused of heresy without good reason, and anyone could accuse anyone else of heresy – except an accused heretic who, whether his heresy had yet been proved or not, could not be trusted. Rather than being assumed innocent until proved guilty, the accused was assumed guilty until proved innocent; and it was extremely rare for anyone accused of heresy ever to be proved innocent. The best the accused could hope for was to go through the process of confession and repentance – even if he had nothing to confess to – and hope for reconciliation under penance. The penance might be merely a fine, or it could go as far as imprisonment on a diet of bread and water. But those accused who refused to confess, or who confessed and subsequently retracted their confessions, were excommunicated by the Church and given to the secular authorities for temporal punishment. This meant that their property was confiscated by the state; their heirs for two generations were barred from public office; and they themselves were burnt. If they were lucky, they were strangled at the stake; if not, they were burnt alive.

Because of the assumption of guilt, it was virtually impossible for a person accused of heresy to defend himself legally; anyone associating with him or her automatically fell under suspicion as well. Almost the only defence open to the accused was to give a list of his known enemies, in the hope that a name on the list would tally with the name of his accuser. Even if it did, though, he still had to prove his innocence – that is, he had to confess and be reconciled; and if for any reason he did not confess, the Holy Office was empowered to use several approaches to persuade him of his (perhaps non-existent) error. The cruder methods were various. The accused might simply be tied down, and a cloth stuffed in his mouth. Water would then be poured either onto the cloth, causing it to swell, or into his nostrils. A little too much and he would drown on dry land. Or he might be placed in a pit no wider than himself, and left to starve until he understood and

admitted his heresy. Or, more expensively, he might be placed on
the infamous rack, and stretched until his thighs and shoulders
came out of their sockets. He might simply be placed in irons,
with shackles around his wrists, ankles and neck; his feet might
be smeared with fat and held before a blazing fire; or, if he was
particularly stubborn, he might be placed in the strappado. This
spectacularly foul invention was simply a rope and pulley. The
victim's arms were placed behind his back, and his wrists were
tied together. From there, he was raised as high as possible into
the air. The rope was then released so that he plunged towards
the floor; but the fall was stopped just before he hit the floor, so
that maximum strain was put on his shoulders and arms. An
optional refinement to this was to hang weights from the
supposed heretic's ankles or navel, or, in the case of a man, from
his genitals.

All these methods, and others, were used to extract confessions from the Templars imprisoned in France. But not all of the
tortures were so crude; de Nogaret and his henchmen had
developed some much more sophisticated approaches, which
were frequently uncannily close to 'modern' systems of interrog-
ation. The victim would be subjected to ceaseless questioning by
relays of men trained in the art; answers would be distorted, and
the victim prevented from sleeping, urinating or voiding his
bowels; he would be held in solitary confinement and told that
any friends of his arrested on the same charges had already
confessed; and when he showed signs of breaking down, a new
interrogator would enter, with a sympathetic and friendly
manner, cajoling the prisoner to confess for his own good.
Through the judicious application of such techniques, almost
anyone could be made to confess to almost anything; the person
who could withstand these tortures to the point of death, which
would be his only release, was very rare indeed. Confessions were
obtained through sheer terror, sometimes merely by showing the
accused the instruments of torture. He might be forced to watch
the torturing of another victim; if that was insufficient, the
agonizing pain of his own torture would usually achieve the
desired result. In some cases it was thought impolitic for the
prisoner to have visible wounds; then the subtler methods would
be used, and in his pain and confusion, as his creature needs were
denied him and his responses were twisted out of recognition, the

victim would admit whatever guilt was imputed to him – and he would believe that he was guilty.

Brainwashing is a word of our century; but its techniques, and the phenomenon itself, are ancient, the bastard offspring of the Holy Office. Therein lies the deepest horror of the Inquisition; for the men who ordered these things to be done, if not the men who actually carried them out, ordered them in the name of Christ, for the love of God, and in the sincere belief that they, only they, were right, that their acts were Christian and were done for the good of their victim's soul. One Templar announced, after his confession, that the men who had tortured him were completely drunk; well they might be, if, in addition to religious belief, they had any human feeling at all. The words of another brother, a man of about fifty, exemplified the utter spiritual defeat and humiliation that such experiences could induce in any ordinary person; he said 'All the errors imputed to the Order were true, and that [he would confess] he had killed the Lord if it were asked him.' Anything – only cease, and let me be. The methods of persuasion used on de Molay to elicit his initial confession were probably of the more subtle kind, but his admission of guilt was not less complete, and apparently no less sincere, for that.

But the support and easy acceptance that Philip seemed to have expected from other kings did not emerge. The replies of James of Aragon and Edward of England to Philip's letters are preserved; both kings – especially James, in whose country the Auto da Fe, or Act of Faith, was the most theatrical manifestation of the Inquisition's cruelty – knew the Holy Office well, and neither was disposed to accept the slanderous reports against the Templars, even when seemingly substantiated by confessions. Edward wrote simply that he found the accusations 'more than it is possible to believe', and James, after expressing 'not only astonishment but also disquiet', added that 'these monks have often offered great and welcome service to our forebears in the exaltation of the faith and the suppression of the enemies of the Cross, fearing neither loss of blood nor death, and incurring many dead from amongst themselves ... and, because we have not been requested by the Church, and no other things have come to our notice in this matter, we have not been able to and we may not proceed against them'.

Nevertheless Philip, in the autumn of 1307, could hope for a speedy conclusion to the turmoil he had unleashed. The weight of the Templars' admissions, however obtained, and the barrage of propaganda from de Nogaret's fluent pen, was too great to admit disbelief, at least to the majority of Frenchmen. All that was required was papal approval and the Order's official dissolution. Some kind of more or less unprincipled solution could have been worked out for the whole reprehensible affair; but, completely unexpectedly – and courageously – Pope Clement suddenly asserted his own rights in the matter. His first recorded reaction was to write a letter, dated 27 October, to Philip, a letter of such indignation and undeniable correctness that even Philip was forced to take it seriously. Beginning with a vigorous affirmation of the inalienable right of the Papacy to lead and judge the Church, Clement condemned Philip's presumptuous defiance in seizing the Templars. 'These acts', he said, 'are the occasion of painful astonishment and sadness to us, because you have always found in us such benevolence compared to all the other Roman pontiffs who in your time have been head of the Roman Church.' Even Philip had to acknowledge the justice of this remark; but nonetheless, he had 'perpetrated these attacks upon the persons and goods of people directly subject to the Roman Church', and worst of all, 'in this action of yours so unlooked for, everybody sees, and not without reasonable cause, an insulting contempt for us and the Church of Rome'.

Clement had gone straight to the heart, in a way that only he, as pope, could do; he had exposed the illegality of the arrests, and had shown that in Philip's action he saw not only an attack on the Templars, but an attack on the Holy See as well. He followed his letter with a Bull, issued on 22 November and entitled *Pastorali Praeeminentiae*, in which he ordered the kings of all Christian lands to follow Philip's example and arrest the Templars in their countries; but it was to be done in the name of the papacy. Yet this did not mean Clement was prepared to accept the Templars guilt as a foregone conclusion, for 'if the premises are proved not to be true, and this is discovered, joy will arise; which is why we propose to investigate the truth of the matter without delay'.

This intervention marked a complete shift in the procedure of the trials. Clement had placed himself at the centre; anything that happened thereafter would have to be in reference to him. And

y taking charge of the trials themselves, he was able to institute
is own commission of inquiry, with the intention of gathering
enuine evidence – evidence based on interviews without
orture.

During December 1307 Clement sent two cardinals to Paris
o begin the examination – a somewhat inept beginning, for the
wo men merely asked the inquisitors and the king's counsellers
or the truth as they saw it. The reply brought back to Clement
vas that all the confessions were acceptable and correct. Clement
romptly sent the cardinals back to Paris with specific instruc-
ions to interview the Templars themselves. They did so; and
heir new report could not have been more dramatic. Jacques
le Molay, Hugh de Pairaud and more than sixty other Templars
ad revoked their confessions.

Battle was joined between pope and king. Philip was already
n too deep to withdraw. The only victory he could afford was
otal victory: for the Order to be declared guilty; for it then to be
lissolved; and for its money and lands to come to him. Anything
ess would be insufficient. If the Templars were proved innocent,
evenge would be easy for them. Even if individual Templars
vere found guilty, but the brethren as a whole were blameless, it
till would not do; if any branch of the Order survived, then
Philip would be in peril, always and wherever he went. That, at
ny rate, was how he understood it; and by this stage, not only
noney, life and land were at stake – there was prestige as well. To
ave revealed and extirpated an international heresy would set
Philip at the head of Christendom; anything else would show him
p as a fanatic, a megalomaniac and a bandit.

At this point one of the more bizarre aspects of the trials
reeps in. The human capacity for self-deception is immense,
erhaps infinite. Possibly sensing that utter personal conviction
night be the only way to ride over Clement's challenge, Philip
eems to have begun actually to believe in the Templars' guilt. He
aid they were heretics; therefore they were heretics. Such mental
crobatics were no more than usual for an inquisitor; but when
hey occurred in conjunction with near-dictatorial power and a
elief in personal divinity, an explosive, deadly mixture was
ormed.

Philip's mind is extremely difficult to sift; his actions,
owever, after de Molay's revocation, have a continuity that

could only spring from a serene conscience and a passionate conviction that all other men were liars and knaves.

In February 1308 Clement suspended the proceedings of the Inquisition in France, determined that all evidence should be gathered, presented and assessed honestly and fairly. Philip, with de Nogaret's masterly aid, immediately began a campaign of propaganda against the pope. In the same month, one of the few Templars in Clement's charge escaped from the house in which he was being held, unintentionally giving the propagandists an ideal opportunity. Scurrilous anonymous pamphlets were circulated through France, pointing to the escape as a further admission of guilt, commenting that if Clement could not keep one Templar captive, he should not demand custody of the thousands of others (as he had done), and suggesting that a pope who sided with declared heretics was no better than a heretic himself. Stinging criticism of Clement's well-known nepotism was mixed with insinuations that he had taken bribes from the Templars; the acid factual comments gave a veneer of truth to the fictions, and all were illustrated with carefully-chosen scriptural quotations that underlined Philip's righteousness and Clement's depravity.

Against such underhand assaults, Clement was defenceless; his training had been as a lawyer, not a liar – in diplomacy, not duplicity. Yet he persevered, placing his earthly faith in legality and his spiritual faith in authority. Philip countered both by submitting a series of seven questions to the hard-pressed lawyers and theologians of the Paris University, questions designed to magnify the correctness of his actions in both spheres. The academics took a month to formulate their reply; and when it came, it must have been cold comfort for Philip, for despite its grovelling tone, the king's 'insignificant clients', as they called themselves, told him humbly and courteously (and probably in fear of their lives) that he had no legal or religious basis to stand on at all. Worst of all, they felt that if the Order was dissolved, there was no legitimate way for Philip to claim the goods, property and money of the Order.

Nothing daunted, Philip summoned an assembly of the Estates General. Typically, this was not the democratic parliament suggested by its title, but yet another implementation of autocracy. Early in May 1308, some two thousand representatives of the nobles, clergy and commons congregated in Tours to listen, for a week or more, to the violent and adept haranguing of le Nogaret and his tribe; and at the end of the ordeal, the representatives dutifully recorded their whole-hearted assent to and support of Philip's opinion that the Templars should die for their sins.

Confident in the support of his subjects, knowing that – in practical terms – Clement was as much a prisoner in France as the Templars, and knowing, too, that feelings towards Clement were hostile, Philip travelled to Poitiers at the end of May to meet the pope face to face. He did not travel alone; his brother, his sons and various barons, bishops and commoners accompanied him, along with a small army of soldiers and archers – a display of power in vivid contrast to Clement's temporal helplessness. Pontiff and monarch met in a transparently hollow show of mutual esteem, and on 29 May sat together in a public consistory. This was a senate of cardinals gathered to deliberate on Church affairs; and though Clement was its president, this particular consistory became merely a vehicle through which he could be overtly attacked by the king.

The main speaker was William de Plaisians, another of the king's lawyers. His speech was heralded with the cry *Christus vincit, Christus regnat, Christus imperat!* – Christ conquers, Christ reigns, Christ rules! It was a consummate display of the persuasive power of emotional language, commencing from a loosely factual base, progressing through a description of the king's horror at the treachery revealed to him and an analysis of the action he had unwillingly been forced to take, and culminating in a direct threat to the pope. No true Catholic could wish to favour heresy by doubting the king's word; and 'therefore, holy father, when the king, prelates, barons and all the population of this realm ask for a speedy issue to this business, it will please you to expedite it quickly! Otherwise we shall have to speak another language to you!'

Clement, astonishingly, listened unmoved. Somewhere this normally compliant man had found a spring of remarkable courage; the main part of his reply was that he would indeed proceed against the Templars, 'but honestly and maturely, not precipitately'. De Plaisians took up the cudgels again, indicting Clement as a sympathizer of the Temple, saying that his delay was casting doubt on Philip's probity, and – once more with scriptual examples – showing that the king could and would act in his own name if necessary. He even hinted that Clement could be deposed if he continued to obstruct justice; but Clement, whose outrage at Philip's presumptuousness seemed to have made him into a new man, blandly shrugged his shoulders and repeated that the law would have its way.

And Philip, the king and demi-god, was afraid of the law. He had always striven to find a theoretical legal basis for his actions. Now he knew he had none. Intimidation had no effect; therefore he tried conciliation. Conceding that the brethren should be under papal supervision, but pointing out that Clement had no means of guarding them securely, he agreed to allow the pope's representatives easy access to the Templars, while actually keeping them under lock and key himself. In practice this meant that his control over the Templars' persons was no less absolute than at the moment of the arrests; but Clement accepted the compromise. At the same time Philip sent seventy-two of the brethren to Poitiers – all hand-picked men who could be relied upon to repeat the full enormity of their crimes to the pope himself. Hearing the confessions, Clement appeared to believe them. So far, Philip may have thought, so good; he had provided the pope with a means of saving face, of acting without seeming to be coerced. But Clement's response was hardly that of a convinced anti-heretic: in addition to his episcopal inquiries against individual Templars, he now set up a commission of eight to inquire into the case against the Order as a whole, and announced that a decision would be given at a general council in Vienne on 1 October 1310 – in two years' time.

Meanwhile, in England and Aragon, the pace of the trials was even slower. After his initial incredulity, James of Aragon made an about-turn. If anything was going to happen to the Order, he was determined to have first refusal on their goods, and in December 1307 he sent an army to occupy the Templar castle of Peníscola. The building was taken over without resistance, but by then the brethren elsewhere were well prepared. The Inquisitor General of Aragon ordered them to appear to answer the charges against them. Naturally they did not; instead they shut themselves up in their fortresses and announced they were ready to defend their good name by force. One by one the

trongholds were besieged; one by one they fell, through
tarvation or, on one occasion, treachery; but the least of them
.eld out for eight months, and the strongest for seventeen, only
urrendering in May 1309. Even then the papal inquiry did not
tart until January 1310 – the bishop in charge was ill. Similarly
1 England, nothing was done until December 1307, when
Clement's Bull *Pastoralis Praeeminentiae* arrived, commanding
King Edward to act at once. Edward grudgingly replied that he
vould do so, in 'the quickest and best way'; but he took his time,
nd did not seem inclined to treat the problem seriously. The
English Templars were arrested in January 1308, almost a full
month after the arrival of the papal Bull; and the English
uthorities, still sceptical, phlegmatic and unwilling to be ordered
round by foreigners, understood the term 'arrest' in a slack and
asy-going way. The detention of the Templars could have been
rranged with an efficiency comparable to Philip's; in the event,
owever, it was done tolerantly and somewhat apologetically.
"he goods of the Temple were not appropriated, and most of the
rethren were allowed to remain in their preceptories. If they
vere actually imprisoned, as the Master of England was, they
vere permitted to keep all their usual clothes and utensils – even
heir weapons; to have two or three brethren with them for
ompany; and to receive funds for their support from Templar
ands. On 13 September 1309 a pair of French Inquisitors turned
ıp in London, ready to take over proceedings. Unfortunately for
hem, English law differed from French, in which the Inquisition
ıad become merely an arm of government. In England the
nquisition was regarded as an unwelcome and unwarranted
ntrusion, and English Common Law stipulated the notion –
arely credible to the Inquisitors – that an accused person should
e tried by a jury composed of free men. These two were the first
nd last Inquisitors in England, and they came away frustrated
nd generally disappointed. In a four-week period over October
nd November 1309 they examined forty-three Templars in
.ondon, using common law techniques, and not one of the
ccused would admit to any guilt whatsoever. The best they
ould do to help the Frenchmen was to agree that a few of the
impler brethren believed the Master was empowered to give
eneral absolution of sins, which he was not. Compared to the
nswers given in the French trials, such an acknowledgement was

trivial; and when the two Inquisitors pounced on the subject o
secret chapter-meetings, reasoning that anything secret must b
nefarious, a brother dismissively said that the secrecy sprang onl
from folly, that nothing had occurred at either receptions o
chapters that was not fit for anyone to see, and that an
confessions made elsewhere were lies. Even the depositions o
the hundred and fifty outside witnesses called from all over th
British Isles were little help; their evidence was either patentl
imaginative, or referred to supposed events decades before, o
was rumour at third- or fourth-hand. By midsummer 1310
progress in England was, from the Inquisitors' point of view, nil
In a plaintive letter to the archbishop of Canterbury, they sai
they were unable to tackle the job in their usual style. They ha
done their best, but they could not even find anyone who knev
how to administer torture; and they were going home. The onl
suggestion they could make was that all the Templars in England
should be shipped over the Channel to Ponthieu, which wa
English territory, but subject to French law. There the truth
would certainly be revealed, for an experienced torturer could b
found without difficulty. Taken on its merits, the idea wa
logical; but it was never followed up.

In France, Clement was becoming confused. In the middle o
August 1308 he had managed to extricate himself from Poitiers
and had announced that, until the case of the Templars wa
settled, he would set up a new permanent papal court i
Avignon. He had also reserved the right to judge the leaders o
the Order personally, and to that end had sent three cardinals t
Chinon, where the senior officers were incarcerated. Betweei
17 and 20 August, the cardinals interviewed the Preceptor o
Cyprus; the Preceptor of Normandy; the Preceptor of Poitou an
Aquitaine; Hugh de Pairaud, the Treasurer and Visitor of th
Order; and Jacques de Molay. Nine months earlier, afte
Clement's first intervention, all of these men had revoked thei
earlier confessions. The revocations had played a large part i
Clement's decision to pursue the trial through scrupulously lega
channels; but by revoking, the brethren who did so place
themselves in the uncomfortable position of lapsed heretics. I
they were now found guilty, they would certainly be burnt alive
and so when the cardinals interviewed them, those five officers al
returned to their original confessions. On one level, this wa

welcome, for it meant the five could be reconciled to the Church. On a second level it irritated Clement; his conscientious legalism was pre-empted, and Philip's reckless freebooting was vindicated. And on a third level, Clement was simply puzzled. Perhaps the confessions were true, after all; perhaps the revocations had indeed been nothing more than malicious insults to the French king. He would have been less confused had he known that two of the cardinals sympathized with Philip, and that during their interviews, three other people were present: the Templars' brutal jailer, and the two lawyers, de Nogaret and de Plaisians. The three together were able to twist the Templars as they chose, simply by being there, for each one played a distinctive role in the slow, corrosive mental and physical torture. The jailer was their daily persecutor, starving and abusing them whenever possible; de Nogaret, they knew, was responsible for their systematic defamation; and de Plaisians – perhaps the most sinister of all – seems to have been the devil's advocate, professing friendship and pleading with them to confess for the sake of their eternal souls.

Despite his confusion, Clement had set his course and was going to stick to it. He discovered that his bureaucratic commission made infinite prevarication possible. Through highly efficient inefficiency, he managed to stave off actually doing anything for a whole year after the officers' confirmation of their confessions. It was not until 8 August 1309 that papal letters went out summoning all witnesses to attend before the commission; and the commission was not going to open its sessions until 12 November. Moreover, it promised to be an utter charade, for out of the eight commissioners, six were known to be more or less directly linked with Philip. Yet Clement accepted this; and the reason is simple. His concern with legality was based not so much on a wish for true justice as on a wish to protect papal rights from encroachment by the French crown, a distinction of which the Templars themselves were unaware, and which for them would ultimately prove fatal.

When the commission opened on 12 November, the promised charade seemed about to be realized. For the first six days, not one witness appeared, either for prosecution or defence. The commissioners were forced to adjourn; and when they re-assembled on the 22nd, the first seven Templar witnesses appeared to have no idea why they were there. On being told they could defend the Order if they wished, they merely mumbled that they were simple men and did not know how.

The remainder of this first session continued in the same sorry way. Altogether, twenty-eight defendants were brought, including Hugh de Pairaud, and Jacques de Molay, who appeared twice. A few of these said that, if they had the skill, they would freely defend the Order; but none actually offered to do so, and one said that he was quite satisfied with the defence given by Clement and Philip. The rest excused themselves on the grounds that they were 'ignoble and obscure' or 'poor and ignorant', and both de Pairaud and de Molay, who the others might have expected to give a lead, refused to say anything except in the presence of the pope. De Molay seemed frightened and confused, and was 'greatly astonished' when his previous confessions were read out to him. The sessions were meant to be secret, but some people could get in anywhere. De Molay's first appearance was attended by the lawyer de Plaisians; and at one point the Master appealed for help from the lawyer, who said that he respected de Molay greatly 'since they were both knights', and cautioned him 'to take care in case he blamed or lost himself without cause'. In his second appearance de Molay protested his belief in 'one God, one faith, one baptism and one Catholic Church'; but this time his escort was de Nogaret, whose presence was quite illegal, and who nonetheless alleged that the Order had made treaties with Saladin and other sultans, and that Saladin had ascribed their defeat at Hattin to their predilection for 'the vice of sodomy, and because they had violated their faith and law'.

It was a bad start to a defence. The commission's second session began on 3 February 1310, and to begin with seemed like a repetition of the first fiasco. For two days no witnesses were brought forward; then on 5 February, sixteen Templars came before the commission, and fifteen of them offered to make a defence. During the recess, the brethren – at last understanding the nature of the commission – had found something of their old spirit, and by the end of March, five hundred and ninety-seven had volunteered to defend the Order. And this was despite de Molay's continuing bad example, for he, by then, had refused for the third time to speak to anyone but the pope.

Over the next week, four brothers were chosen to represent

the Order. Two, Pierre de Bologna and Renaud de Provins, were priests; the others, William de Chambonnet and Bertrand de Sartiges, were knights. All were intelligent and literate; de Bologna may even have had some legal training at the University of Bologna, for his speeches to the commission were couched in the same style of furious rhetoric that de Nogaret himself used, and both he and de Provins displayed considerable familiarity with correct modes of legal procedure. Eloquence and education – they were the only two things that Philip and de Nogaret feared. Their smokescreen of bombast, their dishonesty, stealth and lawlessness could not stand close examination, and would all be exposed if attacked openly, legally and correctly. That was exactly what the four representatives of the Order intended to do; and on Tuesday 7 April 1310, they began.

CHAPTER 16

THE INFERNAL SACRIFICE

France, 7 April 1310–29 November 1314

'I will judge thee ... and I will give thee
blood in fury and jealousy.'

Ezekiel XVI, 38

THE CHARGES WERE READ OUT in detail. The original
accusations in the mandate of Maubuisson had been that
the Templars denied Christ and spat on His image, that
they exchanged obscene kisses and indulged in homosexual relations; and that they worshipped an idol. When Pierre
de Bologna and his three brothers stood to defend themselves
and their Order, they faced not three but seven groups of
charges, itemized in one hundred and twenty-seven articles. The
seven groups were these.

First, and most important, was the denial of Christ. On his
reception a new Templar was forced to renounce his belief in
Christ's holiness, and to accept that Christ was not the Saviour
but a false prophet crucified for his own sins. The new brother
then had to defile the crucifix either by spitting or urinating on it,
or by trampling it underfoot. All the other accusations stemmed
from this; the second was that the Templars were idolaters. Their
idol was a cat, or a head with magical powers. The head could
answer questions; it provided the Templars' wealth and destroyed their enemies; and every brother had to wear a cord
around his waist that had been placed against or around this idol.
Each brother was thus magically bound to the idol, sharing in
and subservient to its power. The third group of charges covered

different aspects of the Templars' unbelief. Since Christ was not the Messiah, the sacraments of the Church meant nothing to the Templars, and their priests did not consecrate the Host while celebrating mass; the Templars' mass was only mummery. The fourth group dealt with the absolution of sins; the Master of the Temple and other leaders heard confession from the brethren and absolved them, even without the priestly qualification to do so. Then came the obscenities within the Order, the kisses on mouth, navel, stomach, anus, buttocks and spine, and the homosexuality which the brothers were ordered to accept. Sixth was the group of charges of cupidity; the brethrens' prime concern at all times was the material enrichment of the Order, by legal or illegal means. Seventh and last, the Order's secrecy was counted criminal, for not only were receptions and chapter meetings held in guarded rooms, with all doors and windows locked and covered, but also any brother who disclosed the secrets of the Temple was imprisoned or murdered.

When these denunciations, elaborated into one hundred and twenty-seven articles, were read out to him, Pierre de Bologna had been in prison for two and a half years, tortured, interrogated and forced to confess to everything. But in front of the papal commissioners, he spoke defiantly and violently for himself and all his thousands of brethren.

'Each and all of us,' he said, 'declare the accusations to be utterly unfounded. It is unbelievable that such scandalous charges should be taken seriously by anyone. It is true that some Templars have admitted them, but only because of torture and suffering .. It is not in any way to be marvelled at that there are those who have lied; what is more wonderful is that any have kept to the truth, knowing the tribulations and dangers, menaces and outrages which those who speak the truth suffer daily and continually.'

A powerful beginning, and de Bologna continued in the same vein, blending rhetoric and level-headed legal accuracy in a potent and apparently successful mixture. He pointed out that all the so-called confessions had been extracted by torture, adding caustically that 'Beyond the Kingdom of France no brother of the Temple in all the lands of the world will be found who says or will speak these lies, from which it is clear enough why they have been spoken in France: those who have spoken have testified when corrupted by fear, prayers or money.' The confessions, therefore, should be inadmissible as evidence; and 'whenever any brothers are examined, no layman should be present who could hear them, or any person whose probity could be doubted' – meaning that the Templars' jailer and the king's lawyers should not be allowed into the commission, since their mere presence intimidated the brethren. Then, fighting fire with fire, he attacked the Temple's accusers, saying that they were 'false Christians and altogether heretics, detractors and seducers of the holy Church and all the Christian faith'. Motivated by greed, these 'most impious propagators of scandal' had found renegade and apostate Templars, and with them had concocted a set of lies that deceived even the Most Christian King Philip. A new brother gave only four vows, said de Bologna, the vows of obedience, chastity, poverty and the continual support of the Holy Land; and the only kiss that was exchanged was 'the honest kiss of peace' – no more than the customary kiss exchanged between any lord and any vassal. Those who accused the Order of moral and spiritual perversions should be examined by the commission as well, and made to state the grounds for their accusations; and in the meantime all brethren who wished to defend the Order should be given a guarantee of safety, for even now the king's men were still threatening them with torture and death if they dared to deny their guilt.

It seems the commissioners were impressed by the vigour and clarity of de Bologna's statement; but they were determined to hear all sides of the case before coming to a decision. Accordingly, the first witnesses admitted before them were the witnesses for the prosecution: twenty-four men, of whom four were not Templars. None of these two dozen was actually named as a prosecution witness, but fifteen of the twenty Templars had been in the group of seventy-two who had confessed to Clement; the other five had never professed any wish to defend the Order; and the four non-Templars were all connected with the King. The first and most prominent of them was actually one of the King's lawyers, a man named Raoul de Presles; he above all might have been expected to produce cogent arguments to condemn the Templars. But though he gave a long speech intended to convince the commission of the Order's guilt, it contained no concrete evidence at all. There was nothing but rumour and hearsay; and he acknowledged that before the arrests he had not heard anything that explicitly defamed the Order. The next witness, closely questioned by the commissioners, could eventually only say that 'he suspected the Order was not good'; and the Templar witnesses merely repeated the confessions they had made to Clement, confessions which the commission refused to accept as evidence.

Things were looking bad for the royal prosecution. Not even a lawyer of the king could provide real evidence; there simply was none to provide. It was becoming more and more obvious that the king's case was based on terror and confusion, and Pierre de Bologna's exposure of this continued fearlessly and inexorably. In his reply to the prosecution's witnesses, he said that the arrests and the trial to date had been 'rapid, violent, unlooked for, hostile and unjust, altogether illegal, utterly injurious, and bearing intolerable error and the utmost malignity'; and, penetrating to the core of the brainwashing techniques, he said that the tortures inflicted on the Templars had deprived them of 'freedom of mind, which every good man ought to have', since without it, a person lost all 'knowledge, memory and understanding'. He wanted to know how any brother could have wanted to join or remain in the Order, if so doing imperilled his eternal soul; and he demanded written copies of all materials pertaining to the case, as well as a promise that all depositions would be secret, and that witnesses who had spoken should be kept apart from those yet to come.

While de Bologna and his three brethren co-ordinated the defence, the commissioners had announced that they were willing to hear everyone who had anything useful to say, either for or against the Order. Some six hundred Templars had said they would speak, and as their confidence mounted with de Bologna's example, it became clear that the hearings would go on for a very long time. Clement had scheduled the Council of Vienne, at which he would give his judgement, for October; it was already April, and so he decided to postpone the Council for another year. Thus, by the end of April 1310, the Templars' position was better than it had been at any time since the arrests in 1307, and de Bologna reported to his imprisoned brothers that their release and complete exoneration could only be a matter of time.

And so it should have been. But in their wave of sudden

optimism, the defenders of the Temple had begun to under-estimate King Philip. As the papal commission progressed in its investigation of the Order as a whole, episcopal commissions con-tinued to investigate charges against individual Templars. The papal commission was implicitly superior to the episcopal ones, but this had never been explicitly stated; and as soon as Philip's lawyers recognized this loophole in legality, they jumped on it.

Fifty miles south-east of Paris lay the town and archdiocese of Sens. For some time it had had no archbishop, and King Philip had managed to extract from Clement the right to nominate a new one. He had bided his time in appointing a successor, and for him the wait proved worthwhile. In April 1310 a young man of twenty-two was installed as archbishop of Sens, a man named Philip de Marigny, whose brother was the king's chief minister of finance. The archbishopric of Sens had authority over the bishopric of Paris, where the Templar defendants were im-prisoned; and the new archbishop was a king's man through and through.

Within a month of his appointment, Philip de Marigny carried out the king's instructions to exploit his legal right of judging individual Templars, and convened a provincial council in Paris for Monday 11 May. Somehow, at the last moment, Pierre de Bologna heard of this. On Sunday 10 May, although the papal commission was not in session, he sent a desperate appeal to the commissioners, begging them to prevent the provincial council. He feared that the worst possible judgement would be given, and if so, it 'would be against God and justice, and would completely overturn the inquiry'; it would make the commission, and the commissioners' activities meaningless and foolish. The commissioners understood, but there was nothing they could do; 'We are deeply grieved for you,' they told de Bologna, 'but since the pope has sanctioned proceedings before provincial councils, we are powerless to interfere in any way.'

On Monday morning the commission resumed its hearings. At the same time, only a few miles away, Archbishop Philip inaugurated his council. Early next day, as it plodded along its judicious course, the commission was suddenly interrupted: Archbishop Philip had given his sentence, and fifty-four Templar defendants were to be burnt alive that afternoon. The com-missioners did their best, but without legal power they could only request the young archbishop to forego his rights and delay action. The request was ignored.

On Tuesday afternoon a procession of tumbrils creaked through Paris, bearing the fifty-four guilty Templars – knights, priests, sergents and serving brothers, all clad in their distinctive uniform – to a field outside the town. Fifty-four stakes piled with brushwood and timber awaited them. A large crowd gathered to watch; any execution was good entertainment, and this mass slaughter, everyone knew, was especially important. When it was over, one of the crowd wrote that 'All of them, with no exception, refused to admit any of their alleged crimes, and persisted in saying they were being put to death unjustly ... which caused great admiration and immense surprise,' and another spectator commented laconically that such resolute persistence could make ordinary people believe that the Templars were speaking the truth.

For the surviving Templars, at any rate, the effect of the executions was immediate and decisive. Their hope, and with it their defence, collapsed. Their lives could only be saved at the cost of their honour; their honour could only be saved at the cost of their lives. Legality was no security any longer. On the day of the burnings, thirty-eight of the brethren refused to continue the Order's defence, saying they would rather confess any heresy and live in degradation than die in the flames. In Paris the burnings carried on; before long nearly one hundred and twenty Templars had been fed to the fires. Not even the dead were safe – the bones of dead Templars were exhumed and burned publicly with the living brethren. Imitating Archbishop Philip, the archbishops of Reims and Rouen held provincial councils and sent unknown numbers of the brethren to their deaths. The archbishop of Rouen was another very young man – he was only twenty-four, and Pope Clement was his uncle.

Six days after the first executions, Archbishop Philip pre-empted the papal commission again. Renaud de Provins, the second priest of the defending representatives, came from Sens, the archbishop's diocese; and, as was his right, Philip called de Provins to be examined by the provincial council. When not even the appointed procurators were safe, the commission became completely farcical. The commissioners sent a tactful message to Philip, pointing this out. As before, he ignored it. The message was repeated, more forcefully, and de Provins was restored; but at the same time, Pierre de Bologna vanished. The commissioners asked that he too should be allowed to reappear; but instead a group of forty-four brothers were sent to them, all of whom said they no longer wished to defend themselves or the Order. The commissioners had lost any control of the proceedings. They gave up. On Saturday 30 May, they adjourned for five months.

Whatever happened to the Templars in those five months, in the dungeons and torture-chambers of Paris, no one knows; but on Tuesday 3 November, when the commissioners reassembled, they discovered a dramatic and near-complete reversal of all their previous experience. Only two of the Order's four representatives were available – the two knights; both the priests, de Bologna and de Provins, had confessed their guilt in the course of the summer, and had been sentenced to perpetual imprisonment. De Provins, indeed, was incarcerated somewhere in Paris, but de Bologna was reported to have escaped. One hopes that this may be true, and that the Templars' most courageous defender found freedom at last; but it was suspected that he had been murdered by his jailers.

Without their educated brethren, the two defending knights lost confidence and asked to be released from their unmanageable responsibility. No one was left to represent the Order; and in their winter session of 1310–11, the papal commissioners heard almost nothing but pathetic, cringing confessions, the confessions of men debased by terror and extreme pain into creatures unable to combat or comprehend the outrageous savagery of their traducers and torturers. No one admitted every single charge, and many tried to pass the blame on to the leaders of the Order; but between them, they confessed to it all: the denial of Christ – yes, they had declared that His mother was not a virgin, and that He was a false prophet and not the Son of God; the defiling of the crucifix – yes, they had spat on it, urinated on it, trampled it underfoot; as for sodomy, that was common throughout the Order, especially in places where women were not available; and idolatry was certain. The confessions were consistent only in the most general way, varying in their details as much as in their accompanying excuses; but when they came again and again, from men who knelt, weeping and trembling, to swear by all that was holy that their words were true, the commissioners could only accept them. On 26 May 1311 the last witnesses were heard: by then, two hundred and thirty-one people had given evidence, Templars and non-Templars, and all but a very few of them had condemned the Order irretrievably. Nevertheless, on 5 June, the commissioners gave King Philip their official verdict that the case against the Templars was not proven. But they did believe that the Order harboured some unorthodox practices, which should be punished; and for Philip, that was quite enough.

Yet even that qualified assent was lacking in other countries. In Portugal, Majorca and Aragon the Templars were declared innocent; a Majorcan Templar, being told that Jacques de Molay had made a complete confession, said the Master 'lied in his gullet'. In contrast, one English Templar priest claimed that de Molay had forced him to deny Christ at his reception; but apart from this, and two or three other damning confessions, nothing more solid emerged against the Order in England than the discovery that some of the simpler brothers had confused the absolution of breaches of discipline with the absolution of sin. The same was true in Scotland and Ireland. The general opinion in the British Isles was that the brethren were innocent; but in order to keep the pope happy, a compromise was worked out. The Templars declared themselves 'so defamed by the articles in the papal Bull that they could not purge themselves'; thereupon, they were absolved by the prelates of England and reconciled to the Church.

In Germany and in Cyprus, where the Order's chief house was located, the authorities were less diplomatic and acquitted the brethren outright. The German acquittal came after two dramatic incidents: in May 1310, a group of twenty-one Templar knights forced their way into the council-chambers of the archbishop of Mainz, armed and in full armour, and with the information that the Order's innocence had been miraculously shown in Paris. It was said that the tunics and red crosses of the brothers burnt there had not been harmed by the consuming fires, and in the midst of the flames had been seen to glow with a supernatural light. The archbishop was sufficiently impressed to postpone his council; and when it was reopened two months later, forty-nine witnesses (including twelve non-Templars) defended the Order in general and de Molay in particular, saying he was 'as good as any Christian could be'. But the subsequent acquittal displeased Pope Clement. The whole business of the trials was beginning to drag upon even his prevaricating soul. He had begun to wish for an end to it all, and he wanted that end to be as uniformly respectful of his authority as possible. Accordingly he annulled the German verdict, claiming the decision as his right alone; and in Cyprus, the Governor of the island, who was friendly to the Order and had found it innocent, was discovered one morning stabbed to death – a convenient murder, for Clement was able to institute a re-trial in which the original judgement was reversed.

Only in Navarre and Naples, ruled by satellites of King Philip, and in the papal states of Italy, was the Order found guilty at once; and only in those countries was torture used from the start. Even in August 1311, with the Council of Vienne only two months away, Pope Clement was still sending out orders to the places where the brethren had been unequivocally acquitted, orders saying that such acquittals could not be correct and that torture should be used everywhere to find the truth.

The ecumenical Council of Vienne opened on Saturday 16 October. It was intended to represent all of western Christendom; more than a dozen kings and several hundred prelates had been invited, from as far afield as Ireland, Cyprus, Hungary, Portugal, Russia and Sweden. But it was unpopular from the start, for the three matters on its agenda were the discussions of aid for the Holy Land, a reform of the Church, and the Templars' trials. To many of those invited, all three topics were unsavoury and unattractive. On 16 October, there were no kings present in Vienne at all, and fewer than two-thirds of the expected ecclesiastics had turned up. Those who did come found Vienne to be a small, dirty city, cold, crowded and extremely expensive. They also found that Clement was far more interested in disposing of the Templars and their goods than he was in Church reform or crusading. The latter questions were dealt with fairly swiftly; but when they arrived at the Templar problem, progress came almost to a stop. Clement had borrowed an idea from King Philip of France: in the same way as the French Estates General were a vehicle not of democracy but of autocracy, the Council of Vienne was not called to advise Clement about the Templars, but simply to accept and approve the decision he had reached. If Clement had had de Nogaret's rhetorical ability and Philip's military strength, such acceptance and approval would probably have been given immediately; but Clement was more experienced in being coerced than in coercing, and to the majority of the Council was not a very terrible figure. He himself had decided by then that the Order should be dissolved, its goods reserved for the Holy See and its brothers either reconciled as repentant heretics and sent to monasteries, or given to secular authorities as unrepentant, and imprisoned or put to death. His one abiding wish over the previous four years had been to preserve papal power, and by 1311 he was past caring for the technicalities of justice and law.

He had gathered copious quantities of 'evidence' against the Order, and on his side in the Council had several vigorous speakers; but the evidence was grotesquely biassed, containing only rumour and gossip, and although his supporters criticized any mention of a proper discussion as 'frivolous and vexatious', the majority of the councillors were not prepared to swallow the Order's dissolution as meekly as Clement had hoped – especially as, in many instances, they came from countries where the Templars had been acquitted.

Since the Council concerned them so intimately, the brethren themselves had been invited to attend. None was expected to do so, and the invitation was only for form's sake. However, the resistance within the Council was suddenly and unexpectedly strengthened in late October – for a group of seven Templars actually appeared, soon to be joined by two more. The nine offered themselves as defendants, and said that nearly two thousand other brothers were still at liberty, and were close at hand. In fact this cannot have been true; but the mere appearance of the nine, like spectres from days of old, was a thorn in the Council's conscience, reminding the councillors that any verdict they reached would affect real people. The Templars' sins were little more than a matter of hearsay; the Templars' deaths, in the dungeons and at the stakes, in Paris and elsewhere, were a matter of definite fact.

Clement's reaction to the sensational sight of nine living, free Templars was to clap them all in prison. Then, dividing in order to rule the better, he ordered the councillors to select a commission from their unmanageably large number. The commission and the pope conferred together, hearing transcripts of the trials; and then a still smaller group was chosen from the commission to assess what they had heard. In spite of this progressive diminution, Clement was still unable to win the prelates over; only four agreed that the Order should be dissolved without more delay, and of those four, one was Italian and three were French.

Christmas 1311 came and went, and the New Year arrived without any resolution. An Englishman attached to the Papal Curia wrote to the bishop of Norwich, saying that 'the larger part of the prelates, indeed all of them, excepting five or six from the council of the King of France, stand on [the Templars']˙behalf ... and the King of France is coming in a rage with a great following. We are frightened of this and ... it is hoped that the pope will transfer himself elsewhere. Everything remains in suspense.'

Philip had indeed made up his mind that a little temporal persuasion was necessary, and was advancing towards Vienne with an army. The hopes that Clement would shift the Council to a site beyond the scope of French influence were disappointed, and on 17 February 1312 a royal embassy arrived in Vienne – an embassy containing the lawyers de Nogaret and de Plaisians, and the royal Chamberlain Enguerrand de Marigny, whose brother was the pyromaniac archbishop of Sens.

The ambassadors and the pope conferred in secret for several days. Attending the Council were secular representatives of various countries, and the Aragonese in particular were intensely suspicious of these secret meetings. They guessed that the French embassy was forcing Clement to agree that King Philip should receive the Templars' property, and so after the ambassadors had left, they in turn began to press the claims of King James. Clement had managed to place himself in the middle of an extremely uncomfortable triangle – Philip, James and the unco-operative Council – and on the morning of 20 March he said he still could not tell whether the Order would be preserved or dissolved. But that very day, in a flash of understanding, his way was illuminated; for Philip, the 'bringer of light', rode into Vienne with his army.

Two days later the pope held a secret consistory with his commission of councillors, and on 3 April the entire ecumenical

Council was solemnly assembled. Three thrones were placed in front of the councillors. In the central one sat the pope; at his sides, and only slightly lower, sat King Philip of France and King Louis of Navarre, Philip's eldest son. Clement's sermon was ready; but before he began, a priest stood up and warned the ecclesiastical audience that any interruption, unless permitted or requested by the pope, would be punished by greater excommunication. Then Clement spoke, and the councillors, muzzled into silence by the papal threat and the presence of the two kings, heard *Vox in excelso.*

'In view of the suspicion, infamy, loud insinuations and other things which have been brought against the Order,' Clement began, 'and also the secret and clandestine reception of the brothers of this Order; in view, moreover, of the serious scandal which has arisen from these things, which it did not seem could be stopped while the Order remained in being, and the danger to faith and souls, and the many horrible things which have been done by very many of the brothers of this Order, who have lapsed into the sin of wicked apostasy, the crime of detestable idolatry, and the execrable outrage of the Sodomites ... it is not without bitterness and sadness of heart that we abolish the aforesaid Order of the Temple, and its constitution, habit and name, by an irrevocable and perpetually valid decree; and we subject it to perpetual prohibition with the approval of the Holy Council, strictly forbidding anyone to presume to enter the said Order in the future, or to receive or wear its habit, or to act as a Templar.'

It was done. It was so simple, Clement discovered, after all. In a few sentences and a few minutes he had succeeded where all the armies of Islam had failed. Two centuries of faith and hardship, of battle and honour, of jealousy and rivalry, of hope and effort and belief – it was all wiped away with a word. In silence the councillors listened, and in silence they departed, 'neither consenting', as an English chronicler commented, 'nor expressly contradicting'.

Shortly afterwards Clement ruled on the disposal of the Templars' property. He decided that, except for the lands in the Iberian peninsula, whose fate he reserved for himself, it was all to go to the Hospitallers, lock, stock, and barrel. But the decision, though made as easily as the decree of dissolution, was less easily put into practice. James of Aragon, Philip of France and Philip's descendants all had their eyes on the land and money involved, and years passed before the distribution was finally sorted out.

There still remained the question of the fate of the Templars themselves. Since they were considerably less valuable than their property to anyone except themselves, this was a much less knotty problem. Clement reserved the right to judge the leaders, but all the other brethren were to be judged at provincial episcopal councils. Those who confessed or were found innocent would receive a pension from ex-Templar property, and would be permitted to live in other monasteries, or in houses once owned by the Order, though only in very small groups; however those who revoked their confessions, or refused to confess at all, would be pronounced heretics, and dealt with as they deserved.

At this point, when the options were finally clear and unequivocal, it is astonishing that, while many of the Templars took the easy way out and chose confession, reconciliation and the degrading pension, many others found their spirit again and accepted death at the stake. And, according to legend, one of these frightful executions led directly to the death of that villainous lawyer, the malignant genius William de Nogaret. He died in mid-April 1313; and it is said that, eight days before, he accidentally met a group of Templars who were being taken to be burnt. On recognizing him, one of them cried out:

'You unworthy minister, ponder the effects of your lies and injustice! We cannot call you to your master, for with the pope he has become our worst enemy; but we call you to appear, eight days from today, before the tribunal of the Judge of the quick and the dead.'

Perhaps to add credibility to the tale, the chroniclers who report it add that de Nogaret died 'without being attacked or struck by anyone'. But whether the story is true or not, it reflects a considerable proportion of contemporary public opinion. Walter of Hemingborough, the same Englishman who described the ceremony of dissolution, felt that the ecumenical Council 'did not merit being called a council, since the pope did everything on his own authority'. One of the Parisian university professors of theology openly expressed his doubts on the Order's guilt, while another French theologian – from the Dominican Order, which never cared much for the Templars – commented, after observing many of the individual trials, that 'more faith was to be attached to those denying than to those confessing'; and in Florence, Giovanni Villani said outright that the whole tragedy sprang from King Philip's greed.

Philip had clearly won a victory of some sort, but it did him little good. His overt coercion of the pope and his fanatical despotism had blackened his name throughout Europe; and as for his extravagant dream of ruling a Christian empire as the 'Warrior King', Clement's decision to pass Templar property to the Hospitallers blocked that more effectively than de Molay could ever have done.

But it may be that Philip's years of tyranny and torture brought their reward in the end. Jacques de Molay, the Master himself, was still alive in a Parisian dungeon, awaiting Clement's judgement. Time and again the pope had delayed a decision and, when he finally acted, he contrived to avoid personal responsibility by sending a commission of cardinals to Paris in his stead. On 18 March 1314 the cardinals summoned de Molay to their presence, along with the three other major leaders – the Preceptor of Aquitaine, Geoffrey de Gonneville; the Preceptor of Normandy, Geoffrey de Charney; and the Treasurer and Visitor of the Temple in France, Hugh de Pairaud. De Molay was seventy years old, or more, by then; de Pairaud was slightly older; and all four of the men had been in prison for six and a half years. At the time of the arrests de Pairaud had said that he would do anything to save his skin. Now he had his chance, and he took it. He affirmed his confession of absolute guilt, was reconciled to the Church as a repentant heretic, and taken away to perpetual imprisonment. Geoffrey de Gonneville followed his example and shared his fate; and it was then that Jacques de Molay and Geoffrey de Charney, understanding at last their betrayal by the pope they had trusted, revoked their confessions, asserted finally and for ever their innocence and the innocence of the Order, and were dragged in chains to their slow and agonizing deaths. Thus was the Order of the Temple destroyed, dying as it had been born and had lived – in blood, and rage, and piety.

And yet it was not quite over: Philip's reward was still to come. When de Molay died, the Capetian dynasty had ruled France for three and a quarter centuries. After his death, it endured for only fourteen years more, and Philip the Fair and his descendants became known as the 'Accursed Kings'. It is said that, out of the flames which killed him, Jacques de Molay's voice was heard, cursing Pope Clement, King Philip and his family, and beseeching Christ Himself to prove the Order's innocence. If the Templars had been unjustly condemned, Clement was to be summoned within forty days, and Philip within a year, to the judgement of God.

Clement died on 20 April, thirty-three days after de Molay; and on 29 November Philip followed him. In his *Divine Comedy*, Dante placed them both firmly in hell. Whether or not one accepts the legend of de Molay's curse, the deaths remain; and in the next fourteen years, as the Capetian dynasty staggered to its end, each of Philip's three sons became king and died. France was then split by internecine struggles; and, in a line as clear and direct as the line of the Capetians, the kingdom's convulsions led to the Hundred Years' War with England.

One may make of it all what one chooses. Those who accept the infallibility of Pope Clement's words must also accept that the Templars were heretics, and justifiably condemned; but one must then forget the circumstances of Clement's election, his character, and Philip's influence upon him. With a similar, carefully blinkered view, one may see Philip as the founder of France, the king who united the nation and encouraged the rule of law; but to do that, one must ignore the way he twisted the law, and the barbarity of his rule. One may see the Templars as innocents attacked by an avaricious king and a despicably weak pontiff, and the deaths of Clement and Philip as divine retribution for their sins; but the truth of the retribution is obviously unproveable, and as for the question of the Templars' innocence or guilt, one can only say that either verdict must be qualified.

In the absence of proof one way or the other – and in our century, which has seen Stalin and Hitler, the Templars' 'confessions' cannot possibly be counted as proof of guilt – any assessment of the charges against the Order can only become a list of possibilities and probabilities. Taken under the broad headings of homosexuality, heresy, and idolatry, the first may be said to be very probably true. In any closed, all-male community, homosexuality is almost bound to occur, even if it would not in normal conditions. It would be straining credibility to claim that, in a period of nearly two centuries, amongst all the scores of thousands of men who took the Templar vows, there were none who made love together. Against that, however, it is equally incredible to claim that sodomy was universal, or even widespread, within the Order. A clause in the Rule specified its punishment; and since the clause was a late addition, and not part of the original Rule, it suggests that sodomy had occurred, and that the Master and his advisory chapter of brothers reacted with strong disapproval. Such disapproval stemmed not only from a heterosexual dislike of homosexuality, but also from general contemporary thought, for throughout the time that the Templars existed, sodomy was closely associated with heresy in European minds – so much so that the Bulgars (whose association with the Greek Church made them heretics) found their name transformed into bugger.

Heresy and homosexuality overlapped in the alleged illegal reception of new brothers – the exchange of obscene kisses, the denial of Christ and the defiling of the Crucifix. This cannot be counted as probable, but it must be allowed as possible. Even then, though, it cannot be interpreted definitely as a consciously anti-Christian action. In anything to do with the Templars, the peculiar nature of their all-male, half-spiritual and half-military Order must be remembered, and, as was suggested at the time, the kisses (if they ever occurred) could have been nothing more than a coarse joke, while the denial and defiling (if those ever occurred) could have been only a crude test of obedience.

After the probability and the possibility comes the hypothesis – a feasible answer to the charge of idolatry. The most striking aspect of the confessions of idolatry is their utter confusion. None of them agrees in close detail, but with one exception – the confession of an Italian brother who said he believed the Order had once worshipped a mysterious cat – they agree in general that the supposed idol was a head. But beyond that, it is difficult to find any unity. Some said the head was coppery in colour; some said it was a small gold picture, something like a woman. Others said it was bearded; others said it had two faces; and yet others claimed it had feet as well, either two alone, or two before and two behind. One knight gave such an exact description to the papal commission that the commissioners ordered a thorough search of the Paris Temple to be made. Nothing more than a silver reliquary in the shape of a woman's head was found, totally unlike the knight's description, and of the sort that could be possessed by any religious community of unquestioned integrity. The confusion is apparent not only in the descriptions; many of the brethren who said they knew of the adoration of a head, or professed to have adored one themselves, seemed uncertain at first whether the adoration was heretical or not.

Since then, innumerable answers, of varying degrees of transparently spurious romanticism, have been given to this question. Among these are the ideas that the head was the mummified head of the Order's founder Hugh de Payens; or a representation of Satan; or one of a devil named Baphomet; or one of the Prophet Mohammed. Even without the additional absurdity, that Baphomet was a corruption of Mohammed, that last is the weakest suggestion of all, since a portrayal of the Prophet would be as unholy to a Moslem as it would be to a Christian. It is worth noting that the original source of accusations that the Templars became more Islamic than Christian was Frederick II; and he was scarcely an honest champion of Christianity.

However, recently, a more sensible proposal concerning the Templar's 'idol' has been made. It is only a hypothesis, but it has virtues which all the others lack – it is simple; it takes all the known facts of the matter into account; and it explains both the confusion of descriptions and the Templars' own confusion. The idea has been ably set out in detail by Ian Wilson in his book *The Shroud of Turin*, but in brief, it is this: the Templars did possess a picture of a head, a picture which they believed had magical powers, and which they guarded with the utmost secrecy and security. The picture came into their possession after the sack of Constantinople, and after the dissolution of the Order, it was publicly shown in France. No tinge of heresy need have been attached to the adoration of this picture – for it portrayed the head of Christ. In this way the Templars' personal confusion is made understandable: if they were worshipping Christ, it could not be heresy. The confusion of description is equally simply clarified. Possessing such a portrait, the brethren would undoubtedly have made copies of it, on cloth or wood, and these would certainly have varied, depending on the skill of the artists and the materials used. Adding weight to the entire argument are the facts that a portrayal of Christ, known as the 'Mandylion' disappeared in the sack of Constantinople, never to be seen again; that in England, in the village of Templecombe in Dorset, a painted image of Christ's head, dating from Templar times, was found in 1951; and, most importantly, that the cloth known today as the Shroud of Turin appeared in France after the dissolution of the Temple, in the family of Geoffrey de Charney – the Templar Preceptor of Normandy who died at the stake with Jacques de Molay.

The hypothesis is worth close examination, for it renders credible aspects of the accusations which hitherto were difficult to explain or take seriously at all. However, the question of serious credibility applies not only to the charge of idolatry, but to the charges as a whole. King Philip the Fair could not have kept five thousand men in prison, and certainly could not have had hundreds of them burnt to death, if the majority of his subjects had not believed in the basic truth of the accusations, and had not approved, at least at the time, of the subsequent executions. For such a reaction to happen today, an entirely different set of charges would have to be devised; but when William de Nogaret wrote the mandate of Maubuisson, he wrote it in full knowledge of the contemporary view of subversion, a view which he undoubtedly shared. At the beginning of the fourteenth century, the worst sort of subversion was not political, but religious. The grip of the Church on people's conscious thought was very strong, but the emotional, subconscious vigour of Christianity had been slipping for a long time. That was largely why the Order of the Temple had grown so quickly: it was acceptable on social, spiritual and emotional levels all at once. And that too was why it could be destroyed so savagely; for when the Holy Knights, with their strength and wealth and pride, were shown actually to be an organized body of Christian apostates, two things were revealed: a mortal threat to the fabric of the social structure, and a scapegoat whose destruction could resolve the struggle between conscious faith and unconscious apostasy.

A further major cause of the charges' credibility at that time was, quite simply, the Templars' secrecy. Suspicion and fear were born of imagination and ignorance; and ever since, the same impenetrable secrecy has given rise to scores of fantastic notions, myths, which, being based on unknown events, can neither be proved nor disproved. Thus, some people like to believe that the original band of Templars searched for, and found, the Ark of the Covenant; that, because the surviving Portuguese Templars were absorbed into a new royal military order, Christopher Columbus was a Templar; that Christ Himself was the first Master of the Order; and that the Order continues in secret today. Another pair of whimsical beliefs are that the Templars introduced chess and Gothic architecture to Europe; but these fancies can easily be disproved, for Gothic architecture existed in Italy before the Order of the Temple was founded, and the playing of chess was expressly forbidden by their Rule.

It is sad that this group of dedicated men, who strove to unite the contrary virtues of monk and warrior, and who gave their lives willingly for their faith, should be mostly remembered as a source of fantasy and fairy-tale. It would be far better, far more appropriate, to remember the honest image of the knights, sergents and humble serving-brothers, clad in their mantles of white or brown, living, farming, trading, fighting and dying with the red cross of martyrdom on their chests and their battle-standard above their heads. In Aragon, in January 1308 a Templar Preceptor wrote to King James and said, 'God knows that I pity you, and the King of France, and all Catholics for the harm which arises from all this – more than ourselves, who have to endure the evil.'

The Templars were not angels or saints; but they were no devils either.

Bibliography

Albon, Marquis d' *Cartulaire Général de l'Ordre du Temple, 1119?–1150.* Paris, 1913.

Albon, Marquis d' *Fascicule Complémentaire contenant la Table des Sommaires des Actes et l'Identification des Noms des Lieux.* Paris, 1922.

al-Qalanisi, Ibn *The Damascus Chronicle of the Crusades.* Tr. and ed. H. A. R. Gibb. London, 1932.

Anglo-Saxon Chronicle Tr. and ed. D. Whitelock, C. Douglas and S. Tucker. London, 1961.

Barber, M. *The Trial of the Templars.* Cambridge, 1978.

Bloch, M. *La France sous les derniers Capétiens 1223–1328.* Paris, 1958.

Boase, T. S. R. *Kingdoms and Strongholds of the Crusaders.* London, 1971.

Boussard, J. M. *Atlas historique et culturel de la France.* Paris, 1957.

Brooke, C. N. L. and Keir, G. *London 800–1216: The Shaping of a City.* London, 1975.

Broughton, B. B. *The Legends of King Richard I Coeur de Lion: A Study of Sources and Variations to the year 1600.* The Hague and Paris, 1966.

Brundage, J. A. *The Crusades – A Documentary Survey.* Milwaukee and Wisconsin, 1962.

Bulst-Thiele, M. L. *Sacrae Domus Militiae Templi Hierosolymitani Magistri – Untersuchungen zur Geschichte des Templerordens, 1118/9–1314.* Göttingen, 1974.

Burchard of Mount Sion *A Description of the Holy Land, 1280.* Tr. A. Stewart. London, 1896.

Burns, R. I. *The Crusader Kingdom of Valencia.* Cambridge, Mass., 1967.

Campbell, G. A. *The Knights Templars – Their Rise and Fall.* London, 1937.

Carrière, V. *Histoire et Cartulaire des Templiers de Provins.* Paris, 1919.

Clifford, E. R. *A Knight of Great Renown: The Life and Times of Othon de Grandson.* Chicago, 1961.

Cohn, N. *Europe's Inner Demons.* London, 1975.

Comnena, A. *Alexiad.* Tr. into French B. Leib. Paris, 1937–45.

Coulton, G. G. (Tr. and ed.) *Life in the Middle Ages.* London, 1910.

Bibliography

de Curzon, H. *La Règle du Temple*. Paris, 1886.

de Curson, H. *La Maison du Temple de Paris*. Paris, 1888.

de Deuil, O. *De Profectione Ludovici VII in Orientem*. Tr. and ed. V. G. Berry. New York, 1948.

de Paris, G. *Chronique*. (Ms., 1313) Tr. into French J. A. Buchon.

Digard, G. *Philippe le Bel et le Saint Siège de 1285 à 1304*. Paris, 1936.

Dubois, P. *De Recuperatione Terrae Sanctae*. Ed. C. V. Langlois. Paris, 1891.

Duby, G. and Mandrou, R. *Histoire de la Civilisation Française*. Paris, 1958.

Duby, G. *The Chivalrous Society*. Tr. C. Postan. London, 1977.

Durrell, L. *Monsieur, or The Prince of Darkness*. London, 1974.

Ernoul *Chronique*. Tr. and ed. M. L. de Mas Latrie. Paris, 1871.

Evergates, T. *Feudal Society in the Bailliage of Troyes under the Counts of Champagne, 1152–1284*. London and Baltimore, 1975.

Farnell, I. *The Lives of the Troubadours*. London, 1896.

Favier, J. *Philippe le Bel*. Paris, 1978.

Finke, H. *Papsttum und Untergang des Templerordens*. Munster, 1907.

Forey, A. J. *The Templars in the Corona de Aragón*. London, 1973.

Fuller, T. *The History of the Holy War*. London, 1840 (first published 1639).

Gabrieli, F. *Storici Arabi delle Crociate*. Tr. E. J. Costello. Turin, 1957, London, 1969.

Gregory IV Dgha Catholicus *Elegy on the Fall of Jerusalem*. Published in *Recueil des Historiens des Croisades, Documents Arméniens*. Paris, 1869–1906.

Grousset, R. *Histoire des Croisades et du Royaume Franc de Jérusalem*. Paris, 1934–36.

Hillgarth, J. N. A. *Ramon Lull and Lullism in Fourteenth Century France*. Oxford, 1971.

Holtzmann, R. *Wilhelm von Nogaret, Rat und Grosssiegelbewahrer Philipps des Schönen von Frankreich*. Freiburg, 1898.

Huxley, J. *From an Antique Land*. Bath, 1972 (1st edn. 1954).

Jeune, R. P. M. *Histoire Critique et Apologétique de l'Ordre des Chevaliers du Temple de Jérusalem, dits Templiers*. Paris, 1789.

Johnston, R. C. (Ed.) *The Crusade and Death of Richard I*. Oxford, 1961.

Lacroix, P. *Military and Religious Life in the Middle Ages and the Renaissance*. New York, 1964 (1st edn. 1874).

Lameyre, A. *Guide de la France Templière*. Paris, 1975.

La Monte, J. L. *Feudal Monarchy in the Latin Kingdom of Jerusalem 1100–1291*. Cambridge, Mass., 1932.

Lane-Poole, S. *Saladin and the Fall of the Kingdom of Jerusalem*. London and New York, 1898.

Lees, B. A. (Ed.) *Records of the Templars in England in the Twelfth Century – The Inquest of 1185 with illustrative Charters and Documents*. London, 1935.

LeFebvre, Y. *Pierre l'Ermite et la Croisade*. Amiens, 1946.

Lizerand, G. *Clément V et Philippe le Bel*. Paris, 1910.

Lizerand, G. *Jacques de Molay*. Paris, 1913.

Lizerand, G. (Tr. and ed.) *Le Dossier de l'Affaire des Templiers*. Paris, 1923.

Luttrell, A. *Two Templar-Hospitaller Preceptories North of Tuscania*. Rome, 1971.

Madaule, J. P. *La Drame Albigeois et le Destin francais*. Paris, 1961. Tr. B. Wall as *The Albigensian Crusade – An Historical Essay*. London, 1967.

Martin, E. J. *The Templars in Yorkshire*. York, 1929–30.

Melville, M. *La Vie des Templiers*. Paris, 1951.

Michelet, J. *Procès des Templiers*. Paris, 1955.

Mountfort, G. *Portrait of a Desert: The Story of an Expedition to Jordan*. London, 1965.

Oldenbourg, Z. *St Bernard*. Paris, 1970.

Paris, M. *Chronica Majora vol IV*. Ed. H. R. Luard. London, 1877.

Parker, T. W. *The Knights Templars in England*. Tucson, 1963.

Pegues, F. J. *The Lawyers of the Last Capetians*. Princeton, 1962.

Perkins, C. *The Knights Templars in the British Isles*. London, 1910.

Pernoud, R. *Les Templiers*. Paris, 1974.

Prutz, H. *Die Geistlichen Ritterorden: Ihre Stellung zur kirchlichen, politischen, gesellschaftlichen und wirtschaftlichen Entwicklung des Mittelalters*. Berlin, 1908.

Pugh, R. B. *Imprisonment in Medieval England*. Cambridge, 1968.

Richard, J. *Le Royaume Latin de Jérusalem*. Paris, 1953.

Röhricht, R. (Ed.) *Regesta Regni Hierosolymitani (MXCVII–MCCXCI)*. Innsbruck, 1893.

Runciman, S. *A History of the Crusades*. Cambridge, 1951–54.

Sandys, A. *The Financial and Administrative Importance of the London Temple in the Thirteenth Century*. Manchester, 1925.

Bibliography

Saunders, J. J. *Aspects of the Crusades*. Canterbury, 1962.

Schlumberger, G. *Renaud de Chatillon, Prince d'Antioch, Seigneur de la Terre d'Outre-Jourdain*. Paris, 1898.

Scott, W. *Ivanhoe*. London, 1906 (1st edn. 1819).

Schnorhali, N., Catholicus *Elegy on the Fall of Edessa*. Published in *Recueil des Historiens des Croisades, Documents Arméniens*. Paris 1869–1906.

Simon, E. *The Piebald Standard*. London, 1959.

Smail, R. C. *Crusading Warfare (1097–1193)*. Cambridge, 1956.

Thrupp, S. (Ed.) *Change in Medieval Society: Europe North of the Alps 1050–1500*. New York, 1964, London, 1965.

Thubron, C. *Mirror to Damascus*. London, 1967.

Thubron, C. *Journey into Cyprus*. London, 1975.

Treece, H. *The Crusades*. London, 1962.

Trevelyan, G. M. *A History of England*. New York, 1942.

Tritton, A. S. (Tr.) *The First and Second Crusades from an Anonymous Syriac Chronicle*. London, 1933.

Walker, A. *The Knights Templar in and around Aberdeen*. Aberdeen, 1887.

Wakefield, W. L. *Heresy, Crusade and Inquisition in Southern France 1100–1250*. London, 1974.

Williams, W. W. *St Bernard of Clairvaux*. Manchester, 1935.

Wilson, I. *The Shroud of Turin*. London, 1978.

Wood, H. *The Templars in Ireland*. Dublin, 1906–7.

Yusuf ibn Rafi ibn Tamin *Saladin; or, What Befell Sultan Yusuf (Salah Ed-din) (1137–1193 A.D.)*. Tr. C. W. Wilson. London, 1897.

Various authors *Le Siecle de Saint Louis*. Paris, 1970.

Index

Abbreviations: b – birth; c – character; d – death; e – excommunicated; I – illustration; KT – Knight(s) Templar; MT – Master of the Temple.

Index

271.79 HOW

HOWARTH, STEPHEN
KNIGHTS TEMPLAR

$24.00

FINKELSTEIN
MEMORIAL LIBRARY
SPRING VALLEY, N.Y.

SEP 2 8 2007

3c 12/14